THE ARTHUR D. LITTLE FORECAST ON INFORMATION TECHNOLOGY AND PRODUCTIVITY:

Making the Integrated Enterprise Work

THE ARTHUR D. LITTLE FORECAST ON INFORMATION TECHNOLOGY AND PRODUCTIVITY:

Making the Integrated Enterprise Work

Norman Weizer

George O. Gardner III

Stuart Lipoff

Martyn F. Roetter

Frederick G. Withington

John Wiley & Sons, Inc.
New York • Chichester • Brisbane • Toronto • Singapore

Unless otherwise noted, all figures have been provided by
Arthur D. Little, Inc.

Library of Congress Cataloging-in-Publication Data
Weizer, Norman.
     The Arthur D. Little forecast on information technology and
  productivity: making the integrated enterprise work / by Norman Weizer.
        p.   cm.
     Includes bibliographical references and index.
     ISBN 0-471-52511-1 (alk. paper)
        1. Information technology.   2. Industrial productivity.
     3. Industrial management.   I. Arthur D. Little, Inc.   II. Title.
  HC79.I55W45   1991
  004—dc20   90-46325
                                                                  CIP

Printed in the United States of America.

91 92 10 9 8 7 6 5 4 3 2 1

This book is dedicated to the founders of the
Arthur D. Little Information Technology Practice

Frank L. Allen and Martin L. Ernst

whose inspiration made it possible.

ABOUT THE AUTHORS

Norman Weizer has over 30 years of experience in the information processing industry, including extensive experience in line management and program management, with three major computer manufacturers. Since joining Arthur D. Little in 1977, Mr. Weizer has been involved in technology forecasting, and the development of strategic and product plans for the participants in the information processing industry. He has also participated in the analysis, specification, and design of large data processing and office automation systems for medium to large user organizations.

Prior to joining Arthur D. Little, Mr. Weizer was a program director of Computer Sciences Corporation (CSC) where he headed a multimillion dollar military, software development, and systems integration effort.

From 1971 through 1976, Mr. Weizer was associated with Sperry Univac where he held several positions including that of Director, Software Strategic Planning. His responsibilities included the development and maintenance of the strategic plans for all Univac produced or supported software. These strategic plans and policies, upon the approval of the Univac Executive Committee, became the guidelines within which all Univac software was developed.

Mr. Weizer has also held several positions at RCA of increasing responsibility starting from senior software specialist (responsible for designing and implementing a virtual storage management subsystem), through second-level management of a group responsible for the design and implementation of the executive and communications systems of RCA's Virtual Memory Operating System (now Sperry's VS/9).

Prior to his RCA experience, he held several positions at Burroughs Corp. in computer design and development. This included supervision of the installation and start-up of the time-sharing equipment for the B5500.

George O. Gardner III is a vice president of Arthur D. Little, Inc. and a member of the Information and Telecommunications Systems Section. His major activities involve the managerial and technical aspects of planning business and engineering data processing systems.

In the area of business data processing, Dr. Gardner has helped several large banks, insurance companies, government agencies, and universities prepare computer systems development plans. These studies have involved determining current and future computing needs, assessing several potential hardware and software solutions, and recommending implementation plans. He also spent three years managing the implementation of new data centers and modern business systems for Saudi Arabia's oil company, Petromin.

Dr. Gardner has helped several large engineering and construction firms prepare their data processing plans. He has also helped design and write a system for automatic structural design that included preparation of working drawings by computer. Dr. Gardner has also assisted several large manufacturing and chemical companies in determining ways to upgrade their support for R&D, scientific and engineering computing.

In addition to his work for computer users, he has completed several assignments for computer manufacturers. These assignments have involved market studies or product evaluations for new hardware and/or software offerings. Recently, he has done technical and market studies for engineering workstation providers and for super and near-super computer manufacturers interested in the university, R&D, and financial marketplaces.

Stuart J. Lipoff is a member of the professional staff of Arthur D. Little's Electronic Systems Section. He is a communications systems engineer with a broad background and exposure to a wide variety of technologies and industries. He has assisted clients in interpreting and applying technologies in activities ranging from conceptual studies to detailed implementation of products.

Prior to joining Arthur D. Little, Inc., Mr. Lipoff was section manager at Bell & Howell Communications Company and project engineer in Motorola's Communications Division. At both companies, he had project design responsibility for land, mobile walkie-talkie and paging products.

Martyn F. Roetter has 15 years of experience in consulting in the fields of information and communications technology and services on behalf of users, suppliers, and regional and international policy-making authorities in North America, Europe, and the Far East. He is currently co-manager of Arthur D. Little's global consulting practice with companies in these industries. He was previously employed in the establishment of the company's information technology consulting practice in Europe following several years of experience in the Electronics and Telecommunications Sections in the United States.

Dr. Roetter was educated in England, Germany, and the United States and holds a doctorate in physics from the University of Oxford. He has lived in the United States and several European countries, and speaks English, French, and German. He has broadcasted and spoken at major conferences on communications and information technology in both Europe and North America.

Frederick G. Withington is an independent consultant to vendors and users of advanced information systems. He applies his 35 years of information system experience to analyses and forecasts of information processing technology and management.

From 1960 to 1986, he was employed by Arthur D. Little, Inc., for the last six years as vice president of Information Systems.

He participated in consulting studies for over 200 of the firm's clients, which included virtually every kind of vendor and user of data-processing products and service. The majority of these studies involved forecasting future information technology. For 20 years, he was responsible for the company's annual reports, assessing and forecasting the data processing industry.

Mr. Withington has written four books and over 70 articles and papers on data-processing markets, technology, and management. Variously translated into eight languages, these have been published in most parts of the world.

Among his professional activities, Mr. Withington has been a Visiting Professor at Harvard Business school, a Trustee of Educom, Inc., a member of the Executive Council of the Society for Information Management, an Advisor to DATAMATION magazine, and a director of Addison-Wesley Publishing Company. He has also served on several federal government review boards.

Prior to joining Arthur D. Little, Inc., Mr. Withington was with the Burroughs Corporation for four years in product planning and marketing support roles. Before that he spent three years at the National Security Agency as a programmer and programming supervisor.

FOREWORD[*]

Technology decisions have never been easy, even for the experts. Just forty years ago, a boardroom debate over a major computer expenditure pitted John von Neumann against Albert Einstein. While the scale of the project (a few hundred gates and scarcely more than a dozen words of memory) appears miniscule by today's standards, the debate itself ran along familiarly modern lines. Neither side had any hard information beyond the system's initial cost and performance specifications. Despite the remarkable credentials of its members, the board voted on little more than gut feelings alone. Von Neumann's optimism was pitted against Einstein's worries about duplicating existing facilities. After all, Einstein pondered, with three comparable machines already in operation in the United States alone, and a fourth under construction in Europe, who could find profitable uses for all those extra computing cycles? In the end, von Neumann's view won out.

Now, with two generations' worth of technology growth and more than one trillion times as much computing power at our disposal, decision making has become far more demanding. Obliged to provide costly services under trying circumstances, and with few objective cost/benefit measures to go by, today's corporate executives must combine technological vision with good business sense as

*Note: The author, Arno Penzias, author of *Ideas and Information*, received the Nobel Prize for Physics in 1978. He is currently Vice President of Research at AT&T Bell Laboratories.

they strive to lead their organizations into the future. Managers need all the help they can get. This timely book provides much of that needed held by alerting its readers to the technological surprises that may lie ahead.

For instance, with supercomputing power and high-speed data access available at the desktop, distributed networked computing will provide a unique platform for new applications. The electronic networking of paper documents appears ripe for integration with mass storage, database technology, and even optical character recognition. As a result, paper documents may soon blend smoothly with other information modalities in the orchestration of work flows.

The authors predict that by the middle of the decade, "the typical PC will evolve into an interface device between a worker and a network of resources." This business workstation will intermediate between human users and a host of cooperative processes and communications capabilities. These systems will accommodate documents, speech, video, text, data, images, and graphics in any combination with the same transparent ease.

The forecasts at the heart of this book span the web of information technology, from semiconductors to supercomputers, from system architecture to applications software, from communications networks to human interfaces. The predictions of the five collaborating authors are fused into a single perspective that leads the reader beyond the technology and into working environments. If there is one message here, it is that in the mid-1990s, organizations will, for the first time, have the tools to build a truly integrated enterprise.

How do you get there from here? Even though the challenges that major corporations face resemble one another on a global level, no two organizations face exactly the same set of implementation problems. As companies strive for greater productivity from human and capital resources, as well as strategic advantage over competitors, they face a complex array of technologies from which to choose.

This book offers help in the form of benchmarks rather than recipes; instead of predicting where your company should be in 1995, its chapters preview the position your technologically aggressive competitors may occupy at that time. The choice of keeping up with the leaders or trying to break out in front, rests with each decision maker. For example, while software techniques such as object-oriented programming will make code-generation processes faster and more cost effective, progress will remain uneven. The authors note that "by the year 2000, many developers will turn to integrated CASE tools and dialects of programming languages such as C++ and Prolog. Still, significant use of Cobol will last into the twenty-first century."

Within the general trend toward the benefits of fully integrated information systems, a variety of architectural options present themselves. To provide every information worker with desktop access to computing through a business workstation, today's simple LAN connections must evolve toward more powerful architectures, such as the client server model, embedded in a layered networking hierarchy as described in the text.

No summary can do justice to the number of topics covered and trends analyzed in this book. The authors do not shrink from making flat predictions when they see themselves on firm ground, as in their views of hardware outcomes. On the other hand, they avoid the temptation to gloss over vexing issues that straightforward extrapolations of present-day technology cannot resolve, such as the lack of a scientific basis for allocating the cost of providing data networking services.

The technology chapters will appeal to the technology implementers within the systems departments of corporations, while the first three chapters offer valuable insights into the upper echelons of management in and out of the information systems. Here the authors dissect the fads of the day, such as the call for a technology-driven revolution in business. This book argues for evolutionary, low-risk technology planning. It is a vision that should appeal to any chief executive concerned with the capital spent on the route to the future.

In keeping with this balance of optimism and realism, the final chapter opens with a provocative list of technologies that similar books would have missed at the start of each of the three preceding decades. What new developments, they ask, are we overlooking today? The trends and projections contained in this book offer the reader a firm base from which to address these questions.

Arno Penzias

PREFACE

The time is the mid-1990s. You are crawling down the interstate (traffic hasn't improved over the past five years) after a long business dinner with your field service managers. Your car phone rings and its display shows that one of your company's most important customers in Japan is on the line. Your office communications system has prescreened the call, found it to be one you are willing to accept at any time, and automatically forwarded it to your car phone.

You answer the call—it is the president himself, whom you met on your visit to Tokyo last year when you signed the deal to be their primary supplier. He tells you that fire has struck his largest plant, knocking it out of commission. He needs all of the parts that were scheduled to be shipped to that facility diverted to another. He also needs an additional emergency shipment sent to the working plant to make up for the parts destroyed in the fire.

Pulling over to the side of the road, you open your briefcase and use the computer inside to access your corporate database through a cellular radio link. You identify yourself to the system with your key-card and PIN number. The system then knows exactly what information you may access and what changes you are permitted to make.

You order the system to redirect the scheduled shipments (even the ones already en route) and to send out the needed emergency parts to the customer's plant by the fastest means possible. Within seconds the system replies with the expected shipment and delivery times. It informs you that some of the needed parts are stocked in

Europe and asks if you want them shipped by international courier. It quotes the extra cost for this service.

You pass the information on to your customer and ask if he wants to pay the costs for next-day delivery. He agrees, and at the same time expresses a great deal of appreciation and admiration for the speed with which you are able to help him. He asks for a fax confirmation of the new delivery quantities, destinations and time, which you immediately transmit from your briefcase-computer.

On the road home again, you feel good about the help that you have been able to give to a good customer. You feel even better a few weeks later when this customer increases the percentage of parts that he buys from your company by more than 10 percent because of the excellent service that you are able to provide.

Science fiction? No! The technology exists today to allow you to do what was just described. But most companies have not integrated their internal systems sufficiently—nor established external links to their outside suppliers and other business partners—to permit field personnel or executives on the road to access information and take the immediate action to meet the customer's needs.

The Integrated Information System (IIS), the coming systems structure of the mid-1990s, will turn into reality what is now just technologically feasible. IIS is the name that we give to the integration of all of a company's computing and communications resources (yes, even those PCs and LANs which are springing up like weeds and are just as hard to control) into a unified structure. This single system will allow all of the information and computing resources of a company to be accessed and utilized by every employee in an organization, to the extent that he or she is authorized to do so. In most cases, a company's IIS will be linked to its equivalent in principal customers, suppliers, and other business partners.

IISs will allow busy executives and knowledge workers to get the information they need and utilize the computing resources they require as a normal part of doing their jobs. And they will not need to learn mystic incantations or become computer literate—as they often must now—to tap the enormous power at their fingertips.

Downward spiraling prices and enhanced capabilities will make such systems practical and indeed necessary for business in mid-decade. The challenge for most companies in the information systems area will be to wisely decide which technologies to invest in and how to integrate them into the normal work flow without their businesses skipping a beat.

However, the even more fundamental challenge will remain that of deciding which business objectives to pursue and how. We have now reached the point where the business "dog" can wag the technology "tail." That is, the technology can be adapted to support the way in which you want to do business. The business no longer must be overhauled—or re-engineered—just to match the technology. It will not make sense to only automate existing business procedures, whether proven effective or not, simply because information systems are now available to do so, or to introduce new procedures on the basis of the capabilities of information systems alone. It is ironic that one of the most valuable consequences of a heightened attention to the roles and benefits of information technology may be a new understanding of the real requirements for success of an organization. These will include, but certainly go well beyond, the necessary information and communication systems infrastructure.

As the technology becomes more powerful and flexible, the less must the optimum way of doing business adjust to technological imperatives. At the same time, the very power of information systems makes it more critical that those people who are ultimately accountable for the successes and failures of an organization clearly and completely understand what that organization is doing, how it is doing it, and why.

Because of the potentially immense coverage and responsiveness of information systems, the rewards which can flow from their effective application, and the damage from their deliberate or accidental abuse in conception or implementation, are immense. Knowledge and wisdom are required to determine the proper role and inherent value of information as well as the technology associated with it. Some of that knowledge, collected from our many clients over the years, is contained in this book.

The route to the world of Integrated Information Systems will not be easy. Most companies will not make the transition in five years and many will not be fully converted in ten. However, all will have been forced to start or face the consequences of not being fully competitive with their peers.

In this book we take a pragmatic view of information and communications technology. We spear the fads and show the directions of the long-term trends. We speak as businessmen as well as technologists. We understand that you cannot continue to put much of your investment capital into a technology which shows little apparent return. We also understand the business problems that technology can solve, and where the technology can assist you in simplifying and speeding-up your critical business processes.

Finally, we understand that people change much more slowly than technology. While it is true that people and organizations must adapt to the new business conditions of the 1990s, it is also true that they must fix their eyes on the business goals while their organizational and information infrastructures are being remodeled under them.

Just as in the case of renovating an existing shopping mall, where all of the stores must remain open and inviting to customers while major changes are being made, businesses must remain functional and fully competitive while the information systems are being reshaped.

Don't expect to find strident calls for a technology-based revolution in this book. We don't believe in it. What you will find is a road map for implementing an IIS, a discussion of the real capabilities that such systems and their components will possess over the next five to ten years, and a description of the business problems that such systems can solve.

The first three chapters are very business oriented. They are written with a minimum of technical jargon so that a business executive can quickly grasp the concept of the IIS, the benefits to be obtained from such systems, the issues involved in implementing them in his company, and the methods to be used in getting from here to there. We include many examples of how companies are dealing with implementing an IIS and the advantages they are already deriving from them. We also discuss the organizational, technical, and procedural problems that companies are encountering, and overcoming.

Chapter 4 forecasts the overall architecture of the IISs of the mid 1990s. It describes the essential components of the IIS, and how they will be interconnected to obtain the desired benefits. You will find that we do not forecast a "one size fits all" architecture. We envision a flexible architectural structure in which multiple types of systems are interconnected in multiple ways to meet the needs of specific parts of an organization.

Chapters 5 to 11 cover the major technologies and subsystems that go into making up an IIS of the 1990s. We predict the technological changes which will occur over the next several years and discuss how these technologies will be used to solve real business problems. These chapters are intended for the technically inclined reader. The jargon gets thick here because the forecasts must be precise enough to prevent you from going down one of the many technology blind alleys that we see opening up over the next several years.

The final chapter, number 12, summarizes the book and looks beyond the mid-1990s to some of the trends that we believe will occur into the beginning of the next century.

So whether you are a business executive, a CIO, an information processing or communications technologist, a planner or implementor of systems for an information industry supplier, we believe that there is something useful and interesting in the book for you. Settle back and enjoy your journey into the future.

But wait! Is that your portable phone ringing? Has your next major business opportunity just kicked off? Good luck!

ACKNOWLEDGMENTS

The authors would like to especially acknowledge the untiring efforts of George Harrar, without whose editorial talents this book would have remained a disparate collection of chapters written by five individuals. We also would like to acknowledge Tamara J. Erickson and Edward T. Choate, the leaders of the Arthur D. Little practices who sponsored the effort; Betsy Showstack Young who handled all of the business aspects of the publication; and Cara O'Brien and a myriad of other Arthur D. Little secretaries and graphic specialists who produced so many copies of the text and figures. Finally, we would like to thank our wives and special friends, without whose forbearance the many nights and weekends required to produce the book would not have been possible.

CONTENTS

CHAPTER 1

THE VISION OF
THE INTEGRATED
ENTERPRISE

By 1995, the much-heralded "Information Age" will finally arrive for companies aggressive enough to have taken advantage of progress in information technology.

These companies will have embedded information systems into their organizational structure as deeply as electricity or phone service. The processing that currently runs the moment-to-moment operations of airlines, banks, and stock brokerages will by then be powering manufacturers, distributors, and retailers as well.

"Information as a major strategic weapon" assumed the status of standard business principle in the late 1980s, yet most companies still do not factor future information technology opportunities into their long-term strategies. Those who overlook information technology will be ill prepared as global, information-based enterprises. To remain competitive in the new decade, companies must be well on their way in the next few years to logically integrating their total computing and communications resources into a corporate Integrated Information System (IIS).

An IIS is characterized by a single data architecture and transparently connected networks of hardware that support the competitive thrust of the company. Mainframes, workstations, departmental computers, personal computers, wide- and local-area networks can

1

form an almost seamless infrastructure that will enhance the operation of all parts of the company. Furthermore, the IIS is a practical, achievable goal—not some computer version of Detroit's concept cars that are never meant to touch rubber to the road.

The most aggressive companies will complete their internal IISs by the mid-1990s, choosing different configurations to match the structures and goals of individual business units. By linking these separate systems, the company creates the overall corporate IIS that unifies the organization. When the company extends its technological reach into both its suppliers' and customers' premises, then it truly becomes the integrated enterprise.

Early adopters of technology already use information systems to speed their processes, from basic manufacturing to report generation. Some have found considerable competitive advantage in tactical systems: McKesson Corp. with Economist, Otis Elevator Co. with Otisline, and The Chubb Corp. with its insurance product, Masterpiece.

Gaining market share through any single information-based application, no matter how innovative, was the 1980s' way of competing. One-time strategic moves simply do not confer sufficient long-term superiority. Rivals can quickly copy such systems, as United Airlines did with its Covia reservation system to match American Airlines' SABRE. Or they buy the same service. Thus, what once was strategic advantage typically weakens within 6 months into simple financial advantage. Not only *can* any application be copied, it *will* be copied by competitors, thus diminishing what seemed at first to be a knockout victory into simply a lead.

Driving organizations toward a full IIS is the recognition that greater fundamental benefits derive from an infrastructure that forges all of a company's information and communications systems into a coherent unit. Potential business improvements—eliminating layers of management and wasted executive time, taking products to market more quickly, spreading out decision making, cultivating flexible customer service—may well succeed or fail based on the enterprise-wide use of information.

To achieve success in the 1990s, a company needs a business- and technology-wise staff, both inside and outside of the information systems department, that knows how to take continuous advantage of the IIS. As Bill Friel, executive vice-president of the information systems infrastructure at Prudential Insurance Co., has observed, "It is more important to build an excellent staff than an excellent application, even if it is strategic." The staff, he recognizes, is an ongoing resource, whereas the strategic application is not. The only sustainable competitive advantage in the 1990s is the ability of a company's people to identify and seize new opportunities more rapidly and effectively than competitors.

EVOLUTION RATHER THAN REVOLUTION

Building a new information infrastructure within an existing company is similar to redesigning a shopping mall. Computers and their databases are the steel, concrete, bricks, and mortar out of which the foundation and walls are built. Networks are the electrical and telephone lines—invisible but indispensable. In a mall, key department stores, like crucial applications, anchor the whole development. Specialty shops—like niche applications—come and go according to how well they appeal to customers, their users.

An aging mall can be repainted only so often to make it appear modern. Yet the developers cannot disrupt the various units of business to reconfigure the underlying structure. Rather than closing up shop to tear down and build again, they must renovate malls gradually. So it must be with information systems.

Some suggest, however, that companies should "jackhammer" or "detonate" old systems, as consultant Michael Hammer has phrased it, then rebuild from scratch. Consultant Michael Treacy told John Hancock Mutual Life Insurance Co. to toss out systems— perhaps $1 billion worth of past investments—over this decade. He declares that fundamental innovation must be revolutionary.

Other observers and academics advise using the "information

weapon" to launch a revolution in American business, with the chief information officer (CIO) as the spear carrier. Old organizational structures must be destroyed, they say, to make way for the information-based enterprise, and old systems must be tossed onto the technological scrap heap to make way for the new.

These voices of apocalyptic change fail to see that the course of business history is much more the story of evolution than revolution. Individuals and companies are both limited in the scale and the rate of change they can accommodate. Sweeping organizational change cannot easily be implemented on the back of information technology. An Index Group study of 35 companies that attempted to do so turned up only 7 that reported succeeding. In the other 28, the fundamental transformation of processes and people that was undertaken failed to materialize into any quantifiable gain, such as market share, earnings increase, cost savings, or stock value. The lesson is clear: The development of increasingly complex information technology should be viewed as the growth of flexible, evolving organisms rather than the sudden introduction of new systems.

The corporation of the mid-1990s will continue to look to research and development, human resources, and new services as areas from which competitive advantage can arise. Information technology has joined this list and is climbing in importance, but it is myopic to declare it the major weapon of every corporation. If information systems are the absolute key to market dominance, why does it seem that every article on "Information as Competitive Weapon" begins with American Airlines' SABRE or American Hospital Supply's ASAP systems? Both are decades old. Both were designed as improvements to business processes, not as information weapons to bludgeon competitors. These companies have spent years refining their systems into what Tobey Choate of Arthur D. Little, Inc., calls "breathtaking breakthroughs." Both companies know that tactical systems evolve out of years of good business decisions and a similarly long commitment to investment, and not from sudden shifts in direction or deployment of corporate resources. AMR Corp., American Airlines' parent company, spent almost 14% ($1.225 billion) of its revenue in 1988 on information systems (IS). SABRE itself returned $134 million in earnings to AMR's bottom line.

Properly used in an IIS, information technology can be a major tactical tool, a lever that propels the company toward its business strategy. Companies such as American Airlines that cannot absorb even a few hours of downtime without serious financial losses spend millions for backup systems, redundancy, fault tolerance, and hot-site emergency support. Evolution is the only way to move such data-dependent organizations into the age of the integrated enterprise.

This realization does not diminish the importance of information systems. Gradual, well-planned changes in the next 5 years can still add up to an IIS of revolutionary effect on the way a company conducts its business.

VIEW FROM THE TOP

Just as the Integrated Information System is becoming achievable, top management is beginning to question the bill for technology, and its payoff. The visible information processing and communications budgets are jumping by an average of 10% or more per year. The actual increases are much greater because personal computer (PC) hardware, software, and related personnel costs are often camouflaged in burgeoning support budgets.

The lack of seeming benefits derived from IS is rooted in the history of every incompatible application that has been developed, patched, and enhanced over the past 20 years, and that is still being used today in most companies. The skepticism also stems from the mass of incompatible third-party commercial applications purchased by companies. Individual applications, each implemented on a different manufacturer's hardware, were originally intended to work in a stand-alone manner. In the age of integration, however, these inharmonious applications are now required to work together. They do so grudgingly, often frustrating users.

Users perceive that new applications take unreasonable amounts of time and money to implement. That is not surprising, since IS staffs spend most of their time maintaining systems, rather than developing new ones. At Mellon Bank in Pittsburgh, Management Information Systems (MIS) Director George DiNardo has said that he assigns 60% of his staff time to the upkeep of the old systems, and only 40% to developing the new. Avco Financial Services in Los Angeles has reported a backlog of new application requests measured in 19 man-years. New projects take a long time to implement because each one requires major changes to existing systems due to data or other forms of incompatibility. Even simple management reports are often difficult to obtain by an executive needing to make a quick decision.

In short, while everything in the world of information systems seems to be changing, little seems to be improving.

The questions being asked in the typical boardroom of America rightfully chill the skin of the CIO: "Where is the promised increase in productivity from past expenditures?" "Where are the expected strategic advantages?" "Why are our investments *not* producing the promised returns?" "Why is there still a 3-year applications backlog?"

Often, the CIO cannot provide satisfactory answers. Analysis by Morgan Stanley & Co.'s Stephen Roach puts white-collar productivity growth in the service sector at under 1% annually for most of the 1980s. By contrast, manufacturing productivity returned to its traditional 3% annual growth rate during the same decade. The problem for American business overall is that more than 70% of all employees work in this lower productivity service sector. While productivity has languished, expenditures on information technology have mushroomed in service sector companies. For instance, the money invested in computers and communications amounts to almost 40% of total capital expenditures for finance and insurance businesses, and 35% for banks.

Faced with meager productivity gains, top managers in some companies feel compelled to slow or even eliminate the seemingly inexorable budget jumps the IS departments have become used to. This financial squeeze often leads to staff cuts, restructuring, or both. In some cases, the amount spent on information systems is merely shifted from the central IS budget to divisional units, where it can be better aligned with business objectives.

THE ROLE OF THE CIO

The concept of information technology leading change in the organization is hindered by the adolescence of information systems themselves. Computers have barely stepped out of the glassed-in back rooms. They are still misunderstood and mistrusted.

That newly created executive, the chief information officer— whether he or she carries the formal title "CIO"—is in no position to declare that the corporation must bend to the imperative of information. If trained in technology, then he or she is still learning the business side of the trade. If he or she came up through the business ranks, then he or she is still learning the capabilities of technology. In either case, the CIO is a newcomer to the boardroom, who should leave any weapons outside the door. What the CIO should take inside are complementary strategies rather than weapons.

Under intense scrutiny from the top, CIOs are being replaced almost as rapidly as marketing vice-presidents when things go wrong. According to John Davis, president of the search firm John J. Davis & Associates, Inc., the life span of a CIO averages 2 1/2 years. In a study conducted by Touche Ross & Co. in 1989, 30% of 538 CIO-level executives revealed that their predecessors had been dismissed or demoted.

The title "CIO" bespeaks control over information. Yet the position is increasingly untenable. The CIO would seem to have authority over who gets which information, how soon one gets information, and what one is allowed to do with it. However, such a position can well impede achieving a main goal of the IIS: dispersing information, processing, and communications resources throughout the corporation. Companies see little sense in hiring someone to be chief electric officer or chief telephone officer; so, too, it may not make sense to put control of an equally basic resource—information—in the hands of one individual.

In the past, the MIS chief directed all of the basic data processing that ran the corporation. As applications move into end-user departments, however, there is much less central data processing to govern. The newly anointed CIO of the last decade is, ironically, ending up with diminishing functions to rule. So often, the CIO can be found extending his or her influence into the divisions, essentially into other people's business. To avoid this problem, a few companies have decentralized information systems so far that the final act of the CIO is to eliminate his or her own position.

Some view this trend as "empowering" the managerial lieutenants with the control taken from the IS group, but such a word scares every vice-president or chief executive officer (CEO) who must act the role of captain. In the IIS of the 1990s, information should be viewed no longer as the instrument of power or control, but rather as the means to improved profitability through integration of corporate resources.

The savvy head of IS will realize that he or she is a service provider, not a control agent. "You have 100 bosses," said Carl Dill, McDonald's Corp.'s vice president of information services. "To keep them happy, you have to deal with their immediate problems while still being a visionary."

Most companies will not decentralize the CIO out of existence for one primary reason: The network is becoming more important, and someone must manage it. In the 1990s, that function may well become the principal role of the CIO, who will create the consistent interfaces and connectivity standards that enable users to access and negotiate the network. Also, the CIO will establish an environment in which applications can be added, removed, or modified to facilitate the company's business initiatives or responses to external forces, such as government regulations, without jeopardizing other applications or causing systems failure.

Maintenance and enhancement of the structural elements of the IISs, such as a company-wide transaction processing system, will remain the responsibility of the CIO. Central IS, in conjunction with a user oversight committee, will originate and maintain necessary corporate systems standards. The CIO will be in the key position to implement, monitor, and enforce cross-functional system standards, such as those involved in electronic data interchange (EDI).

Research and development of new products and services will fall primarily to data processing professionals working within the end-user functional organizations. Alternatively, end-users may sub-contract the work to central IS or to outside system integrators. In either case, end-users gain more control over the products and services developed.

In the midst of unsettling organizational change involving his or her responsibilities and status, the CIO must hold on to a long-term perspective. However, a chief executive demanding results from technology investments does not want simply to hear the promise of future returns. He or she wants results this quarter, as well as the promise of them in the future. Therein lies the dilemma for the CIO: To ensure a sound technology foundation for the company in the long term, he or she must construct the Integrated Information System block by block over the next 5 years. Until the structure is fully built, however, there may be no dramatic benefits to point to. Some companies, in fact, may not survive financially to see the future if all benefits from technology expenditures are delayed.

The CIO can maintain credibility for the long-term vision by choosing every opportunity along the way to implement "quick-hit" systems that deliver immediate, visible impact. For instance, a tool such as Easel (see Chapter 3) from Interactive Images, Inc., can give the appearance of integrated systems even though that reality may be years away. With Easel, a user can search and retrieve information from multiple applications and databases from a single screen. He or she makes only one request for information through a simple graphical user interface. Any service representative handling a complex business account can be made more productive through the ability of Easel to bring information quickly to the screen from any of hundreds of databases, while the representative talks with the customer. Workers get a taste of what integrated systems can do for them, and therefore actively support the long-term effort.

ADVANTAGES OF AN IIS

In the 1980s, computers primarily processed text and numbers. In the 1990s, image and voice will become common on networks, allowing human communication to take the form most natural to the message and most comfortable to the user. According to IBM estimates, 95% of information used by the average business is not yet coded and, therefore, not manipulable by computers today. Image processing and multimedia applications are aimed at this huge, hard-to-handle amount of paper-based information.

Information is a basis of all decisions. The flow of raw data out of which information is built increases at a phenomenal 30% annually at some companies, such as Du Pont Co., which spends about $1 billion annually on systems to access, control, and use data. An IIS can facilitate the movement of important information, whatever its form or amount, to executives by significantly cutting the delay of review and handling.

Faster decision making contributes to a quicker introduction of new products, which can lead to increased profits. In the late 1980s, Xerox Corp. realized that the only way it could compete against Japanese companies in making photocopiers was to compress time to market by 50%. One economic model explores the tradeoff of bringing a product to market late but on budget versus on time but over budget. High-tech products delivered 6 months late earn 1/3 less profit over 5 years, according to the McKinsey & Co. research. Products delivered on time but 50% over budget diminish profit by only 4%.

Clearly, information systems can maximize a bottom line when they are part of the corporation's time-based competition philosophy.

In a typical company today, it may take 3 weeks of moving paper to effect a price cut to match a competitor, and 5 weeks to propagate an engineering design change to correct a defect. Such time scales will seem glacial to aggressive companies in the mid-1990s.

Even mundane administrative matters, such as travel authorizations, hiring requests, and expense reports, can cut into the productivity of an organization when paper is the medium. At Hughes Aircraft Co., "The cycle time for documents is horrendous," admitted Peter Donaghy, designer of a new forms-routing system. The prototype electronic system aims to automate the document review and approval process, then eventually extend to all 15,000 electronic mail users spread over 275 buildings in southern California. "We believe that the increased efficiency will be so shockingly large that we won't have to cost-justify it document by document," Donaghy said.

A simple purchase order can take a week to process in many companies. Most of that time is consumed by the paper's traveling in a mail cart from one office to another. In an electronic purchase-order (PO) system, as soon as one individual approves the PO, it can be moved into the next approver's electronic "in box." This setup allows all sign offs to be obtained within a few hours, even when the approvers work miles, or even states, apart. The time saving can be justification enough; however, the system also can reduce the number of local personnel whose major function is to approve routine requests.

The equivalent of paper in the office is people in a warehouse. Ford Motor Co. found that 70% of the work done in its huge parts distribution centers involved people walking to various bins and picking out items. In 1987, the company applied information technology, such as bar-code scanning, automated carousels, and central mainframe databases, to transform the process, not just simplify it. Conveyer belts move the parts from stock shelves to traveling carousels, which in turn take the items to the shipping area. The system virtually eliminates the time workers formerly spent walking, keeping paper records, and keyboarding information. Ford also eliminated 600 jobs and 1.5 million square feet of inventory space while increasing shipping volume at its eight distribution centers by 45%, and cutting rush-order delivery from 72 to 48 hours.

In the communications arena, the standard business card can no longer accommodate all of an executive's "address"—his or her postal address, voice telephone number, voice mail number, FAX number, Email identifier, telex number, car phone number, and perhaps internal corporate phone extension. Each locator allows a person to receive and send communications under different conditions in the particular format that suits the message. The IIS will help to coordinate these forms of communications so that an individual will be notified of and be able to receive all forms of communication at his or her "desk," wherever it may be—at a company location, on the road, or in a home. The system will determine the appropriate form of communication and automatically make the necessary connection.

On a broader scale, international companies such as General Electric Co. and Du Pont are extending integrated networks around the world. In December 1989, General Electric switched to a private network designed to provide voice, data, and video services to offices in twenty-five countries. Du Pont considers its global network "the nervous system for the whole corporation." General Motors Corp. announced in May of 1990 that it would link its 9,700 American dealers by 1992 into what it called the world's largest private satellite network.

As information spreads throughout the enterprise in distributed databases, electronic mail, and universal file sharing, each part of the corporation more easily sees the inner workings of the others. In this way, each worker becomes more reachable and more able to reach. Each person's role becomes more understandable to others. Instant communication allows professionals to go beyond their specific departmental functions and feel more a part of a single corporate entity. Work teams can form and dissolve, reform and dissolve again, in combinations of members spanning functions, buildings, even countries. These teams, rather than being collections of specialists, are dynamic groups of pragmatists, people who must think of themselves foremost as bankers, auto makers, or retailers more than as financial analysts, design engineers, or marketers. The pragmatists bring their special expertise to the mix, but their understanding of the broader context is what enables the company to act as a whole.

A COMPANY OF PRAGMATISTS

Some believe that the organization of the future should divide into specialists who each play their part as in a symphony orchestra, eyes upon the conductor's baton. They know the score and what the music should sound like, but no player takes responsibility for any but his or her own notes. The violinist does not know how to coax music from the trumpet or the keys of the piano. He simply runs his bow across his violin night after night, doing his job as he expects others to do theirs.

In the true Integrated Information System of the mid-1990s, technology will not only permit but demand that each member of the team go beyond his or her narrow specialty. Each person must understand the roles of other team members and take responsibility for their success, because it is his or her organization's success as well. The human "nodes" on which the networked enterprise depends must be able to generate actions and send understandable signals to other nodes, as well as simply respond to stimuli emanating from a corporate conductor. The information-driven organization must be interactive, not simply reactive.

The traditional corporate structure, which disenfranchises most workers from taking responsibility for inventing means to accomplish a company's ambitious ends, is not challenged by the orchestra model. Even where middle ranks are thinned, the hierarchical model still frustrates innovation in favor of, at best, incremental improvements that fit current conventional wisdom as seen from the top. The challenge in achieving the information-driven enterprise is to establish and nurture peer-to-peer relationships within the hierarchy in order to stimulate creative ideas. The environment must provoke people throughout the organization to invent new forms of competitiveness. This challenge cannot be met by a company of autonomous specialists, however brilliant the individual players.

The hierarchical chain is, of course, being broken as many organizations decentralize and flatten. The new information infrastructure will indeed enable slimming the levels of middle managers, but not devastating them, as some predict. Each level of management views and understands the company and its markets differently. Mid-level managers possess both functional and technical expertise. They do not simply act as filters for information heading up or down the corporate structure. In fact, they combine information with their intimate knowledge of products, services, and manpower to make important localized decisions. They pass those decisions up to executives who are thinking on a more strategic, enterprise-wide level, and down to workers who lack the experience and insight to decide for themselves.

The number of employees per manager will grow up to 20 to 1 or more, depending on the industry. The well-designed information infrastructure will provide technical or entry-level workers with much greater insight into the whole enterprise and more information about their own jobs, reducing their need to seek understanding from a supervisor. Thus, the lowest level of management, the caretaker supervisory posts, can be eliminated.

In those companies still maintaining eight or nine layers of management, improved information flows will lead to weeding out those managers whose control spans only two or three people and whose jobs are primarily repackaging data for others to act on. As these middle managers are erased from the organizational chart, their support staffs will disappear as well.

Beyond a certain point, however, eliminating intermediate-level supervisory positions produces an anorexic organization starved of its muscle as well as the nutrient ideas that it needs to generate initiatives. Most middle managers spend from 35 to 70% of their time doing valuable individual contributor work, not simply overseeing others or repackaging information. Thus, several ranks of these managers will be necessary, in part to handle scheduling, personnel matters, and planning for the larger groups of people for which they are responsible. These direction-setting and "human factors" matters will not disappear simply by a change in the way information is used.

Then, too, CEOs will not entrust profit-and-loss responsibility to specialists in the divisions. The business units must be run by generalists who are learning how to run all functions of the enterprise, for where else will the company turn when it seeks to replace its president? In a hospital, the chief of staff does not train for the position by spending 25 years as a doctor. Longevity does not prepare the first violinist to take over as conductor. The professor's classroom lectures do not provide the skills to run the university. In all three cases, so often cited as the models for the future, the head of the organization trains for the position outside of the profession itself.

This arrangement cannot apply, however, to profit-making companies. There is no other place for an executive to learn the business other than in the business. The models for the nouveau information-based enterprise—the hospital, orchestra, and university—fail to capture the realities and subtleties of business in the 1990s.

Corporate effectiveness hinges on cross-functional cooperation, understanding, and communication. Companies must cultivate the bonds among pragmatists across the organization, not the straight links of specialists to a single director. Japanese companies have achieved substantial competitive advantage by ensuring close ties between product development and manufacturing. Engineers incorporate consideration of manufacturability into their designs from the concept stage because in many cases they have actually worked for a time in a production plant. They have seen beyond their specialty. Rotating fast-track executives into different business areas can help break down barriers, but it will not be enough to train a specialist for the role of CEO. Generalists are needed to assume responsibilities for guiding the information enterprise, and it is from the ranks of middle managers that they will grow.

CHAPTER 2

THE EVOLUTION OF
THE INTEGRATED
SYSTEM

The Integrated Information Systems of the mid-1990s will be the culmination of systems evolution over the previous 40 years (Fig. 2.1). That is not to say that information technology has progressed along the simplest, quickest, or most desirable route to

Figure 2.1   Functional Evolution and the Integrated Information Systems

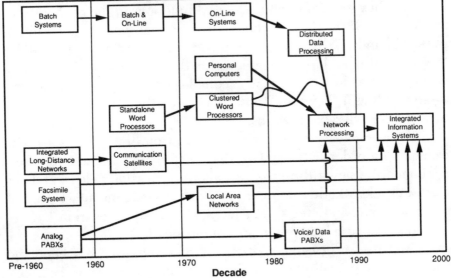

Figure 2.2   Evolution of Application Solution Functionality

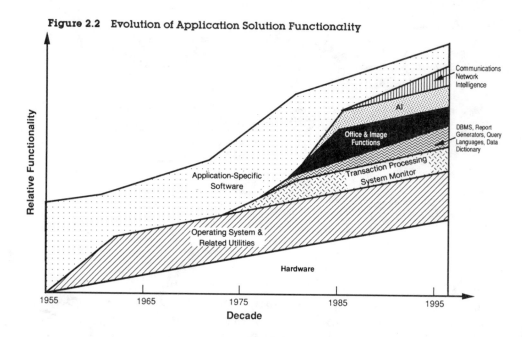

integration. The various components—telecommunications, local and wide-area networks, software, and hardware—matured separately as they were applied to isolated functions in the corporation. In the late 1980s, these technological siblings were bonded into a physical family. What remains to be done in the early 1990s will be the trickiest part: logically integrating the components so that they will work as a unit. This task is so complex that many companies will avoid tackling it; however, those that avoid the challenge will also miss the considerable rewards.

The complexity of integration arises from several sources. For example, an order entry system that once merely accepted and totaled an order now fills in the customer information fields; validates credit; checks whether items are stocked; triggers manufacturing, if necessary; and initiates shipment. Such an expanded role has required a dramatic increase in program code.

But an even greater contributor to complexity has been the incorporation of utility software systems into the fabric of the application. Operating systems, database management systems (DBMS), and transaction processing systems already have been absorbed into the function (Fig. 2.2). Over the next 5 years, office automation, AI, desktop publishing, intelligent networks, and document image processing systems will likewise be knitted into the general application environment.

ARCHITECTURE AND FUNCTIONALITY

By the mid-1990s, large companies will implement IISs embodying the overall architecture shown in Figure 2.3. This configuration is network- rather than mainframe-centered. Because communications networks are ubiquitous, there are no "islands of automation." Although the glass-house systems located in major complexes retain more importance than other computer systems, application programs run at all locations. Up-to-date data are simply a button press

Figure 2.3   The Integrated Enterprise of the Mid-1990s

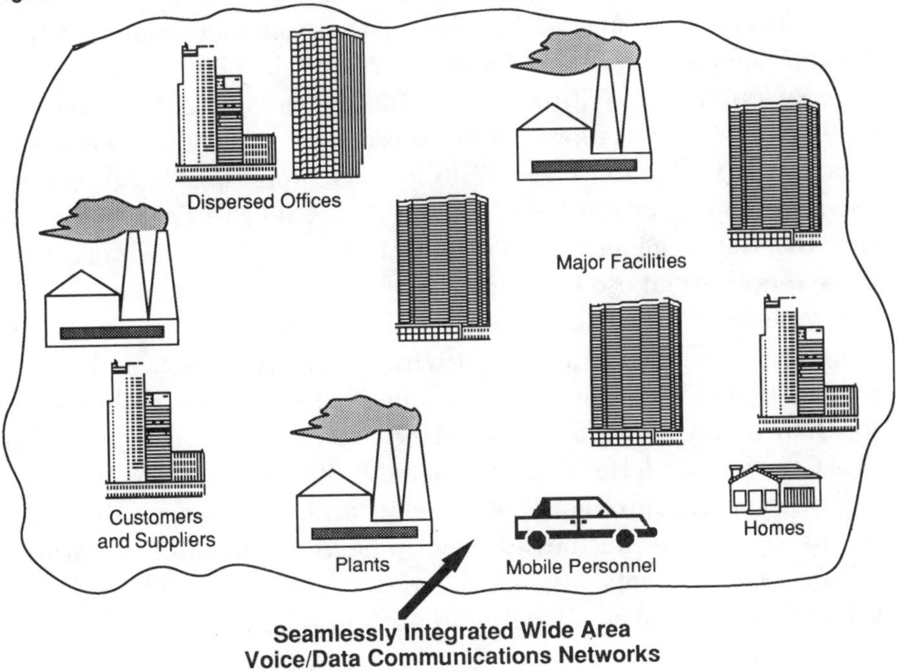

Dispersed Offices

Major Facilities

Customers and Suppliers

Plants   Mobile Personnel   Homes

**Seamlessly Integrated Wide Area
Voice/Data Communications Networks**

away for those authorized to obtain the information, no longer weeks away, buried in a welter of insignificant computer printout.

Aggressive companies of any size will closely integrate portions of their systems with those of customers and suppliers. Levi Strauss & Co. already has taken a giant step in that direction in deploying LeviLink. This integrated system was designed in the mid-1980s to speed and simplify the ordering, stocking, receiving, and invoicing of Levi Strauss' products. LeviLink pretickets merchandise with bar codes so that retailers can display the clothing without tagging it themselves. This innovation alone saves retailers 3 to 14 days in the time it takes to display products for purchase. LeviLink generates electronic packing slips that arrive before a shipment, giving retailers advance notice of coming merchandise. The packing slips double as electronic invoices, thus reducing paper handling. Additionally, the system automatically tracks sales to quicken reorders. To accomplish these tasks, LeviLink incorporates bar-code scanning, electronic data interchange, point-of-sale data collection, and electronic funds transfer.

Most of the country's 12,000 apparel manufacturers are $20 to $30 million founder-run businesses that are reluctant to buy into new ways of operating. With a budget for technology and the taste to match, Levi Strauss tailored business processes to meet the needs of its retailers, as well as to its own best interests. More than 3,500 retailers use some aspect of the LeviLink services. CIO Bill Eaton estimates that the system generates 20% more business for Levi Strauss from those retailers that use LeviLink than from those that do not.

Another retailer, Dillard's Department Stores, shocked its suppliers in the summer of 1989 by giving them until February 1, 1990, to hook into electronic data interchange (EDI) or find another outlet for their merchandise. In July of 1990, the CEO of Sears Merchandise Group sent a letter to an estimated 5,000 suppliers saying, "EDI will become a requirement for doing business with Sears." EDI—the means by which businesses electronically communicate orders, billing, and payments—is considered so important by Dillard's executives that they risked alienating their 800-plus suppliers.

FAx has become
` Poor Man's EDI ´

Du Pont connects to 800 customers and suppliers through **EDI**, and can be reached by 2,000 firms through electronic mail. The company has even opened up its technical databases to some customers seeking product information. Wal-Mart Stores may surpass any company in the number of standard **EDI** trading partners, with more than 1,800.

DOWNSIZING SYSTEMS

Most aggressive corporations are already facing the issues involved in planning and implementing their future IISs. One major concern is downsizing. Many mainframe-based applications are too cumbersome to be effective in today's rapidly changing business environment. Two- to 3-year backlogs exist everywhere for new systems as well as enhancements. Maintaining current systems can absorb 60 to 75% of the IS staff's time. A staggering 80 billion lines of Cobol code may be running in American businesses, all patched, repatched, and patched again.

The price–performance disadvantage of mainframes (despite the rampant deep discounting) encourages the implementation of new applications on minicomputers and personal computer (PC) networks. User acceptance of local-area networks (LANs) and the adoption of high-speed workstations have accelerated this downsizing.

Echlin, a $1.3 billion automotive parts manufacturer, switched from a single mainframe to networks of PCs over a 3-year period. Enhancing end-user applications was a major goal, along with reducing the size of the IS department. Ironically, end-users opposed any change, while IS supported the downsizing.

Eastman Kodak Co. is moving its critical applications to LANs more slowly. The $18 billion multinational corporation is targeting the year 2000 as the date by which it can fill orders, bill customers, and do most office work on PC networks, rather than on more expensive mainframes and minicomputers. Kodak's go-slow policy stems from a technical deficiency (the means to centrally manage multiple LANs in such a large company probably will not exist for 3 more years) as well as an internal organizational debate (determining how much of the support, maintenance, and management functions should reside in the business units).

Operating group managers at many companies rightfully feel that if they bear profit and loss responsibility for their units, they should control the computing and communications resources that support not only their competitiveness, but also their survival. Even some typical "mainframe bigots" (e.g., large systems application designers, analysts, and programmers) are recognizing the inherent advantages of downsized solutions, such as the new minicomputer-based application alternatives. As servers and departmental systems, minicomputers support multiple office automation and personal computing tasks, as well as departmental applications that are being produced in large numbers by third-party suppliers. Minicomputers are appearing in organizations where they have not been used before. A survey by the research firm Computer Intelligence Corp. shows that from 1987 to 1989 the average Fortune 1000 company increased its installed base of minicomputers from 34 to 63. By contrast, the number of on-site mainframes decreased slightly, from 8.9 to 8.6. Dial Corp., for example, embarked in 1990 on a 5-year conversion from a centralized IBM 3081 mainframe environment to a network of Digital Equipment Corp. VAXs. The three divisions responsible for foods, household cleaners, and personal care products ultimately will generate and control their own processing power on site.

The death knell is being sounded for proprietary minicomputer operating systems, particularly those developed by Data General Corp., Prime Computer, and Wang Laboratories. Because operating systems typically retain a strong hold on their users, however, even those from second-tier minicomputer companies may stay in use through the end of the century.

The promise of Unix as a standard operating system is being spread like the old-time gospel. Applications can theoretically be moved with little effort from one computer generation to another and from one vendor's systems to another's. Although Unix does not yet meet this potential, whispers of "soon, soon" from Unix vendors carry the fanatical believers onward.

PCs, workstations, and LANs are multiplying beyond count. Cheap MIPS (millions of instructions per second), office automation applications, personal database-based applications, shared group applications (groupware), and executive information systems promise major productivity improvements, as well as new and better services for customers.

DISTRIBUTING FUNCTIONS

Large companies will distribute several mainframe-centered complexes around their organizations, splitting the work load among them. Each should be equipped with sufficient computing, storage, and communications capacity to take over the critical functions of another in the event of a system failure. In addition, most companies will contract with "hot standby" service providers. In the event of a disaster that incapacitates the major corporate center, these hot sites will pick up the corporate mainframe computing load within minutes. Such a quick reaction can occur when the standby site is fully integrated into the company's own network and critical data are continuously updated.

Most sales offices and geographically isolated company locations will be equipped with servers and/or application-specific departmental systems with their associated LANs to handle the local information needs of the employees. These dispersed systems will generally connect via public digital communications lines to the various mainframe centers. Many new applications will be constructed in two to three parts to allow for network processing (also called cooperative processing) among several computers in the IIS: The primary interface code segment of the application will be implemented to run on a workstation; local data-related code will run on local servers or departmental systems; and data-intensive processing will be carried out on a remote, larger system, either a departmental system or a mainframe. This distribution of functions will permit faster processing of interactive applications while minimizing the hardware investment by taking advantage of the cheaper processing power embodied in the workstations.

MAJOR CENTER ARCHITECTURE

The major center complex portion of the IIS (Fig. 2.4) will be physically based on two to four tiers of computers. The top tier (central mainframes) and bottom tier (workstations or PCs) will be present in almost all companies utilizing IISs. The middle tiers, comprising departmental computers and servers, will be utilized in companies having specific business-oriented needs, such as special

Figure 2.4 Major Center Complex of the Mid-1990s

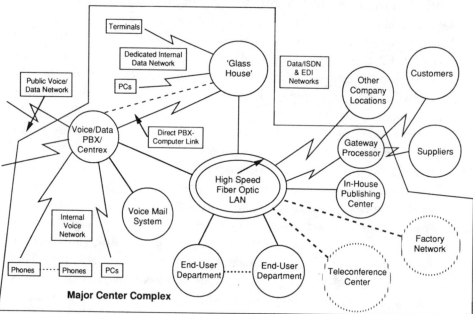

- - - - *Optional*

application systems. Hardware from multiple vendors will almost always be included. Servers will be much more heavily employed than application-specific systems.

Computer systems within a single location will be interconnected by a multilevel LAN complex and by a voice telephone network centered around a voice-data PABX or CENTREX system. The LANs will consist of the following:

- A fiber-optic, high-bandwidth backbone that interconnects the major processing and information consumption nodes in the system,
- Multiple PC-level and/or local fiber-optic (where image or engineering drawing message traffic dictates) LANs that link local workstations.

Bridges and routers will tie together the various LANs to permit communication among all workstations and computers. Long-distance public or private communications networks will connect LANs in one location to LANs elsewhere in the company. It will be possible to share information among workstations in different parts of the world almost as easily as between machines adjacent to each other. PABXs also will be used as intermediaries for accessing external electronic mail or data services.

In the mid-1990s, mainframes will serve primarily as the corporate document and information repository. Although some people call this role "database server," the name undervalues the mainframe's actual role. Most batch processing and information retrieval tasks will still be carried out by a central large system.

Many transaction processing applications, however, will move to application-specific departmental computers. Most of the current time-sharing applications will move to workstations. Nevertheless, growth in mainframe MIPS will continue into the mid-1990s, averaging about 20% per year for the average U.S. company, less than the traditional 25 to 45% growth rate in MIPS capacity by U.S. companies. Aggressive companies will increase their MIPS capacity somewhat faster than 20%—by an additional 5%, perhaps—

because of their support of workstation applications that also have mainframe components.

Advanced companies by mid-decade will operate "lights-out" computer centers in which processors and direct-access storage devices (DASDs) run unattended. Input and output peripherals will be located remotely, near the users. Archival media will be delivered electronically to backup sites. Control consoles will reside centrally, often near network control consoles. Lights-out centers will house mainframes and application-specific departmental systems, while servers will be on user premises. Lights-out centers will be facilitated by the use of fiber-optic channels and will foster responsiveness, efficient use of staff, and security.

Two types of small- to mid-range shared systems will be used in IISs of the mid-1990s: servers and application-specific departmental systems. Microprocessor-based servers (Fig. 2.5) will normally employ high-end business workstations or workstation-derived systems. These systems will act as LAN hubs; local document-processing

Figure 2.5 Server System of the Mid-1990s

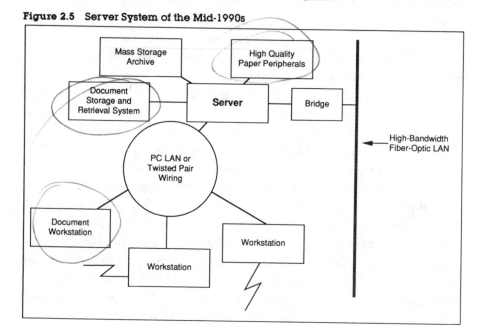

input stations and repositories; local electronic mail hubs; attachment points for high-cost peripherals; and local repositories for calendars, schedules, and so forth. Most of the work to be handled by these servers will be infrastructure related rather than application specific.

The larger application-specific departmental systems (Fig. 2.6) will be purchased primarily to serve a community of interest around a single application that is not necessarily prescribed by organizational boundaries. Manufacturing and engineering, for instance, might join a community of interest around a product design. That is why the adjective "application specific" applies better than the more common "departmental" systems. In addition to their primary application, these systems will carry out all of the functions of the servers, especially when directly connected to workstations.

Workstations will absorb an increasing percentage of the overall work load over the next 5 years, primarily in the form of local

Figure 2.6   Application-Specific Departmental System of the Mid-1990s

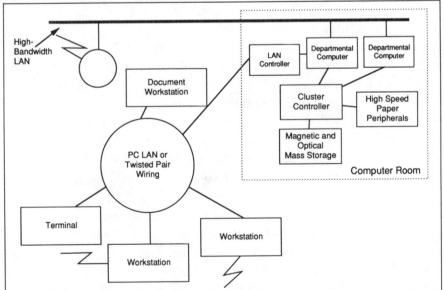

PC-level applications and the response-time sensitive portions of larger applications.

SYSTEM SOFTWARE

By the mid-1990s, IBM's System Applications Architecture (SAA) will be adopted by the majority of users and supported by most third-party software suppliers. To attain their backing, however, IBM will modify its proprietary products and standards so much that SAA will resemble the open standards of the time.

The major changes in systems software (Fig. 2.7) will be evolutionary—improving existing systems in user friendliness, self-measurement and self-management, security, and self-protection.

Mainframes will almost always use MVS/ESA; by mid-decade, its advantages over earlier operating systems will be overwhelming. DB/2 will be the most common database manager, but users satisfied with the structure of IMS will continue to use it to achieve high throughputs. When they do, they will employ a bridge to the structured query language (SQL) intercommunication standard.

Departmental systems will often be based on superminicomputers, but they will usually be application specific (i.e., contain the application programs and files for an application or region, but interoperate with the network). IBM's AS/400 product line probably will be the most widely used, despite the continued growth of Unix.

Servers provided to the entire organization as part of the centrally controlled network will usually employ OS/2 (probably as LAN manager as well as operating system), and its version of the DB/2 Database Manager. These two products will be the primary server system programs of SAA.

Servers in non-IBM environments, as well as those in IBM environments that have been brought into the organization without central MIS support, will most likely employ Unix as their operating system. In fact, Unix's use in servers will represent its major inroad into business information processing, except in Europe where the operating system will be heavily employed in business application

Figure 2.7 System Program Use in Typical Manufacturing Company in the Mid-1990s

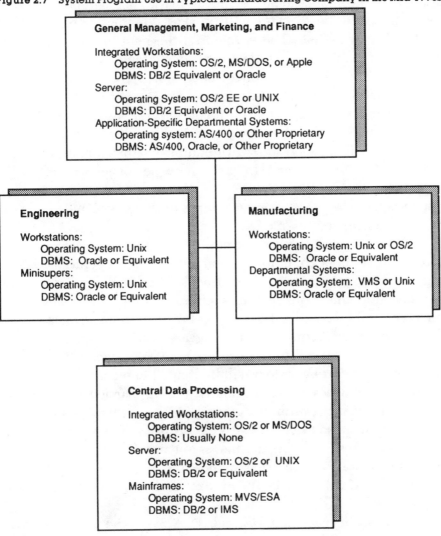

processing. Because few, if any, applications in U.S. companies will be implemented on this class of system, any operating system incompatibilities, except those relating to data communications, will be inconsequential.

Although the majority of PCs will use OS/2 as the operating

system, for a combination of technical, marketing, and political reasons, the evolution to OS/2 will be slow. Foremost, no important application in the late 1980s required the multitasking and other advanced capabilities that OS/2 provides. Many users of PCs will remain indefinitely at the spreadsheet, word processing, and electronic mail level of use. Secretaries and clerical personnel, for example, do not need the capabilities found in OS/2, or in Unix for that matter. Planners, therefore, will find it difficult to justify the expense of providing such staff with equipment that supports the advanced operating systems. In fact, these personnel will often be supplied with "hand-me-down" PCs that cannot support the new applications. Therefore, many machines in the early 1990s will still run evolved versions of MS/DOS.

OS/2 will form the basis of new multimedia applications which combine sound, video, graphics, and data in their operation. Training, sales presentations, and executive information systems are now envisioned as the major uses of such applications, but many other purposes will be found as the systems become commonly available.

As more cooperative processing applications appear that require SAA compatibility, the use of the Apple Macintosh with its proprietary operating system will be limited to settings in which its distinct capabilities are particularly useful, particularly desktop publishing and other primarily graphic environments. The incompatibility of Macintosh machines with the majority of PCs in the organization will cause a problem when a Macintosh user wants to pull down a cooperative processing application. Switching to a different, compatible PC will often be the only means for the user to access the application.

Database management systems (DBMSs) of the mid-1990s will possess significantly greater distributed database capabilities than those of today. These capabilities will be delivered in three forms:

1. Within the DBMS itself, which permits queries to be automatically passed among cooperating databases until the data necessary to answer the queries are found.

2. Within application programs that are built in the form of distributed cooperating processes based on geographically segmented databases (usually under DB/2 or Oracle). These applications will have a database allocation and segmentation algorithm built into them and have the ability to parse queries into a form in which data from the various databases can be combined to answer the original queries. The IBM SAA Distributed Data Management (DDM) architecture with its OS/2 Query Manager and mainframe-based QMF compatibility will assist significantly in the development of such applications.

3. Within the improved resource-sharing infrastructure provided by IBM's evolved Advanced Program-to-Program Communication (APPC) facilities and Apollo's Network Computing System (NCS) facilities, which permits sharing of resources among several geographically distributed computer systems on an ad hoc basis.

By the mid-1990s, advanced companies will rely on all three types of facilities; however, most companies will make some use of the first facility and be at the point of developing applications that tap the potential of the other two.

INFRASTRUCTURE APPLICATIONS

Most office automation functions will be integrated into the infrastructure of the various systems by the mid-1990s. Mainframes and their associated communications controllers will generally act as hubs for document storage and retrieval systems, electronic mail networks, and corporate-wide databases. PABXs will serve the same function for the voice mail systems. Departmental systems will contain local calendars, project schedules, and local databases, and will control local electronic mail systems. Where workstations are connected directly to the mainframes, the latter will also take on the normal departmental system functions.

Electronic mail systems will be hierarchical in nature, taking on many of the characteristics of the U.S. mail system. Most corporations will set up corporate-wide addressing and routing schemes. Although a great deal of discussion will have taken place about a universal addressing scheme, most likely based upon the X.500 standard, it will be only at the initial stage of implementation by 1995.

In most large companies, office automation, document image processing, AI, and perhaps information retrieval elements will be integrated into a main-line data processing application. All of these elements will be accessed through a single user interface and will be integrated into a single seamless application using Computer Aided Software Engineering (CASE) tools.

By the early 1990s, the client–server model of computing will be supported by advanced resource-sharing protocols that will allow dynamic allocation of many processing functions. Users will be able to make more effective use of the processing resources contained in an IIS.

APPLICATION SOFTWARE ARCHITECTURE

In the mid-1990s, many large applications will be designed and implemented for network processing. Applications containing program modules will operate where they are needed, in the mainframe, departmental system, or workstation. Response-time–critical functions, especially those that involve only routine editing and next-screen generation, will generally be allocated to the workstations. IBM's SAA and the other vendors' equivalents will permit modules to be allocated to systems in accordance with each specific customer's architecture. SAA will also allow modules to be moved and reallocated to meet performance, load leveling, and other customer needs.

Work-flow languages, now just starting to appear as a part of document image processing systems, may become the backbone of most complex application systems by mid-decade. These languages, and their associated run-time systems, are designed to specify and control the flow of information objects around a large IIS. They can be used to specify the movement of an electronic document through a complex processing and approval environment. Procedural language programs calls (e.g., in **COBOL, FORTRAN, SQL**), as well as actual procedural program segments, can be embedded in such systems. The program calls also can trigger one or more predefined, simultaneous, independent processes in multiple computers as a result of an individual's actions in the IIS.

Approval cycles, for instance, can be dramatically shortened and the approvers spread out geographically without incurring any time delays. In addition, by using a workflow language as the basis of an application, "paper" flows and job responsibilities can be easily altered without the need to carry out time-consuming and expensive major rewrites of supporting computer application programs.

These languages will provide one of the major new functionalities of IISs in the mid-1990s. Most other new capabilities will result from the integration of currently independent functions.

HARDWARE TECHNOLOGIES

Each large company will forge a variety of computer systems into its unique Integrated Information System. In terms of **IBM** and plug-compatible mainframes, the expected price–performance improvement is shown in Figure 2.8. The price of the high end of the 390 Series systems, which were announced by **IBM** in September of 1990, will decrease to $50,000 per **MIP** by 1993, and smaller machines (such as the **DEC VAX 6000** series) should exceed this rate of improvement. The price–performance ratio of supercomputers, which will be more widely used in the 1990s for mainstream business applications, will increase nearly tenfold. Improvements in **DASD** will be comparable.

By experiencing the cutting edge of technology in the late

Figure 2.8   Computer Price/Performance Forecast

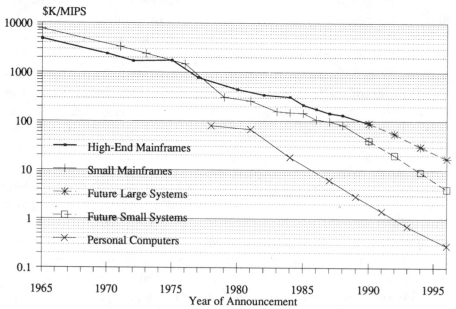

1980s, aggressive companies will have become more comfortable there in the early 1990s. Thus, they will be more willing to take greater risks on new technologies. Nonmainline systems (e.g., supercomputers, minisupercomputers, file processors, and AI-component processors) can be technically integrated into an IIS relatively easily, but it takes vision to see where they will do the most good for the business. This vision may be the CIO's, but to become reality, it must be shared and publicly backed by the chief executive officer (CEO).

Chairman Robert McDermott of USAA in San Antonio demonstrated his commitment to ridding his insurance company of paper 20 years ago. He burned files, he has said, "to show there would be no turning back." In the mid-1980s, USAA became the first test site for IBM's ImagePlus, which helped the company to stop using 99% of its original documents and retrain 160 paper-handling employees for other duties. Along with networks and expert systems, imaging reduced USAA's cost of writing policies by enabling the work of five people to be done electronically by one.

In the 1990s, the aggressive company will routinely integrate such nonmainline technologies as imaging into its overall IIS, treating them as everyday, rather than fringe, components. The steep up-front costs make such efforts risky. As John Hammitt, vice-president of IS at United Technologies Corp., has noted, however, there is no prescription, or even pattern, for gaining competitive advantage from information technology. What is needed is the spirit to try. "For the last 20 years," he has said, "our goal has been simple: Keep out of trouble. We have encouraged people to be afraid to do anything strange. We have to start rewarding people for falling on their faces so that they'll try again."

USER INTERFACES

For these systems to be usable by and useful for the average non-computer-literate worker, a much better user interface for PCs will be developed. By the mid-1990s, the Desktop Metaphor (similar to that used on the Apple Macintosh) will be the interface of choice for all workstations except those dedicated to old applications. The interface image is made up of a main desktop window upon which application windows can be placed in any position, possibly overlapping others. The command interface will also have been generally standardized, with scroll bars, window sizing, and some frequently used function keys standard across the industry.

There will be no standardization beyond this level of detail in the visual interface. Variations in interfaces will not be sufficiently great, however, to prevent users of one from easily switching to another. Changing PC interfaces now can be like trying to steer a tank after learning to drive a Mercedes. Interfaces will migrate to-ward each other sufficiently that, in the future, changing from one to the other will be like sliding behind the wheel of an unfamiliar car at night: You may fumble for a moment looking for the headlight switch, but soon you will be driving away confidently.

Two major camps will develop, one for the scientific and engi-neering community and one for the business community. Scientific users will employ interfaces based on the MOTIF (X-Windows) standard, whereas business users will choose interfaces based on the Microsoft Windows (OS/2 Presentation Manager) de facto standard. The difference between these two, although noticeable to application program developers, will seem very slight to the casual user.

By the mid-1990s, live-action sound and video will be mixed with digitally generated text and graphics on one or more of the windows in a high-end business or engineering workstation. Other advances will be much less noticeable to end users. In fact, they may notice only that their systems run a little faster, that almost all of the applications use the same controls for common functions, and that the sharing of data among individual applications has become possible and often easy.

The seamless interface will have been implemented, but only in aggressive companies. It will require a great deal of local programming to achieve and a similar investment of programming support to maintain well beyond the 1990s.

THE NETWORK INFRASTRUCTURE

To become a reality, the integrated enterprise will depend upon corporate-wide networking. In the 1990s, aggressive companies will make substantial progress toward creating networking management databases to provide a common interface to data and information, and a directory of user names and resources. Several organizations will probably implement their own proprietary designs because the sophistication of existing network management products will likely not be sufficient for their purposes, at least not before 1993. To permit flexibility and growth in the future, these companies will design their databases so that they are compatible with, for example, IBM's SAA.

Bandwidth available to users in these organizations will continue to increase as a function of applications, such as imaging and compute- and graphics-intensive workstation-based design systems. T3 (45 megabits per second) links will be in use in addition to their

T1 cousins that became popular in the late 1980s, and even higher bandwidths will begin to enter operation.

As the peak-to-average traffic flow ratio becomes much larger in these kinds of applications than in traditional networking, aggressive companies will tend to avoid fixed channels and fixed multiplexing in favor of networks that can allocate bandwidth dynamically on demand. This requirement will provide an opportunity for the major public telecommunications network operators to become more competitive against private network or leased-line alternatives than they have been in the 1980s. Their vast pools of bandwidth, when coupled to the flexibility inherent in their new Signaling System 7–based networks, should enable them to provide a level of reliability, availability, and capability of coping smoothly with peak demands that no private (or leased-line) network can match. At the very least, many organizations will be looking at hybrid public–private network solutions to satisfy their overall requirements for bandwidth, coverage, and reliability.

Aggressive organizations will also have achieved substantial progress by the mid-1990s in providing connectivity at the applications level, not only at the physical and systems levels. This connectivity will span different wide- and local-area networks that grew up in the 1970s and 1980s, such as Systems Network Architecture (SNA), DECnet, and Transmission Control Protocol/Internet Protocol (TCP/IP), as well as Ethernet and token-ring LANs. They will also have begun to make use of LANs based on the Fiber Distributed Data Interface (FDDI) standard that have significantly higher bandwidths than products more closely comparable with the speeds of mid-1990s workstations.

ALTERNATIVE WORKING ENVIRONMENTS

Demographic factors, such as low birth rates and an aging population, will combine to significantly limit the growth of the white-collar workforce in the United States over the next 5 years. Companies will compensate for the lack of personnel and reduce expenses by closing very small offices and using call forwarding to maintain the appearance of a local presence.

These factors will significantly increase the utilization of work-at-home and work-on-the-road technologies. A significant number of employees in larger corporations will work away from the office at least part of the time. A well-planned combination of all of the technologies described above will be required to support these independent people. Since many will work in the office part time in order to maintain social and business relationships, the desired home computing environment should mirror the office setting as closely as possible.

The portable workstation of the mid-1990s will actually be an "office in a briefcase." The system will include the capabilities of today's average office PC: a color, high-resolution display; 8 to 16 megabytes of RAM; more than 100 megabytes of nonerasable secondary storage; and communications capabilities to interface with corporate systems as well as to originate and receive standard facsimile messages. Optional features, such as cellular telephone, nonimpact printer, and extended-use batteries, will transform the system into an "office in a carry-on suitcase." Although compact at 4 to 6 pounds (not including printer), the basic portable will support traveling workers in the technological style to which they have become accustomed in the office.

THE CONTINUOUS CYCLE

The overall information infrastructure will necessarily grow more complex in this decade to support the integrated applications that will be required to meet a business' needs. A far richer variety of data types, emphasizing graphics, images (both moving and still), and voice, will be implemented, permitting richer forms of interaction between the system and its users.

Cost is not the issue in achieving an Integrated Information System. Almost any company can spread the investment in technology over a long enough period to make the expenditures feasible. What separates the aggressive from the hesitant companies is the vision to see where the technology can lead them, to realize the long-lasting systems benefits from their investments.

Aggressive companies also will not let security concerns hold them back. They have two possible courses: spending the corporate resources, including money and time, to secure the IIS before opening it up, or getting an open subsystem up and running as quickly as possible to capture business advantage, but isolating it. The vulnerable, stand-alone system in the latter course will be maintained separately from the company's master files until it, too, if desired, can be secured and brought fully into the IIS. Banks, for example, process ATM transactions twice, once on the less secure ATM network itself as the customer conducts business, and again at night in batch mode as the day's activities are officially posted on the master network under strict controls.   ?? Never

Of course, the evolutionary development of information systems will not be complete in the mid-1990s. By that time, even newer technology will be on the horizon, such as self-healing computers and AI executive assistants. Changing user needs and competitive pressures will fuel the demand for newer and better systems, and the overall development cycle will continue unabated.

Conservative companies will be even further behind their more aggressive competitors. Many will have been absorbed or gone out of business. Just before they close the doors and turn off the lights forever, they will shut off the last computer and disconnect the last telephone line. The IIS is not the only key to success for the integrated enterprise of the mid-1990s, but the lack of such a system will be one of the surest ways to guarantee failure.

CHAPTER 3

MANAGING THE INTEGRATED ENTERPRISE

Almost all aggressive U.S. corporations foresee the same major challenges in the 1990s. They understand the need to market their products or services globally, particularly the opportunities selling to the unified Europe of 1992. They recognize the necessity of linking themselves electronically to customers and suppliers. They know they must customize products in ever-decreasing lot sizes. They realize that technology will continue to shorten product life cycles.

Similarly, these corporations have identified the general long-range means to meeting these challenges, such as flexibility, speed, innovation and connectivity. These strategies must be based, at least in part, on a complex, reliable information infrastructure—namely, the Integrated Information System, (IIS). Each specific strategy can be supported in several ways by the IIS. For example:

- *Streamlining the business*—Universal, easy-to-use data communications, electronic mail, electronic conferencing, and databases will permit instantaneous dissemination of information as well as more effective control of geographically disbursed workers. The number of middle-management layers and information-collection groups can be reduced.

- *Responding rapidly to changing market conditions*—Closer communications-based interactions with customers and suppliers

41

coupled with more complete integration of marketing and production control systems will permit faster ramp-ups and ramp-downs of the production line and less buffer stock in the warehouse. Such tightly coupled relationships will also facilitate the rapid identification of fast and slow moving items, thus allowing companies to revise their product mix in time to adjust to market trends.

- *Responding more rapidly to customer requests*—Customer requests spend an estimated 95% of the time between receipt and fulfillment simply being moved as paper from one individual to another. Document image processing systems and other automated processes can cut this wasted time to a minimum.

- *Using resources more flexibly and economically*—Computer-based conferencing, standardized electronic information formats, and universally accessible databases will allow ad hoc project teams to form and function with a minimum of travel. These teams—which can consist of sales, engineering and industry-specialized marketing support personnel—might coalesce around a specific small proposal or broad large project. They can cooperate via electronic media to get the job done without having to suspend their current assignments to travel.

- *Innovating more quickly*—Teams of marketing, engineering, and manufacturing personnel working in parallel on the same sets of electronic files and documents will make dramatic improvements in time-to-market for most products. Every stage—product conceptualization, design, development, and manufacturing—will be accelerated through the use of electronic communication and approval facilities.

  New computer-based tools, such as significantly enhanced workstations, will improve the productivity of engineers (a must in an era in which fewer new engineers will be graduating from college) and significantly reduce the chronological time required to produce new designs.

- *Expanding breadth of product line*—Increased ease of data communications among a corporation's operating units will encourage product-line offerings that incorporate components and/or services from multiple divisions. This ability will permit companies to strengthen existing product lines or add new ones, which a single operating unit would be unable to develop and/ or support on its own.

  Easy data communications and computer-based conferencing between customer and vendor's personnel will permit the more rapid and more economical development of customized products. In addition, a vendor's relationship with its customers will strengthen, leading to increased volume and often profitability.

- *Improving total product quality*—The concept of ensuring quality in the corporate processes involved in making the product as well as in the product itself has gained currency over the past few years. Computer-based processes ranging from statistical manufacturing control to standardization of data definitions using a corporate or divisional data dictionary will go a long way to improving the quality in all corporate processes.

- *Competing and serving customers on a global basis*— Competing worldwide requires coordination among geographically scattered personnel. The IISs of the mid-1990s will allow timely, cost-effective communication. For instance, a design project being worked on in New York can be transmitted at the end of the day to a team in Tokyo, where the sun is rising. Neither group wastes any of its crucial work hours waiting for responses from the other.

  Universally accessible, distributed databases containing such information as project design and status files, inventory files, and software bug files with appropriate "work-arounds" will permit a company to service its worldwide customers more effectively.

RESHAPING THE ORGANIZATION

Over the past twenty years, information systems technology has transformed the way in which business is conducted and will soon transform the organizations as they conduct the business.

In the late 1950s, small groups of data processing "wizards" and their computers began to replace large groups of clerks in accounting departments. Since the new data processing employees almost always reported to the same vice president of finance as the clerks did, the change was generally isolated to a single department.

But as automation spread to the secretarial pool, the marketing group, the engineering department and elsewhere, so did change. It became, in effect, endemic to the function of information systems. The typist became a word processing operator; the order entry clerk became a customer service representative; the draftsman became a designer. Along with the new titles came enhanced responsibilities—and the necessity to work with computers. People suddenly found themselves handling stacks of punched cards, which they were not to fold, spindle or mutilate. Terminals popped up on desktops throughout the corporation. For the first time in more than 50 years of American business history, a new technology was introduced that could potentially affect every employee, from clerk to chairman.

In the early years, professionals and managers used electronically generated reports but otherwise were not personally involved with computers. The chief executive remained the CEO with no change in title or role. The CFO retained his financial responsibility for the corporation, but with the help of a fast-growing group of data processors.

Though they were rarely visible in the halls of upper management, information systems personnel were making an impact. Executives could not escape noticing that computers were enabling the business to run faster. For example, the monthly financial totals, which were not ready until a month after closing in the 1960s, became available within a week in the 1970s and then within a few days by the 1980s. This diminishing information delay allowed decisions to be made more rapidly. Action could be taken on problems while they were still minor, not after they had festered into major issues affecting profitability.

Then in 1981, IBM introduced its aptly named "Personal Computer," launching the PC into mainstream business use. First white collar professionals, then supervisors and upper-level managers, found box-like machines crowding onto their desks. The terms "spreadsheet," "database," and "word processing" began to be used freely in the company cafeteria. The means for the average worker to complete his job changed dramatically.

TECHNOLOGY-RELATED CHALLENGES

Throughout the 1980s, it was fashionable to decentralize corporations. "Lean and mean" and "Put the authority where the action is" were just some of the catch phrases. Using the portfolio style of business organization, many companies created autonomous units that could be easily divested if, and when, necessary. Although information technology didn't precipitate this tend, developments in the computer industry were certainly compatible with it. Of foremost importance, systems became available in small and medium sizes—at small- and medium-size prices affordable by all.

The drive to form autonomous business units has, in fact, gone too far in many instances. The financially driven compartmentalization of companies often leads to their being unable to act upon (or in some cases even recognize) the strong connections that may develop among business units as a result of changes in technology, competition, and customer demands. Compartmentalized companies often overlook:

- Technologies from consumer electronics that may later be applicable to information systems

- Benefits from corporate-wide relationships with suppliers that autonomous divisions refuse to develop
- Efficiencies from forging multi-product sales teams.

In order to overcome the territorial mindset of compartmentalized companies, different financial incentives and measurements must be used. Divisional vice-presidents must understand that their salary and performance reviews are tied to their developing a long-term integrated information architecture.

The CEO's attitude is crucial here. He or she cannot just talk up technology publicly, as so many do today, and then berate divisional managers in private for not meeting this quarter's numbers. The long-term development of an IIS may well include investments that diminish short-term earnings. The unwritten attitudes and policies are what truly govern every company—the system dynamics, as MIT computer pioneer Jay Forrester phrases it. A CEO who refuses a request for cellular phones by his regional sales managers or allows his secretary to work on an electric typewriter instead of a PC connected to the IIS sends a much clearer signal about the status of information technology in his company than any of his pronouncements highlighted in the annual report.

To observe that information technology needs a champion in the CEO is not to say anything unique. R&D, marketing, human resources and every other function can make the same claim. The CIO need not urge that information technology demands any greater attention of, or backing by, the CEO, just that it now should get equal and knowledgeable treatment after so long being ignored or treated as a necessary evil.

Peer-to-peer communications capabilities contained in IISs can play a role in breaking down barriers by fostering the kinds of interchange of information and ideas that may lead to the early identification and flowering of inter-business-unit opportunities. Once identified, such projects can be pursued by team members cooperating across departments and facilities without these valuable employees being taken away from their usual workplace and work.

Enhanced means of communications allow people to work through the concept stage remotely, giving the ideas time to germinate before formally reassigning personnel to the project.

As such networking capabilities develop, the logical or organizational architecture of a company's information systems can, in principle, be decoupled from its physical implementation. A widely distributed information processing network, for example, could be controlled in a centralized and hierarchical framework. Thus, the information technology that so often is viewed as the means of corporate restructuring is actually becoming less and less a determinant of the optimum business structure. Technology is, in fact, an enabler, not a determiner. As such, it will now support almost any structure appropriate to the business—whether a large, centralized mainframe-centered company or a downsized, distributed operation running on PC LANs.

The Integrated Information System of the mid-1990s will present quite a different set of management challenges and issues than the stand-alone systems of the past. They are:

- Deciding on investments
- Using outside resources
- Managing the transition
- Managing the architecture
- Governing and controlling
- Developing personnel.

DECIDING ON INVESTMENTS

Decisions on new information technology spending will be made in one of three contexts:

- As individual expenditures that stand or fall primarily on their unique merits and payback times
- As investments made in a corporation's overall future

- As part of the costs required to develop and offer new products and services.

Much has been written about justifying specific IS applications on their own merits. This subject is not addressed here since the predicted changes in technology and business practices will only minimally affect the validity of current methods.

Much less has been written about viewing the general IS function as part of the corporate infrastructure, like a new building or a new telephone system. These decisions often begin with a major subjective element, such as corporate image, employee morale, survival, ease of communication inside and outside the company, and overall business efficiency. Because they precipitate enterprise-wide effects, IIS investment decisions must be made for these subjective reasons, rather than by attempting to analyze precise payback.

Although such major systems proposals will always undergo financial scrutiny, they will not live or die by the numbers. Traditional or alternative accounting analysis will compare the likely cost of the system with the projected payback. Then, the expertise of a management committee comes into play. The members, drawn from the CEO's office, IS department, and major business units, will judge whether the intangible, subjective factors are likely to be worth enough to cover the spread between projected cost and anticipated payback.

Increasingly, IS investment decisions will be made in the third context—as part of the costs of developing and offering new products and services. Whether a company is creating innovative financial instruments, faster distribution channels, or new engineering-intensive products, the investment necessarily includes spending on information systems. In the mid-1990s, no product or service proposal will be considered complete unless this information technology investment is factored into the equation. Admittedly the equation becomes increasingly complex as the information technology variable is broken into its capital and expense parts. But as management grows more familiar with information processing, the financial analysis of its costs and benefits will become commonplace and spending decisions will be easier to make. A major role of the CIO in the 1990s will be to help the corporation identify and value the second-order effects of technology investments, such as customer satisfaction.

Robert Kaplan, an accounting professor at Harvard University, says all IS spending decisions fall somewhere between two extremes: a straight machine-replacement decision on the one end, and basic research and development on the other. On the machine-replacement side, costs and benefits are well known. On the research side, however, costs are typically fixed according to how much a company has available to spend; specific benefits are unpredictable. "The purpose of analysis," Kaplan says, "is to move the investment decision as far as you can to looking like a replacement decision, so that the amount we are spending on gut feel is as little as possible."

USING OUTSIDE RESOURCES

In developing the IIS of the mid-1990s, two major "make or buy" decisions will become increasingly important: hiring system integrators and outsourcing operation of facilities. System integrators may be traditional vendors such as IBM, consulting companies such as Andersen Consulting, or technology packagers such as Electronic Data Systems Corp. (EDS). They bring to bear skills and experience that even an aggressive company normally does not accumulate in-house. They are most effective at solving problems that involve multiple brands of computers and local- and wide-area networks, the specific areas that often give the most difficulty to an internal IS staff. Those integrators that provide total solutions also absorb some of the implementation risks by offering time and performance clauses in their contracts, albeit at a significant cost.

In the mid-1990s, integrators will be important resources for managers of information-intensive companies. By using outside services, companies will be able to maintain smaller head counts of highly paid technical experts. They will also be able to focus internal resources on the applications critical to the company's success, those too important to be trusted to outsiders. Integrators can be assigned relatively mundane tasks, for example, implementing a new technology, such as image processing, that is unfamiliar to the in-house staff. Companies will also turn to integrators to handle large one-time projects that would strain the company's resources.

Outsourcing, which is an offshoot of facilities management, appeared in the late 1980s. Companies contract with service providers to take over their mainframe data centers and/or corporate communications networks. Outsourcing can free capital tied up in data center hardware and save ongoing operating costs, two factors that first attracted troubled companies to the service. Annual charges are normally negotiated for a specified period, such as 5 years, which allows the user company to know precisely what its IS costs will be in the near-term future. Outsourcing makes less financial sense, when the user operates a multivendor environment or is powered primarily by less costly minicomputers.

In 1989, Eastman Kodak Co. turned to outsourcing in order to concentrate management and technical resources on the strategic, rather than utility, aspects of information processing. Kodak reaffirmed that its business was developing and selling photographic products, not trying to run four enormous, outdated data centers. The company hired IBM Corp. to operate its facilities. (IBM subsequently formed a new organization, Systems Services, specifically to seek outsourcing opportunities.)

Later, Kodak hired Businessland to support its personal computing resources and, in January 1990, turned over management of its voice and most of its data communications networks worldwide to Digital Equipment Corp. The $17 billion photographics company retained IBM to manage Systems Network Architecture (SNA) based communications, but assigned DEC to operate the underlying physical and transport layers—essentially tossing IBM and DEC onto the same field and telling them to play together, not against each other.

Kodak hopes that this unusual relationship will encourage the two competitors to move toward open systems, one of Kodak's goals.

American Standard, Inc., tried centralizing IS in the late 1980s, selling processing power to the various business units much as a utility does. Although Gary Biddle, the vice-president of information and systems technology, felt that he had achieved an efficient operation, he still chose to outsource data processing to Genix Enterprises and McDonnell Douglas Computer Systems Co. The savings were estimated to be 20 to 35%. "We got rid of the hardware," Biddle has said. Now he buys processing power incrementally, as his company needs it.

The trend to outsourcing shows that information processing facilities are becoming important, yet replaceable, commodities that do not have to stay under the direct control of the user corporation. Hibernia Corp. hired IBM to provide plug-in computer service, much as if it were buying electrical power. Merrill Lynch & Co. sought outside help from MCI Communications Corp. in 1989 to run its telecommunications services, partly because experts in that technology were more prevalent in vendor companies. On a smaller scale, JP Foodservice, Inc., of Hanover, Maryland, transferred data center and network management responsibility to Infonet. The remaining IS staff will concentrate on applications development and end-user support. In a new wrinkle on outsourcing, Dial Corp. turned over interim responsibility for its data center to Andersen Consulting while switching from a centralized mainframe to a distributed minicomputer architecture. With only so many technical resources at its command, Dial chose to concentrate its management on the complicated conversion process.

Not all operations or applications can or should be contracted to outside groups, whether permanently or not. The following model can help companies analyze the appropriate opportunities.

Information processing facilities (hardware, system software data center, operational staff, etc.) may be roughly classified into three groups based on their impact upon the effectiveness and competitiveness of the organization:

- Base—Facilities essential to being in the business, which are readily available and widely exploited by most participants in it; thus, they have little competitive impact.
- Key—Facilities well embodied in products and processes which have a high competitive impact.
- Pacing—Facilities under experimentation by a few organizations, and thus likely to have an important competitive impact.

No company can count on a technology-based advantage to endure. An essential characteristic of information processing facilities, like other technologies, is that over time they move from being pacing to key and finally to base as they become pervasive.

For example, a few aggressive U.S. banks used automated teller machine (ATM) networks to gain market share at the expense of slower moving competitors. But since all banks now can access these networks, ATMs have become an essential, or base, requirement for the retail banking business. It will take a new generation of ATMs (or perhaps self-service terminals that allow customers to fill out, for example, their own credit applications on screen) to provide another window of opportunity for innovative banks to expand—for a time— their market penetration.

Organizations should keep most key and pacing aspects of information processing under their control, applying their own human and other resources to directing facilities and applications that fall into these two categories. On the other hand, it makes economic sense to contract out base facilities.

A wide-area digital telecommunications backbone network, for example, may well be a base facility appropriate for contracting to one or more network operators. Doing so allows a user to take advantage of the greater redundancy, backup capabilities, and inherent flexibility of modern public networks. The operators of these large public networks also offer price advantages because of their economies of scale and the competition among them. Even the largest private networks lack flexibility and expandibility. If, however, the user wants to establish logical networks across the same wide-area digital backbone to improve, for example, the speed and effectiveness of product development or the responsiveness of customer service, then the organization should operate the backbone itself, since these are key or pacing facilities.

Payroll illustrates a base application for which third-party service contracting is a well-established and successful practice. However, the development and implementation of a new document image handling system, such as that introduced by American Express in the late 1980s to handle charge receipt records, should not be left solely to an outside vendor. Such systems have too large a potential for significant competitive impact in terms of cost saving and/or enhanced customer service for a company not to devote its own management and technical resources to their growth, enhancement, and modification.

MANAGING THE TRANSITION

Top managers in companies today find themselves in a state of confusion and transition in terms of their information processing organization and management. Many central information processing groups are losing much, if not all, of their application development role. End-users are demanding, and taking, control of software development for local applications, aided by information centers scattered across the company. Downsizing allows many more applications to be developed on minicomputers and PCs, a development area in which central MIS lacks expertise. Sometimes MIS abets the distribution of application development by transferring programmers into individual business units. Commercial software packages and semi-custom applications supplied by system integrators further confuse the roles of the central organization.

Kendall Co., in Cambridge, Massachusetts, set on a path of decentralizing 2 years ago that led to the decommissioning of the entire corporate IS group, including its director. The estimated savings in salaries was $500,000. Divisional IS directors have taken on day-to-day operations of the networked minicomputers, but with substantial help from outside sources. One of those sources is a new firm founded by Kendall's former IS chief.

Achieving an IIS involves incorporating some radical technologies that will not easily fit into the current systems running the company. Many organizations have taken halting steps toward integrating the new with the old. Patchwork communications link departments and divisions across incompatible technologies and products, but such after-the-fact connections cannot support a fully functioning IIS. Accomplishing a useful integration will require undoing some, but not a major amount, of what has been done.

During a transition to a different IS structure, a company is at risk. One large manufacturer in the heavy equipment industry, a leading user of information technology, fell significantly behind the state of the art as it decentralized application development responsibility. The reason can be traced to myopia in those business units that acquired the new role. When unit managers felt pressure to increase margins and lower overhead, they immediately saw software development as a place to squeeze out savings. The workforce was allowed to shrink through attrition. Any new application or technology investments that could not demonstrate payoffs within a year or so were indefinitely delayed. With few new systems or technologies coming on-line, the company soon found itself unable to match the products and services offered by competitors. It lost considerable market share before realizing that mishandling information technology was at the core of its problem.

As companies come to depend more upon information technology, making major changes in their systems will become increasingly difficult. Dry runs using test data and parallel operations will continue to work at the back end of the process. The more difficult portion will be the job redesign and staff retraining that must take place, especially when very new and different technology, such as document image processing, is introduced.

One emerging interface tool can show the immediate productivity results that management so often demands when migrating to new technologies. Easel, a product from Interactive Images, Inc., and strongly promoted by IBM, allows a graphical user interface to act as a front end to existing applications and databases. Should a customer delay the delivery date for a month on a major order, a salesman can enter the change on one graphic interface screen. Easel then conveys the change throughout the multiple sales, manufacturing, and inventory databases that are affected.

In the reverse situation, a telephone company service representative might need information spread over a dozen databases in order to respond to a customer's request to rewire a corporate campus. Easel can pull the data about available services, pricing, the customer's existing networks, etc. onto one screen.

A product such as Easel can be a major migration tool from old-style applications to the graphic user-interface based applications of the IIS. Users notice instant benefits while the long-term conversion of old applications and databases takes place invisibly in the background.

As in other areas of business, information gathering and planning will be central to preparing for the changes required to implement and effectively use the IISs of the mid-1990s. All major consultant groups and IS suppliers have created methodologies for assisting companies to go through the process. Arthur D. Little, Inc., has developed its System Information Value Analysis (SIVA) methodology for planning and implementing these major changes. The SIVA approach, like other methodologies, allows a company to determine:

- What information is required to perform various business functions
- Who performs the various functions and how they measure their achievement
- How the information should be structured and used in the future
- What overall information system architecture and technologies are required to support the business in the future.

Based on these information-use and system-architectural patterns and requirements, formal implementation plans and schedules can be developed.

In addition to a planning methodology (e.g., SIVA), CASE and CASE-related tools, such as workflow languages, can ease the transition from the old to the new architecture. Applications that are designed and implemented with modern CASE tools are easier to modify than the infamous "spaghetti-coded" systems. Almost all companies will have to redesign and reimplement some old applications that do not fit into the new architecture; however, the number will be significantly reduced when CASE tools are used.

A new form of CASE tool, similar to the workflow language used in document image processing, may be very important in the mid-1990s. With this type of tool, the control skeleton of an application can be defined and implemented independently of the actual processing code. Doing so will permit applications to be built in a very flexible form, in which processing codes can be rearranged with little effort to meet new job definitions and processing requirements. This type of architecture will allow applications to be developed with change in mind. Companies will be able to slowly alter their mode of operation by refining the application in small, incremental steps instead of overhauling it all at once.

There are three major challenges to getting ready for change:

- People—getting them to do new things in new ways
- Business—making large investments with medium- to long-term returns
- Technical—building a new infrastructure while keeping the business group functioning.

Although all of this change may sound daunting, it can be effectively implemented if executive management clearly sees what it wants the corporation to become. This vision, which is in essence a business strategy backed by a technology architecture, becomes the framework within which all information decisions are made. With the appropriate framework and leadership from top management, the necessary changes can and will be made by the aggressive companies of the 1990s.

MANAGING THE ARCHITECTURE

The architecture of the Integrated Information System—the network, the standards for interoperation of activities at its nodes, and the characteristics of the computers on it—must be managed independently of the applications it supports. Of primary importance in this regard is the selection of standards, both in-house and external, that emerge over the next few years, and the network management tools, which exist much longer than the individual applications supported.

Architecture management will be largely a technical matter delegated to a central architecture committee. But this group's decisions and plans are so important that they should be reviewed by a management oversight committee in which user representatives dominate. Most organizations will have difficulty communicating highly technical network and standards issues to nontechnical managers. The discussion must rise above the jargon and details of the technical debate so that the crucial issues can be understood by all.

An organization's overall architecture must necessarily incorporate communications, data processing, office systems, and at least part of engineering and manufacturing support. The central architecture committee should be composed of members from a relatively high level in the organization and be supported by a staff that can represent all elements. Participants should include the heads of the IS function in each business unit and the chief IS architect or planner. The CIO, or an assigned deputy, should chair meetings, which need not be more frequent than monthly, or even semiannually, because they deal only with matters that affect the architecture, not with user-specific applications.

An agenda for such a meeting might include the following:

- Discussion and approval of a preferred vendor list for suppliers of distributed database systems
- Discussion and approval of guidelines for integrating document image processing systems into the overall IIS
- Discussion and approval of revised distributed database interface standards
- Formation of a task force to investigate solutions for a major deficiency uncovered in the current architecture.

Grumman Corp. created an information resource council composed of division presidents, key users, and the company chair. This committee, which Tom Kelly, vice-president of Information Resource Management, calls "my board of directors," approves the policies and plans of the systems group. Grumman is shifting from justifying systems projects based on their abilities to meet local needs to viewing any proposed projects in terms of how they further corporate strategic goals. Current policy states that the aerospace and electronics manufacturer will become a computer-integrated enterprise based on a data-driven architecture. "To be honest," Kelly admits, "that day is a long way off. But we've outlined the steps."

The transition from the existing stand-alone applications to the integrated architecture will be accompanied by the challenge of managing major conversions, as existing applications are reimplemented for the new data-independent architecture and new system programs. Many organizations will employ outside systems integrators to perform these conversions rather than incur the ongoing costs of maintaining integration experts on their staffs.

GOVERNING AND CONTROLLING

One common method of limiting exposure to unknown risk will be compartmentalization. Instead of being accessible to anyone on the network, sensitive master files and local networks will be separated by human-monitored gateways. Each access to sensitive files will require the on-line approval of a security monitor. Particular controls will be focused on connections between the corporate network and uncontrolled networks belonging to others, as arise through electronic data interchange. Every type of transaction crossing the gateway between such intercorporate networks may first be subjected to human review.

Modifications of master records in financial files will need to be controlled. Tight accounting controls have always been applied here, and they will necessarily become tighter as chances for fraud increase along with the number of people having access to the system. This trend implies that more companies will use the memo file approach used by banks (where files are updated on a pro forma basis during the day, and official changes are made only at night under batch controls).

A positive offshoot of compartmentalization is that the spread of distributed databases will be carefully controlled. When a corporate database of importance is segmented, a central authority will exercise control over standards, updating authority, and procedures.

In the age of the IIS, companies will be increasingly sensitive to overuse or misuse of their information resources. Software packages will monitor and report use. Over time, expert system capabilities will be added. Slowly, expert systems will become system managers with approval authority.

Budgeting will become more difficult in the future integrated information enterprise because the true costs of information processing will be harder to determine. Users will be preparing or procuring many of their own programs to run on the network, making it increasingly difficult to assign portions of the network's expense to individuals or even departments. Meanwhile, the costs of systems purchased to implement corporate-wide electronic mail and conferencing systems or other corporate infrastructure systems cannot be allocated to individual departments.

Many organizations will give up trying to charge back the services of the network and the remainder of the infrastructure and distribute only those portions of the costs that users specifically, and identifiably, incur. This elimination of a general charge-back mechanism is appropriate as information systems are established in the company.

Just as budgeting becomes increasingly difficult, so does measuring the cost-effectiveness of information processing services. Yet it will become clear that budgets are indispensable. Rather than being set by objectively determined need, budgets will be to a large degree incremental: In the 1990s, budgets may range 7 to 10% greater or 3 to 5% less annually, compared with the 12 to 15% annual increases of the late 1980s. Budgeting should not work this way, but it already does in many organizations. Incremental funding tends to lead to bloated organizations in which unneeded personnel are assigned to unnecessary jobs. Compartmentalization of budget requests and careful scrutiny of indirect support and administrative personnel budgets will be required to prevent overweight IS organizations from developing.

Organizations may experiment with "flickering authority," where decision-making power automatically resides with the employee working closest to the problem, supported by information systems. This setup allows a company to react more quickly to customer problems and provide much better service. Experiments with flickering authority will be conducted cautiously, with the review of a human supervisor usually being required before a junior employee's decision takes effect.

Another issue is who controls the resources that comprise the IIS. These resources will remain divided among the corporate entity and the various business units. The corporation will control and maintain the infrastructure (communication networks, shared mainframes and databases, and other shared computing resources). The individual business units will govern and maintain the computing and communication resources that specifically support their operation. The corporation will also retain responsibility for the basic financial accounting applications, such as payroll and accounts payable/ accounts receivable, while the business units control business-specific applications, such as Material Requirements Planning

(MRP.) Some areas of responsibility will overlap or be fuzzy, rendering it unclear who is in charge. In these cases, the corporate architecture committee, not the IS director, will assign control. In rare cases of critical corporate importance, the CEO will decide. The committee will also set the guidelines and interface standards that must be met by the business unit resources to ensure that the overall architectural goals are met.

DEVELOPING PERSONNEL

Operating an integrated information business requires substantial changes in the roles of IS people and their mix of skills. The need for general and IS managers to focus on issues of architecture instead of application will typically necessitate their taking technical courses to learn the capabilities of architectures and the effects of their decisions about them.

Computer system suppliers such as IBM and DEC already emphasize these issues in their executive seminars. The general business press will soon follow, leading to a gradual building of awareness in the ranks of general managers. In aggressive companies, executives will even take the time to attend specially designed 1- and 2-day seminars on the major issues involved in the design and development of the IISs that will be required to support their business strategies.

Within integrated networks, new controls must be put in place and exercised by a kind of technician that barely exists yet: a person skilled in data security technology, network management, and financial control. A burgeoning of professional seminars and training courses in the area can be expected. A shortage of such people will probably induce many smaller firms, especially in highly networked industries, to hand over design and operation of their networks to outside system integrators. (In the financial industries, specialized network service companies already play a major role.)

In decentralized organizations with infrequent corporate-wide applications, central data processing will need fewer application programmers. Organizations operating complex transaction processing applications that serve the entire enterprise, however, may actually hire more programmers.

End-users will need even more on-call help in the 1990s as they take on increased responsibility for their own applications. Transferring programmers from central IS to user departments will help disperse expertise where it is needed, and sometimes enough on-the-job training by local programmers will meet the need.

The introduction of Integrated Information Systems will change the jobs of almost all employees in a company to some degree. Careful piloting, training, and phasing-in will be needed. Most of the organizations that are aggressive in the use of information systems are already reasonably adept at these tasks. Still, an increased emphasis on ergonomics and training will be needed.

PITFALLS AND UNCERTAINTIES

Most managers underestimate the costs of implementing and maintaining the technology that they bring into their corporations. Basic misunderstanding of how to assess tangential costs is the major reason, but sometimes IS managers deliberately underestimate to better their chances of getting the systems they want. The biggest area of underestimation is in support. Hardware, software, and even communications costs are fairly well known and accepted; however, support (maintenance, training, enhancements, etc.) costs are underestimated, or even ignored, especially by the "Power to the Users" advocates.

The equivalent of one full-time person is currently needed to support every 10 to 15 PCs or workstations attached to a LAN. This personnel cost of about $60,000 must be added to the regular hardware and software maintenance charges, about 10% of the purchase price per year. Thus, the total ongoing cost can reach $500 to $700 per month for each PC or workstation.

Hiring a support person, however, is always cheaper than having the more highly paid professional users of these systems solve their own technical problems. When end-users train or troubleshoot for each other, they usually take longer to diagnose the problems and often come up with only patchwork, roundabout solutions. They also are helpless when faced with a system-wide failure. When the costs of lost productivity—their own as well as general downtime during even one system failure—are counted, the costs for planned central support will seem trivial.

Technological advances will also reduce central support costs. Improvements in the interfaces will make it easier for end-users to learn about their workstations and programs on their own, and improvements will make the machines themselves less likely to break down. By the mid-1990s, companies will need only one full-time equivalent person to handle every 40 to 60 PCs. This increased ratio will cut costs to under $200 per month per PC or workstation.

A major concern of senior management will be unintended exposure of the organization to changes caused by the new system environment. For example, in an industry interconnected by EDI, competitive roles are likely to change. In an organization with distributed databases, junior employees may usurp authority simply because greater access to information gives them the ability to do so.

Realizing that they cannot foresee all that will happen, some managers may deliberately put constraints on new systems, thereby limiting the pace of innovation, so that they are comfortable with their degree of exposure to the unknown. Yet while their timidity to innovate may save them from stumbling in the short run, they may end up in the long run crippled by their unwillingness to act on the potential of information technology.

CHAPTER 4

OVERALL
ARCHITECTURE

No single architecture of the mid-1990s will fit the needs of every business. This statement should not be surprising since it reflects the status quo since the introduction of on-line terminals in the late 1950s. What will change in the next several years will be the increased variety and number of viable architectures implemented in a single company. The types will range from the classic "star," two-layer, mainframe-centered configuration to the "mainframeless," totally distributed, minicomputer and PC arrangement.

The two most common modes of computation—the client–server and network processing arrangements—will complement each other within any architecture. They differ in how software systems are implemented within the overall infrastructure of computing resources. The client–server mode allocates functions of the underlying infrastructure to specific systems in the IIS. Print servers control the users' printing resources; file servers govern shared files and backup files for single-user systems; database servers control shared databases; and name servers control the names and network locations of files as well as users, permitting those with proper access to navigate the IIS without knowing exactly how to do so. In the network processing mode, portions of applications operate simultaneously on multiple computers, which cooperate to carry out the overall function. The most advanced form allows application modules to be dynamically allocated to different computers as the need arises. An early example of network processing can be seen in software development, where compilations of modules that make up an application are dynamically allocated to currently unused workstations. For instance, 100 compilations might be needed to generate a new version of a software system. If each compile takes ½ hour, the process on one machine would require 50 hours. In network processing, however, the companies can be dispatched to any number of workstations. If 33 stations are used, for instance, the job would take only 1 ½ hours.

THE ARCHITECTURAL PRINCIPLES

Despite the existence of two or more very different architectures within a corporation, anarchy will not reign. Six technology-based principles will guide companies in choosing the specific architectural types that complement each other while adapting to ever-changing business needs at a reasonable cost:

1. *Complete connectivity*—All workstations must easily communicate with all computers and other workstations.
2. *Information consistency and integrity*—All applications must use a common set of data definitions; information must pass validity checks before it is used to update databases.
3. *Resource sharing*—Wherever possible, scarce resources, such as trained communications and data processing personnel, communications networks, and specialized computer resources, will be shared by all users.
4. *Computer input/output (I/O) bandwidth sizing*—Computers intended to support an application or a specific set of applications must be chosen more on the basis of the amount of I/O activity that they can accommodate rather than on their computing capacity.

5. *Disaster resiliency*—Mission-critical systems must rapidly re-
cover from all levels of disaster, ranging from the loss of a data
file to the loss of a major computing center.

6. *Appropriate security*—Systems must be reasonably protected
from threats ranging from malicious employees to hackers to
industrial spies.

These principles are only guidelines. The specific architectures that
a company implements will stem from how these principles apply to
the organization of the business, its geographic layout, its management style, and the nature of its products and services.

THE IIS ARCHITECTURE

By the mid-1990s, advanced medium- to large-sized businesses will
implement IISs based on the overall architecture shown earlier in
Figure 2.3. All but the smallest locations will be continuously linked
to the remainder of the company through circuits provided by public
network carriers (or, in some cases, privately owned facilities) on a
dedicated or virtual network basis. These links will be used for both
voice and data communications, with the bandwidth allocations dynamically changing as the proportions of voice and data traffic vary
during the day.

Large corporate locations, and several locations within physical
proximity, will be served by systems based on the architectures
shown in Figure 4.1. Such systems will be founded on multiple (generally two to four) tiers of computers. The top tier (mainframes) and
the bottom tier (workstations or PCs) will almost always be present.
Some companies composed of generally independent business units
will utilize minicomputers and PCs as their main processing resources. In these cases, minis will take the place of the mainframe;
however, a centralized communications control point will usually be
associated with the corporate minicomputer.

Figure 4.1   Large Corporate Location Architecture of the Mid-1990s

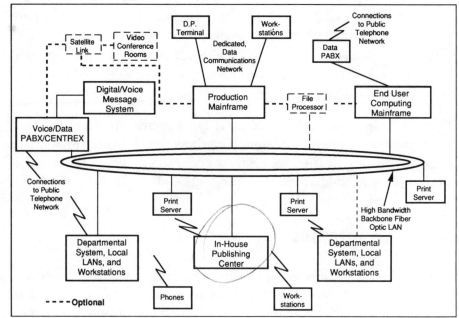

A middle tier of departmental computers will be utilized when business-oriented reasons dictate. The following are examples of middle-tier functions:

- A fault-tolerant computer to control an ATM network
- A centralized computer to handle the order-entry and order-processing functions of a specific business unit
- A factory–floor computer to control an entire production line
- A project-control computer that contains all of the information that must be shared among team members.

In the middle tier will reside the various forms of servers necessary to implement the client–server mode of computing. The IISs of the mid-1990s cannot operate without these servers. Typically, servers will be physically small computers with the computing and I/O capacities found in the large minicomputers of the late 1980s.

Most IISs will contain a mixture of two-, three-, and four-tier architectures. The three-tier setup will generally predominate, with server-class departmental systems being much more heavily employed than application-specific systems. Computer systems (including workstations) within a single location will be interconnected by two or more levels of LANs, as well as by the telephone network centered on a voice–data PABX or CENTREX system. The PABX and LAN will be interconnected, but LAN functions will not be provided by the PABX.

Workflow languages, just starting to appear as part of document image processing systems, will become widely used in the more complex application systems by the mid-1990s. Aggressive companies will find them critical for building large application programs. These languages and their associated run-time systems are designed to control the flow of information objects around a large IIS. They can be used to specify the movement of an electronic document through a complex processing and approval environment. Procedural language program calls (e.g., in COBOL, FORTRAN, or SQL), as well as actual procedural program segments, can be embedded in such systems. The calls can also trigger in the IIS one or more predefined, simultaneous, independent processes in multiple computers as a result of an individual's actions.

Use of these languages will permit companies to redesign workflows and individual job functions in an incremental manner to suit new business and operating conditions without the need to rewrite large amounts of application code. Thus, much of the expense and confusion currently engendered by such changes can be eliminated, allowing companies to become much more flexible and reactive to changing business needs.

THE COMMUNICATIONS ARCHITECTURE

Integrated Information Systems will be communications-intensive systems. All individuals will be able to send multiple forms of information to all other individuals without having to know anything more than a single identifier for the intended recipient. A conceptual view of the overall communications architecture is shown in Figure 4.2. The enterprise is connected via wide-area networks (WANs), often a mixture of public and private or leased-line networks. These WANs carry all forms of information, including normal voice telephone traffic. Communications bandwidth is dynamically shifted among the various forms of communications (voice, data, images, etc.), sometimes on a minute-by-minute basis. All facilities within the same region will interconnect via a metropolitan area network (MAN) that interfaces with the corporate WAN at one or more points.

The primary facilities within a major site or complex of buildings will be LAN-based by the mid-1990s, and multiple levels of networks will be used:

Figure 4.2   Conceptual Overall IIS Communications Architecture of the Mid-1990s

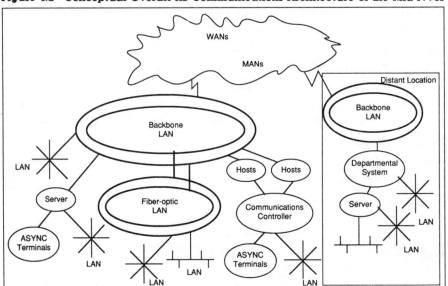

- A main backbone, fiber-optic, high-bandwidth LAN, which will connect the major processing and information consumption nodes in the system
- Multiple PC-level (or fiber-optic, when necessary) LANs, which will link local workstations.

PABXs will be dedicated primarily to voice communications, including voice mail, in the mid-1990s. At times, they will carry digital communications (mostly between workstations and mainframes, or distant servers) for workstations that are not permanently connected to the IIS. PABXs will also serve as intermediaries for accessing external electronic mail or external data services.

On the technical side, the pace of introduction in the 1990s of the overall IIS communications architecture illustrated in Figure 4.2 will be governed primarily by the availability of effective network management systems. The aggressive implementation of distributed applications requires not only a sound network infrastructure, but a way to manage it.

Most, if not all, networks and IISs of any complexity will be hybrid and multivendor, a mixture of public and private (owned or leased) facilities. With so many network operators and equipment suppliers involved, the challenge of network management is formidable. Many users already have a variety of management capabilities. Some are linked to particular suppliers (host or modem based), whereas others are add-on, self-contained systems (often minicomputer based).

The ideal situation for users would be an integrated network management structure that allows them to make use of their existing partial capabilities within a more powerful facility. Such a complete solution would offer fault diagnosis (or even anticipation), network reconfiguration, and the other core elements of management across the hybrid IIS environment.

Standards thus become particularly important in the realm of network management products to permit the cohesive, consistent interworking of diverse facilities. Aggressive companies will employ integrated network management systems, such as those being developed by IBM and AT&T. IBM's NetView might govern mainframe-centered networks, whereas AT&T's Unified Network Management Architecture (UNMA) would handle transport services and facilities within the same company.

Fully logical integrated network management is unlikely over the next 5 years, but substantial progress is expected in the integration of reporting systems. The status and performance of diverse facilities and equipment will be increasingly monitored for availability and fault location. The most successful broadly based network management systems will be those that stress an open systems approach and are supported by vendors whose resources as well as pre- and post-sales support give them high credibility in the eyes of the customer.

Aggressive companies will make significant use of full-motion video teleconferencing systems, primarily for intracompany meetings. The main function of such systems will be to facilitate working sessions among corporate personnel who are dispersed geographically. Research into human factors shows that people are uncomfortable working with a video image of a person unless they have personally met and worked with the person. Even people who have met before become uncomfortable working with only images of each other after a period of weeks. Thus, human factors, rather than technology, will inhibit wider acceptance of teleconferencing. Even in the mid-1990s, people will continue to meet person to person, especially with customers and suppliers, even though teleconferencing technology will provide a cost and time savings alternative, and will be used as a substitute for some meetings.

DISTRIBUTION OF FUNCTIONS

The distribution of functionality within an IIS will be determined primarily by two factors: the location of data and the desired response time. Data location will determine where the primary data accessing and manipulation functions occur. In applications involving corporate data or data that can be stored in only one location, the major processing will take place in the mainframe or an application-specific departmental computer. Where users require rapid response time, and the amount of data to be accessed stays within the limits of the system, workstations will assume the major processing.

For example, engineering workstation-based computer-aided design (CAD) applications are increasingly able to handle all functions that must be carried out as part of a design application. Only the most computationally intensive parts of the process, usually involving simulation, must now be moved to larger systems. In the next few years, workstations will handle even these functions, except in exceedingly complex designs.

By the mid-1990s, most large applications will be designed and implemented for network (or cooperative) processing. Each of these applications will include program modules, enabling it to operate on the mainframe, the departmental system, and/or the workstation. Human interface, control, and response-time critical functions, especially those that involve routine editing and next-screen generation, will generally be allocated to the workstations. IBM's SAA, and other vendors' equivalents, will permit modules to be allocated to systems in accordance with each customer's architecture. SAA will also allow modules to be moved and reallocated to meet performance, load leveling, and other customer needs.

Many on-line transaction processing applications will take particular advantage of such an environment; however, there is some cost versus response time tradeoff. Rapid-response network applications will cost more to implement and maintain because they are harder to design and more complex to manage. To offset the extra cost of the application, users should concentrate on network applications where faster response time would result in a noticeable productivity improvement.

With the resource sharing (remote procedure call) protocols that are already being standardized, dynamic allocation of many processing functions will be possible. Such allocation will allow users to make more effective use of the processing resources contained in an IIS. There is no need to size a central system for the highest load imaginable if distributed resources can be marshaled as needed to handle the application.

MAINFRAME FUNCTIONALITY

In mid-decade, mainframes will still carry out the same variety of functions that they now accomplish. In an advanced company, a mainframe will also become the major corporate document and information repository. Some people label this role "database server"; however, this name does not capture the mainframe's much greater role. Most batch processing will still be accomplished on the mainframe, as will most information retrieval tasks. The mainframe will also carry out certain server functions, such as name server, print server for large runs (e.g., payroll), and so on. Mainframe MIPS will increase by about 20% per year overall, but the cost for this added processing power will rise only 5% per year.

   Many transaction processing applications, however, will move by the mid-1990s to the application-specific departmental computers. Most, if not all, of the current time-sharing applications will also move to the workstations.

DEPARTMENTAL SYSTEM FUNCTIONALITY

Two types of departmental systems will be used in IISs of the mid-1990s: servers (Figure 2.5), and application-specific systems (Fig. 2.6). Servers will be microprocessor based and often contain high-end business workstations or workstation-derived systems (those configured with additional RAM disk and I/O gear). These systems will act as LAN hubs, local document processing input stations and repositories, local electronic mail hubs, attachment points for high-cost peripherals, and local repositories for calendars, schedules, and so forth. Most of the work administered by these systems will be infrastructure related (e.g., electronic mail, LAN control, and management) rather than application specific.

Application-specific departmental systems will generally be larger than their server-class cousins. The mid-1990s' descendants of IBM's mid-range products (the AS/400, 9370, and 4381 systems) or of DEC's 6000 line will be chosen for most application needs. These systems will be purchased primarily on the basis of a single application. They will each serve a community of interest around that application, which may well cross organizational boundaries. In addition to their primary role, these systems will regularly carry out all of the functions of the server-class systems, especially when directly connected to workstations.

Many companies will set up application-specific systems first as combined servers and application-specific systems. They will then add server-class systems when their loads begin to build. Other companies will start bottom up: They will set up the servers, and then define new applications and get application-specific departmental systems to hook the workstations and servers. When one or more server-class systems intervene between the workstations and the application-specific system, the latter will act as the next higher node in the electronic mail system and will be used to store data concerning project schedules that are used by the entire community of interest.

WORKSTATION FUNCTIONALITY

Workstations will absorb an increasing percentage of the overall workload over the next 5 years for three major reasons:

1. Already more workstation MIPS are installed in the United States than mainframe MIPS. This ratio will continue to tilt in favor of the workstations for the foreseeable future.

2. Workstation MIPS are much cheaper than mainframe MIPS and will become even more so over the next 5 years.

3. End-users are becoming increasingly accustomed to subsecond response times for simple operations. This response time will continue to be much less costly on workstations than on mainframe-based systems.

The workstation load will primarily take the form of local PC-level applications and the response-time sensitive portions of larger applications. Another major task will be supporting the seamless user interface with the IIS. This latter load alone will absorb between 20 and 40% of the processor cycles, even taking into account the special-purpose support chips that will be included in the workstations of the period.

PC LANs or twisted-pair wiring will generally network workstations, as shown in Figure 2.6, except for engineering workstations, which will often require wide-band fiber-optic networks.

DECIDING FOR YOUR BUSINESS

Into the life of each chief information officer comes the time when a decision about what architecture to use for the corporation must be made. Although only one member of the management's architecture committee, the CIO must be the catalyst of the decision. It is an opportunity for the CIO to step forward, express the value of IS, and lead management toward a competitive information technology structure. A series of technological, financial, and business factors must be considered in making a rational decision.

Vendors will often compare the raw processing power (MIPS) of small machines with that of larger ones to show how much cheaper the small ones are to operate. It is well known that PC MIPS are more than an order-of-magnitude cheaper than mainframe MIPS. These figures alone are misleading, however. In increasing numbers of applications, it is the I/O bandwidth of a computer, not the raw

MIPS, that eventually limits the speed of application. In the mid-1990s, mainframes, minicomputers, and PCs will be differentiated primarily by their I/O throughput capacities, rather than by processing power. Some large transaction processing applications, or batch applications needing to be done quickly, will continue to require the I/O capacity of a mainframe, thus, at least in part, dictating the form of the architecture.

The cost of purchasing and supporting a corporation's information processing system will remain a major deciding factor of an architecture. Increasingly, the majority of this cost will be found in the software, communications, and support portions of the equation. Many people touting the financial advantages of distributed systems gloss over the additional expenses that such systems engender, especially in terms of maintenance and operational support, compared with centralized systems.

But decision makers must carefully consider these "soft" costs when making an architectural design. Using a 5-year cost-of-ownership method will often help a company gain perspective on true costs. The rule of thumb is that initial costs represent only 20 to 30% of 5-year cost of ownership, whether considering hardware, software, or communications.

The cost of conversion from the current architecture to a new one is the other major financial cost that must be considered. In most companies, such conversion will be carried out over a period of years. Some existing applications can be moved intact or with little change, whereas others have to be reimplemented, possibly in a stepwise fashion. This conversion effort may be so time-consuming and expensive that consideration of alternative solutions is well worthwhile.

For example, the decision to build a mainframeless architecture could necessitate reimplementation of all existing on-line transaction processing (OLTP) systems. On the other hand, deciding to maintain these systems on the mainframe and implementing code to carry out the preliminary edits on workstations might produce the same desired improvement in response time while greatly reducing the amount of code that must be reimplemented.

The two major business factors influencing architectural decisions are the following:

1. *Business stability*—Fast company growth calls for the use of smaller modular systems, whereas slow growth argues for the use of larger systems. Growth resulting from frequent buying and selling of portfolio companies requires modular systems. Growth from within requires larger systems to allow small units to take advantage of existing applications.

2. *Relationship with suppliers and customers*—A close relationship necessitates tight interconnection of systems, whereas a loose association requires only good on-line query capabilities. Close relationships call for the use of somewhat isolated systems interacting via EDI networks, which customers and/or suppliers are permitted to access. On-line query can be handled by normal systems, often mainframes that contain the entire set of customer files.

The units within a holding company normally exchange very little information. The sharing of processing resources becomes primarily a matter of economics rather than business functions. Such a corporation will generally choose a distributed architecture that, in the extreme, will not even include a central mainframe. Minicomputers will be the main computing resource for most of the units. Some smaller sized divisions will operate their information processing functions on a series of LAN-linked PCs.

Entire companies running few engineering or transaction processing applications may also take advantage of PC networks. Units of such a firm will normally share a corporate communications network that will support an electronic mail system and other communications functions.

Separating the information processing functions of various business units is especially important when these divisions are frequently sold or acquired. Entanglement in a divestiture or incompatibility of a business unit's information processing infrastructure often hinders a deal, and sometimes precludes it. Even after the deal is done, intractable problems can arise from incompatible systems. For example, 5 years after Baxter Healthcare Corp. merged with American Hospital Supply Corp. in 1985, the integration of these two companies' information systems still was incomplete. Michael Heschel, then vice-president of information resources, reported tremendous difficulty converting American Hospital Supply's celebrated ordering system, based on Burroughs Corp. equipment, to Baxter's IBM architecture. The systems difficulties contributed to financial problems at Baxter, which led to general personnel cutbacks in March 1990. After 300 of his 800-member IS group were laid off, Heschel left Baxter for the position of chairman and chief executive at Security Pacific Automation Corp.

In a company that has few diverse units, a more centralized overall architecture should be chosen. Most often a three-layer architecture will be put in place, with minicomputers and workstations interposed between the mainframes and the standard PCs to handle special applications and act as servers. Sharing of information, processing resources, and even applications often allows these companies to be more responsive to their customers and to changing business conditions, while holding down costs.

In summary, with the proliferation of architectures now becoming feasible, the choice among them can and should be driven from fundamental business considerations and not solely, or even primarily, from technological tradeoffs.

CHAPTER 5

UNDERLYING TECHNOLOGIES

Semiconductors, displays, and secondary storage media are the foundation technologies that support all computer systems (Fig. 5.1). As the most universal computer technology, semiconductors drive the cost, size, and performance of all other products, machines, and applications. For example, only in the last 5 years have advances in semiconductors allowed the complex processing in Group 3 facsimile machines to be realizable in a desktop product that sells for under $1,000.

Figure 5.1 Technologies Are the Foundation Underlying Products, Systems and Applications

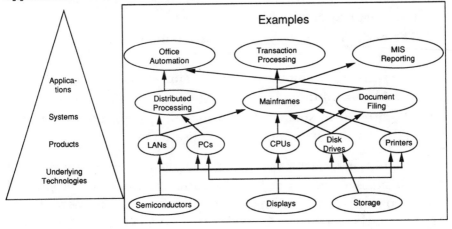

Because no machine is useful without an effective human interface, displays are the second basic technology. Existing displays are large and expensive, and they cannot match the resolution that the human eye can discern. Thus, displays remain in need of significant improvements. Higher quality monitors will facilitate multitasking and expanded use of color and will allow portable computers to be more usable.

Finally, advances in storage technology will make feasible a host of memory-hungry image-based applications that will move into the mainstream of general-purpose business computing by the mid-1990s. At present, storage media needed for developing image applications for desktop systems are too expensive, too unreliable, and too low in performance.

SEMICONDUCTORS

The general demand by users for improved computer speeds (Fig. 5.2) is forcing cost–performance shifts. Faster chips with wider bandwidth (i.e., higher speed or wider word length) are required to support:

- The growth in data-intensive image based computing to allow the visualization of scientific analysis
- The proliferation of image processing in general business applications
- The increased complexity of programs with extensive self-help and AI capabilities
- The growth in simulation and modeling applications now migrating from supercomputers to desktop machines.

In addition to faster speeds, semiconductors are being reduced to much smaller sizes in order to occupy less space on the printed circuit board. Devices will move from the 0.6 micron linewidths of the state-of-the-art very large scale integrated (VLSI) devices of the late 1980s to 0.3 micron linewidths by 1995. This size reduction

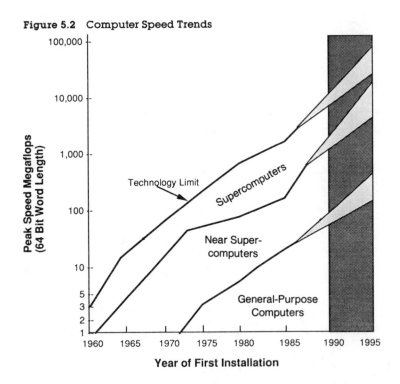

Figure 5.2   Computer Speed Trends

will permit complexity to exceed 100 million devices per chip (Fig. 5.3). To realize these densities at reasonable production yields and to allow the increased complexity simultaneous with improved cost–performance ratios, semiconductor manufacturers must develop revolutionary design concepts and manufacturing processes, such as fault-tolerant and self-repairing chip architectures.

Density increases beyond 100 million devices per chip will be achieved by the use of three-dimensional fabrication technologies that stack multiple layers of integrated circuits onto a single chip. Manufacturers will continue to employ high-density packages suitable for surface mounting, but, to accommodate longer word sizes, will also need to make innovative use of high-speed serial optical buses to reduce pin-outs while not compromising the required high-speed chip-to-chip communications within the computer.

The increase in commercial digital logic speed will permit the the required advances in overall computing power and fast memory

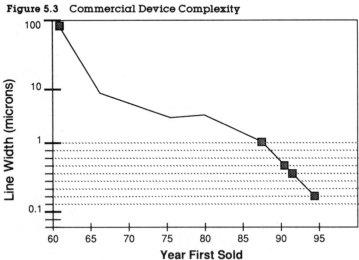

Figure 5.3   Commercial Device Complexity

access to meet user needs. As Figure 5.4 shows, the duration of gate delays for silicon chips will drop from 50 picoseconds to almost 40 in 1995.

History reveals that computer memory needs increase in proportion to computer speed (Fig. 5.5), so primary semiconductor RAM will be made available using the smaller, lower power chips of the future. In one example of anticipated advances, IBM joined with Siemens A.G. of West Germany early in 1990 to develop a D-RAM

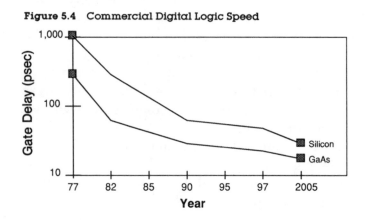

Figure 5.4   Commercial Digital Logic Speed

Figure 5.5   Computer Primary Memory Trends

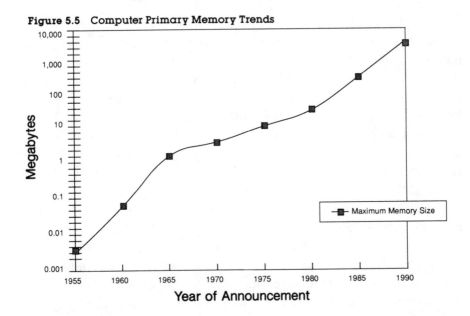

chip capable of storing 64 million bits of information. This capacity, equivalent to about 10 novels, would be placed on a silver of silicon the size of a fingernail. Commercial manufacture is targeted for 1995. In June, Hitachi Ltd. announced it had developed the first working prototype of a 64 megabit chip.

Silicon technology will remain dominant for several decades in general commercial computers. Although the first commercial semi-conductor devices were fabricated from germanium, silicon soon replaced it and became the mainstay of electronics machines. However, the ever-present drive toward increased processing power is encouraging experimenting with other materials as possible successors to silicon. One such promising material is gallium arsenide (GaAs), now widely used in analog applications in radio and microwave communications systems. Because the physics of GaAs allows for higher electron mobility than silicon, this material has the intrinsic potential to support a new class of integrated circuits with shorter gate delays.

For a number of reasons, however, GaAs will not rival silicon for mainstream applications. Although electron mobility is an important intrinsic limit on device speed, silicon excels over GaAs in other critical characteristics. For example, silicon devices can be realized in compact and power-efficient complementary metal oxide semi-conductor (CMOS) structures. GaAs, on the other hand, is less dense, requiring the one-chip silicon circuits to be split up on several chips, which lose speed in the interconnections. GaAs is a brittle, low yield, and costly material for use in integrated circuits. Although GaAs is a well-known substance, insufficient research has been done on the efficient fabrication of GaAs. Fewer gates can be fit on a GaAs chip than on silicon. Also, the thermal resistance of GaAs is much higher, making it more difficult to dissipate heat.

Silicon technology is so well developed and supported, and its manufacture so low risk, that GaAs faces difficulty replacing silicon in the marketplace. Nevertheless, a role remains for GaAs. In the highest performance machines, such as supercomputers and signal processors, some independent and very fast arithmetic and registers will be implemented in GaAs for interface to slower supporting con-ventional silicon circuits. GaAs will also be useful in a military signal processor, which would recognize a particular airplane or sub-marine rather than only a blip, and in a natural language font-end processor or voice typewriter.

More importantly, however, process technologies will develop to integrate GaAs and silicon on the same substrate. Their purpose will be to support on-chip special processing, as well as to allow the GaAs circuitry to support the optical interfaces and signal condition-ing for high-speed serial optical buses.

While basic chip speed will increase for silicon circuits over the next decade, the speed–power product will decrease to approach the fundamental theoretical limit (Fig. 5.6). This coming reduction of some five orders of magnitude will enable systems that today must plug into the wall to run for years on a battery. To understand the impact of the historical improvement in the speed–power product, consider the Toshiba 1100 portable. It can run battery powered for 2 hours, an acceptable, if not desirable, length of time. In 1970, it could run for less than a second. The speed–power product improvement underlies the progression of computing devices from the desktop to the suitcase to the briefcase and even to the vest pocket.

Figure 5.6   Speed Power Product for Commercial Silicon

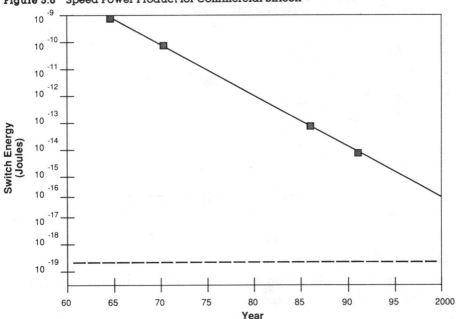

The decreased speed–power product is also important for high-performance machines that will continue to operate from the power line. Without such an improvement, it would be impossible to keep the machines cool enough without making them much larger in size. With the advances, however, it will be possible to actually reduce size while increasing performance.

The effective speed of microprocessors will continue along the constant slope indicated in Figure 5.7, which means that the fivefold increase in clock speed in the last 5 years will be repeated in the next 5. It is not clear if wider word lengths will remain the primary means of achieving this performance. Experimentation over the next few years with very wide words as well as parallel architectures and reduced instruction sets will demonstrate which technique is most suitable and cost-effective to meet the higher performance computing needs of the 1990s.

Optical computing is a much-publicized technology, but it will never achieve the speed and density of silicon. Optical circuits will

Figure 5.7   Microprocessor Performance Trends

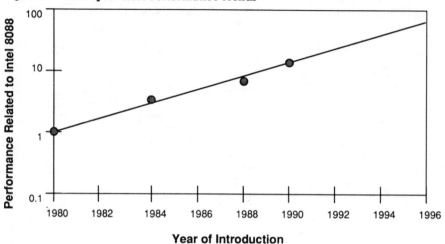

Year of Introduction

not be used in mainstream computers per se, but rather will be applied to switching and routing. Optical interconnects will be used for intrachip, chip-to-chip, board-to-board, and machine-to-host communications. GaAs and its alloys are the preferred materials for implementing integrated optical circuits.

DISPLAY TECHNOLOGY

For general-purpose computing, the resolution of high-contrast displays must be increased from the current level of 128 thousand pixels to one million in order to match the limits of the human eye. Although color will not be a requirement for most professional computing, displays will need eight levels of gray scale to facilitate advanced human interfaces with pointing devices and full-screen editing (Fig. 5.8).

To visualize the needs of the mainstream business user of the future, we need only look at the "power user" of today, the Wall Street trader. Using multitasking capabilities on a large screen, the trader might display seven or more different windows. One window may show a motion video of general activity on the stock exchange

Figure 5.8 Performance Requirements for Information System Displays

	1990		1995	
	General Purpose	High End Workstations	General Purpose	High End Workstations
Type	Emissive	Emissive	Emissive	Emissive
Size (inches)	4x10 to 8x10	8x10 to 15x20	4x10 to 8x10	8x10 to 15x20
Resolution (pixel)	640x200 to 640x400	1,150x900	640x900 to 1,150x900	2,500x2,000
Resolution (lines/inch)	50 to 75	150	75-150	250
Luminance (ft-L)	>20	>20	>20	>20
Gray Scale	None–4	8–10	8–10	8–256
Color	Desirable	Not Needed	Desirable	Desirable
Refresh Rate	1/60 s/field	1/60 s/field	1/60 s/field	1/80 s/field

floor, while others allow the trader to see stock quotes, do financial modeling, graph market trends, enter trades, check on a client's account, and write up his or her monthly activity. In each window, the trader needs resolution of one million pixels, capability not yet available.

Color will grow in popularity for business computing where the resolution limits of the technology are not stressed, such as for report graphics, business presentations, and financial analyses. For those high-end workstations where an intense level of high-resolution viewing is performed (e.g., scientific visualization and engineering design), most users will desire the high-quality monochrome display.

Many areas of the consumer electronics industry have become strategic to the development of the Integrated Information System. In the case of displays, this fact is particularly noticeable. Already the highest performance flat screen technology is required by, and being developed for, television (TV) applications. The state of the art is being pushed in color, display quality, speed of operation, and physical size. Over the next 5 years, the emphasis will shift to increasing resolution and larger size as displays are required to support high-definition TV.

While these improvements are being achieved, the needs of general-purpose computing for document image processing, portability, smaller size, and graphics-intensive advanced human interfaces will drive display technology toward higher resolution, flat screen, and low-power dissipation (for battery operation). The most common displays will remain flat panels and cathode ray tubes (CRTs). Liquid crystal displays (LCDs) have developed rapidly in consumer products for watches and calculators, and more recently in small TVs. As their price and performance improved, they began to be employed in portable laptop computers in larger sizes, up to 640 by 400 pixel resolution. By the use of backlights, LCDs can mimic the features of other emitter displays, and every indication is that they will supplant all other competitive flat panel technologies during the next 5 years. Because small size and portability are becoming increasingly important, there is considerable reason for manufacturers to explore flat panels in general. LCD technology is rising to the challenge.

First-generation twisted nematic (TN) LCDs with static matrixing provide only a fair image quality. However, supertwist birefringence effect (SBE) and active matrixing (AM) offer the promise of a flat panel LCD display of comparable performance to a CRT. When the displays are viewed in a price–performance context (Fig. 5.9), the CRT shows a broad range of coverage. High-end workstations have typically offered 50% greater resolution than general-purpose machines. By 1995, general-purpose workstations should achieve resolution of one million pixels—the limit of the human eye for a 13-inch diagonal display. The high-end workstations will provide the same resolution over a greater area by using more pixels on their larger screens.

CRTs, the oldest display technology that still serves most user needs, are the high-performance baseline by which all the other technologies must be measured. They fall short only in terms of size and power dissipation.

CRT and flat panel technology will improve significantly in price and performance over the next 5 years. Although plasma and electroluminescent (EL) displays will remain comparable in

Figure 5.9   Performance-Price Comparison for Electronic Displays

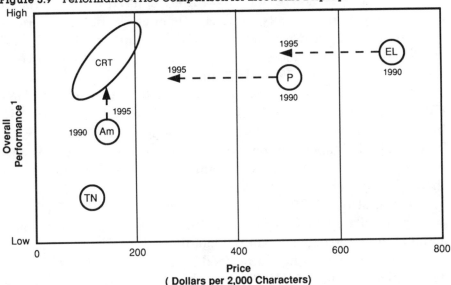

[1] Brightness, contrast, viewing angle, resolution, etc.

CRT = Cathode Ray Tube   AM = Addressable Matrix   P = Plasma Panel
TN = Twisted Nematic   EL = Electroluminescent

performance while halving in cost, the active matrix LCD display will overlap with the CRT and preempt these other rather expensive flat panel technologies for all but the most severe military and aerospace applications.

The current state of the art in CRTs falls short of providing adequate high-resolution color performance at a reasonable luminance. In fact, costs increase disproportionately faster than improvements (e.g., $64 for a 0.6 millimeter dot pitch TV CRT compared with $350 for a 0.15 millimeter CRT). Although this cost premium is caused partly by the difficulty of achieving this performance, it is also strongly influenced by how different the large-size, high-resolution display is from the large-volume, low-cost consumer TV application. As high-resolution displays are required over the next 5 years to support high-definition TV, industrial and consumer high-resolution applications will converge.

Increases in color resolution will be achieved mainly through evolutionary improvements in CRTs themselves, but innovations such as flat tension mask and beam index technology will also be employed. Brightness and efficiency are also expected to improve at the historical rates of 17% and 9% per year, respectively.

In addition to normal rear-projection CRTs, various flat panel CRT designs are being explored. Side gun flat CRTs are currently being shipped by both Sony and Sanyo in consumer TV receivers. These flat CRTs alleviate the size problem of conventional TVs but do not achieve the low power-drain performance of LCDs, and therefore have a more limited application.

The cost of CRTs is expected to decrease at about 7.2% per year, primarily by means of manufacturing yield improvements and automation of testing and material handling.

Few technologies have advanced as rapidly as LCDs. The early TN displays of the mid-1980s were barely adequate on portable computers (Fig. 5.10). Today, supertwist displays with backlights rival the performance of monochrome CRTs at a fraction of their size and power. By the use of active matrix displays with thin film transistors (TFT) on glass, resolution and contrast ratio should improve by 1995.

Figure 5.10   Monochrome LCD Displays Performance Forecast

	—— 1985 ——	——1990——	—— 1995 ——
Pixel Pitch	14 mil	14 mil	10mil
Pixel Matrix	640x200	640x400	1,200x900
Contrast	2:1	4:1	6:1
Technology	TN Matrix	SBE and NTN Matrix	Active Matrix

TN = Twisted Nematic
SBE = Super Twist Birefringence Effect
NTN = Neutral Twisted Nematic

Flat panel display technology will begin to seriously challenge CRTs for more than portable applications by 1995. Even non-portable products will become more attractive for both home and office use as size and power drain are reduced.

LCD technology significantly affects the manufacturing process. Currently, the light and compact electronics inside the CRT-based displays are built in overseas plants, shipped to the United States, and installed into the large and heavier system. The smaller, easier to manufacture LCDs will give the advantage to those vendors who perform all the product assembly in one place rather than in two stages. A result could be the movement of some offshore jobs back to the United States.

SECONDARY STORAGE

The latent desire of users to process image-based documents is one of several trends driving cost–performance shifts in secondary storage. A typical page of text and numbers requires only 2 to 4 kilobytes of memory. If text is stored as image, the memory requirement goes up to 40 kilobytes. A page that includes a photograph requires 1 megabyte of memory. Manufacturers are pushing the storage technology, believing that once users understand the attractiveness of processing images (as pioneering companies such as American Express has done), they will demand the capability.

Engineers working on color displays will place a tremendous load on memory. In a high-resolution, 1,000 by 1,000 pixel screen, each of the one million pixels, requires 8 bits of memory. The memory needed to support such a black-and-white display is multiplied by 3 if color capability is added. Rotating such a color screen image by 90 degrees would require a tremendous amount of processing power.

Greater density and speed in high-performance primary memory will allow for more use of primary/secondary memory partnerships (e.g., caches and bulk semiconductor storage) to enhance system performance.

Achieving faster sequential and parallel processing power will require three things: higher capacity secondary memory to keep the performance ratios constant, faster transfer times to ensure that the secondary storage access does not slow down the system bus, and dual or multiport access to facilitate the use of parallel architectures.

Advances in digital signal processing within consumer electronic products will drive volumes up and costs down for products such as image processors, erasable audio disks, digital videotape recorders, and home computers. In fact, consumer products are driving technology in the MIS area. Traditionally, IBM's highest performing disk drives were the state of the art in terms of information density. Now, however, videotape recorders are. With their high volumes of consumer products driving research, vendors such as Sony will increasingly transfer their advances into the IS area.

Secondary storage products retain very long life cycles compared with other computer and electronics subsystems. Even punch cards and paper tape still find some specialized uses. Therefore, significant changes will take place in the next 5 years in those technologies in the emerging and growth stage, particularly optical storage of all kinds, as well as floppy and hard disks used on small- to medium-sized systems.

Optical storage is particularly interesting because of the combination of low cost and medium to high performance that positions this technology to compete with magnetic disks for both working and archival file storage. Applications include storing of images and local databases and acting as a delivery media for publishing. Today, optical disks can contain in excess of 550 megabytes of data. A central optical drive can read reference material stored on disks and make it available over a LAN to any PC.

Although the historical 33% per year increase in bit-packing density of magnetic media should continue for the next 5 years, there will be an important change (Fig. 5.11). In the past, the highest performance devices were first introduced in low-volume, top-of-the-line mainframes (Fig. 5.12). In the next 5 years, state-of-the-art storage technology will become available in both desktop

Figure 5.11   Forecast Secondary Storage Density

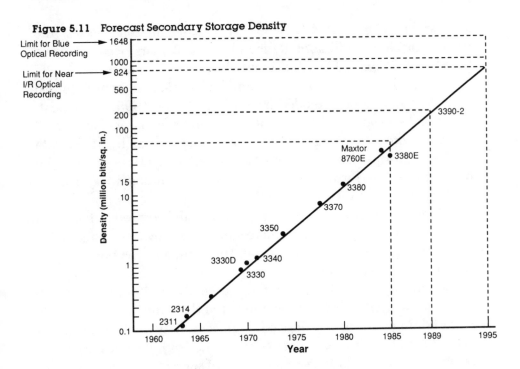

Figure 5.12   Early 1990s State-of-the-Art Secondary Storage Cost and Performance

	Optical			Magnetic			
	14" WORM	12" WORM	5.25" WORM	3390 Disk	3480 Cartridge	3420 Reel	5.25" WD Maxtor 8760E
Capacity (Bytes)	6.8g	2.0–4.6 g	0.23–1.0 g	3.78 g	200 M	165 M	765 M
Access Time	150 msec	150–200 msec	150 msec	18 msec	48 sec	60 sec	18 msec
Transfer Rate (MBytes/sec)	1	0.328–0.4	0.250	4.2	3	1.2	1.9
Error Rates (Corrected)	10^{12}	10^{12}–10^{13}	10^{12}–10^{13}	10^{14}	10^{14}	10^{14}	10^{12}
Cost (Drive w/o controller)	$42K	$11–14K	$1.5–$9K	$90–$275K	$39–$43K	$11-$19K	$3.5K
Cost - $/megaByte (System)	$6	$5	$4	$24	$200	$90	$5
Cost (Media)	$500	$200	$60	–	$6	$6	–
Cost - $/gigaByte (Media)	$75	$75	$75	–	$30	$36	–

and larger systems at nearly the same time; in some cases, the smaller machines will actually lead by 1 or 2 years because of the transfer of advances from consumer electronics products.

Also, the theoretical maximum (diffraction) limit for optical recording should be extended by a factor of 2 by 1995. At present, all optical systems employ near-infrared solid-state lasers in the 0.78 to 0.84 micron wavelength range. The demonstration by Matsushita of blue solid-state lasers in the 0.42 micron range offers the promise of continued performance improvement, which should appear in leading products by 1994 or 1995.

Increases in magnetic storage capacity, and cost reductions, will come from both evolutionary and revolutionary advances (Fig. 5.13). Continued progress will show up in thin film and composite heads with narrow gaps under 30 microinches (millionths of an inch) and reductions in head height from the present 15 to 20 microinches to under 10, as well as in the development of thin-film, high-coercivity materials in excess of 900 oersted (high coercivity refers to the property of a material to resist change in magnetism). Revolutionary improvements will include the application of substrates, such as glass to replace aluminum, and the use of advanced servosystems and signal processing. IBM's Almaden Research Center in San Jose, California, announced early in 1990 the squeezing of 1 gigabit of data on 1 square inch of magnetic disk storage.

In terms of floppy disk drives, magnetic media augmented by optical servotracks will be introduced and compete with other advanced floppy drives to provide capacity approaching 20 megabytes per disk. The overlaid optical tracks can pick up the 20 to 30% overhead typically found on the floppy disk. By moving the fixed information, space is opened up on the read–write floppy.

Secondary storage systems should decline in cost on the average, but some selected high-volume products, such as Winchester and floppy drives, will decrease far more rapidly. For magnetic systems for PCs, the average annual decrease will be about 35% per year, compared with 50% per year for Winchester drives. Semiconductor memory will not become cost-effective competition to magnetic or optical storage for general-purpose applications.

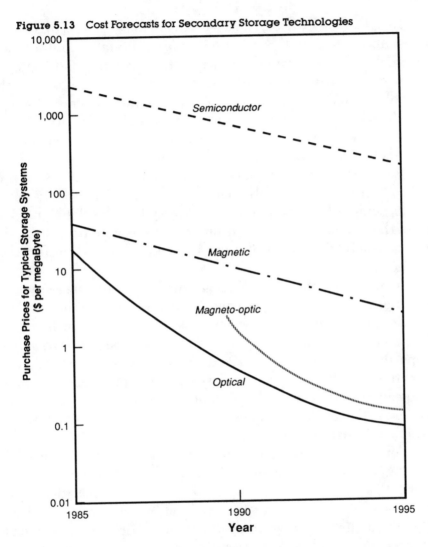

Figure 5.13   Cost Forecasts for Secondary Storage Technologies

By 1995, the typical data transfer rates of hard magnetic disk drives will increase from 3 megabytes per second to more than 6 megabytes per second. Some high-performance specialized systems will exceed 100 megabytes per second using parallel drives. Access time will improve as well, from typical performance of 25 milliseconds today to 10 to 15 milliseconds.

In optical disk drives, capacity will top today's levels by 1 1/2 to 2 times. Access time will drop to the order of 25 to 50 milliseconds, comparable to the capability of magnetic disks today. Optical disks will work in partnership with magnetic media, each handling the tasks best suited to it. Erasable disks will be introduced (initially in the 3.5 and 5.25 inch desktop size) of comparable capacity and cost to WORM (Write Once Read Many) but at a slightly lower transfer rate, about 150 to 200 kilobytes per second.

Rapid advances in performance and reductions in cost of secondary storage systems will change their status from being a barrier to being a facilitator in large-scale system development. The use of these technologies in consumer products will drive down the cost, a benefit that will spill over into industrial and professional products.

In terms of physical size, high-performance storage systems for large machines must be considered separately from low- and medium-performance systems for desktop machines. In large machines, secondary storage system volume will decrease in size in proportion to increase in storage density. In desktop systems, however, the size decrease will be less since the drive and controller overhead is a much larger fraction of the total volume. These small systems will see a 50% increase in information density, but only about a 25% size reduction.

For large systems, magnetic technology will predominate for working storage because slow access and data transfer times will limit optical systems to an archival role. In certain applications, however, such as image storage and retrieval, optical systems will become the on-line working storage, with magnetic systems serving as a buffer. For small desktop systems, optical systems will begin to serve as the primary working storage for image and other large data sets. This trend will accelerate as write–read–erasable optical storage becomes more available in the first half of the decade. Already, the NeXt machine (from NeXT, Inc.) comes from the factory with a Canon optical read–write drive as a standard feature.

The introduction of optical media and image data types will complicate storage management, maintenance, and backup.

Specialized software will be developed to deal with complications, such as the index to databases residing on the faster magnetic media while the referenced images themselves are located on the higher capacity optical disks. For instance, a user might say, "Show me all companies in the manufacturing section that had 18% return on investment last year and revenue of $100 million to $200 million." Acting as a pointer, the magnetic disk could direct the user to optical disks five, six, and ten, wherever the information is spread out.

By 1995, all systems, from the smallest to the largest, will automatically stage file objects up and down a hierarchy of storage devices according to demand. All widely used systems will also offer a range of options from integrity control (mirroring or journaling, with automatic backup) and some of the security features discussed in Chapter 11, notably access control, cyphering, and monitoring.

CHAPTER 6

THE INTEGRATED SOFTWARE INFRASTRUCTURE

The Integrated Information System requires a set of "infrastructure applications" that not only will underlie the major new business applications of the mid-1990s, but will bond them.

- *Office automation*—once the realm of clerical workers, will unite the entire company into a close-knit whole with its complex, but easy to use, mail, conferencing, and scheduling facilities.

- *Information retrieval technology*—with its promising electronic libraries and hypermedia capabilities, will be the foundation for executive information systems and advanced personnel training, as well as news wire scanning systems that can bring to a manager's attention important news as it happens. (NOTES)

- *Software engineering systems*—will allow the millions of lines of application code utilized by aggressive companies in the mid-1990s to be generated in much less time, at a much lower cost, and with far fewer bugs than in the late 1980s. These systems will automatically enforce the standards that will be required to pass meaningful information from one part of a company to another.

- *Artificial intelligence*—will finally come into its own after years of overpromises and underachievement. AI systems will

101

be incorporated into most business applications to reduce the mind-numbing rote work of many professionals, freeing them to apply their knowledge and skills more profitably to other operations.

- *Document image processing systems*—will rid an average company of literally tons of paper and shorten from days to seconds the delay in moving an important letter or report from one desk to another.

Infrastructure applications are analogous to the water pipes, electrical wiring, and telephone lines of the IIS edifice. These behind-the-walls systems will be indispensable for the proper operation of the complex. By making room in their information systems plans for long-term infrastructure projects, aggressive companies will, in effect, be building the basis of a modern skyscraper. Non-aggressive companies that implement only business applications, to the partial or complete exclusion of the infrastructure, will, in effect, be building the equivalent of an 1890s-style water-power mill.

THE LONG-TERM VIEW

Three marking points occur along the evolutionary path that all infrastructure application systems follow:

1. Stand-alone product stage
2. Utility stage
3. Infrastructure stage.

Each system starts as an independent product purchased by users for its ability to meet some special-purpose function. Slowly, the system becomes integrated into larger application solutions in the form of one or more utility programs. It is sought as much for its ability to support the larger solutions as for its own individual capabilities. Finally, the program's functionality is integrated into the overall system infrastructure. At this point, the program's capabilities are often distributed among several hardware and software modules, which are then packaged in the form of features or options of a larger system. By 1995, this third phase will be reached for most of the current components of IISs.

Investments in such infrastructure applications will be justified by companies as a basic cost of doing business, or as part of other, economically justifiable applications. Many CIOs recognize the need for building this infrastructure, but express frustration at the way in which priorities are set. For example, McDonald's Corp.'s Carl Dill, vice-president of information systems, has observed, "We CIOs face an ever-increasing need to integrate our systems, technology, and data. And yet we spend the bulk of our time on urgent delivery of isolated applications. Our future contributions depend on a sound systems architecture."

The current emphasis on local rather than enterprise-wide systems decisions will be reversed by aggressive companies in the 1990s. They will realize that, without an appropriate infrastructure, the technological and organizational changes required to be competitive will be impossible to achieve. Therefore, they will shift the balance of their resources toward projects of long-term importance.

Several developments will shape infrastructure applications in the next few years. First is the impending shortage of entry-level personnel to staff U.S. industry. According to the Census Bureau, the number of 18-year-olds in the population will drop by 8% during 1990 and not climb back to the level of 1989 until the year 2003. The "birth dearth" causing this worker shortage will lead to user pressure for additional productivity from automation of such clerical tasks as calendar maintenance, resource scheduling, moving paper, taking telephone messages, and checking engineering drawings. Second, highly cost-effective signal processing and image processing chips will be developed, permitting easier use of noncoded information in normal office environments. The cost of long-distance communications will fall very rapidly because of intensifying competition in the industry and the rapid increase in capacity as fiber-optic networks are installed. The lower costs will encourage companies to make greater use of these networks for transmitting documents, images, and other complex forms of data, as well as voice and coded (American Standard Code for Information Interchange [ASCII] or Extended Binary-Coded Decimal Interchange Code [EBCDIC]) data communications. Finally, the almost universal use of personal computers by white-collar personnel will make electronic mail and electronic conferencing far more acceptable to everyone. Despite these anticipated changes in infrastructure applications by the mid-1990s, there will be one notable absence: a breakthrough in machine comprehension of human natural language.

OFFICE AUTOMATION

The stand-alone stage of office automation ended in the late 1980s as systems passed into the utility phase of development. IBM captured this transition in its promotional brochures and interviews under the catch phrase, "Office Automation Is a Utility." By the mid-1990s, office automation will have entered the third (infrastructure) stage of development in advanced commercial installations, with almost all office and data processing functions integrated into a single logical system.

The term *office automation* includes a number of systems and technologies that assist workers in carrying out their functions in a business environment. The following functions typically fall under this definition:

- Word processing, document publishing, and desktop publishing systems
- Voice and data communication systems for the office environment, including electronic mail systems, electronic bulletin boards, teleconferencing systems, facsimile systems, and voice mail systems

- Personal productivity aids, such as spreadsheets, calendars, personal database management systems, and project management systems
- "Groupware" systems which facilitate the interaction among individuals in a group working environment.

These office systems evolved from many sources. Along the way, some predecessors, such as stand-alone word processing systems, disappeared, while new systems, such as PCs, suddenly appeared. Until recently, most office automation system components were sold as relatively stand-alone elements on their own technical merits.

By the early 1990s, the scope of office automation will change dramatically. For example, a document image processing (DIP) system will be able to scan a paper insurance application form and store both the image and the textual information. A clerk will review the form image and the database file to fix any incorrect data and to input any data not successfully scanned. He or she will then access internal or external databases to fill in additional data, if any; trigger the generation of a letter to the applicant; and send an electronic mail message advising the agent of the application's status. The clerk will then set up a tickler transaction to reactivate the file when the additional information is received or when a certain period of time has elapsed. When the information is complete, the worker will then route the electronic file (which now contains the image of the scanned application form, other external documents, pointers to the appropriate database records, word processing files of any letters generated, and voice-annotated memos) to a policy rater or actuary. This individual, with the assistance of an AI policy rating assistant, will decide on risk acceptance or refusal, precipitate the generation of the appropriate letters and policy documents, update the appropriate database files, and initiate any follow-up actions, such as premium bills.

Thus, office automation, document image processing, AI, and perhaps information retrieval will be coordinated into a mainline data processing application. Using CASE tools, the diverse elements will be integrated into a seamless application that can be accessed through a single user interface.

Some office automation functions will still be handled by a mainframe, such as the following:

- Control of the corporate communications facilities
- Storage and processing of the master electronic document image and database files
- Overall control of the corporate electronic mail system, including the master name, electronic address, and routing table information.

But the mainframe will not be the center of all communications or the repository for all electronic mail files except in pure, two-level architectural systems in smaller companies. Peer-to-peer connections via the local or backbone LAN will be the major communications mode, rather than the mainframe-centered systems now in place. PABXs will act as the hubs for the voice mail systems.

Departmental systems will contain local calendars, project schedules, and local databases, and will act as hubs for local electronic mail systems. They will also contain the major code modules for the groupware systems. In two-tier architectures, where workstations connect directly to the mainframes, the latter will take on the normal functions of departmental systems.

Electronic mail systems will be hierarchical in nature. Most corporations will set up corporate-wide addressing and routing schemes. Although a great deal of discussion is taking place about universal addressing schemes based upon the X.500 standard, none will be implemented until the mid-1990s.

Many political and institutional barriers block the realization of truly global directory services. For example, some divisions may not wish to change their telephone numbering systems to fit a corporate standard. Another problem is who will control giving out new numbers. Such questions will eventually be overcome by the same factor that favors EDI, namely, the operational efficiencies gained. Also, common carriers will be increasingly squeezed out of messaging markets unless they find a way to implement easy universal connectivity.

In non-IBM installations, X.400-based protocols will predominate; in IBM installations, IBM electronic mail protocols will be used. All suppliers will be able to easily handle both protocol stacks and exchange messages transmitted with one set of protocols to a receiver with the other set.

Servers or departmental systems will act as the primary hubs for local traffic. They will generally store local traffic until accessed by the intended receiver and will forward nonlocal messages to the nearest hub. They will also inform the users of available mail (electronic, FAX, telex, or voice) as soon as it arrives and, upon request, route the message to the facility nearest to the user, no matter where he is. Traffic coming from nonlocal sources will also typically be stored in the local departmental system.

By the mid-1990s, the International Standards Organization's (ISO) Office Document Architecture (ODA) and IBM's Document Content Architecture (DCA) will have been fully specified. They will permit coded data, voice, graphics, and images to be combined into a single document object, which can be stored, communicated, and processed as a single entity. Users will be able to mail any data object by simply moving it to an "out box" and supplying the name of the recipient. Pure data files will be sent using an evolved file transfer, access and management (FTAM) protocol stack, whereas compound documents will be sent using IBM's Document Interchange Architecture (DIA) protocols or the ISO functional equivalents.

Where users need to work closely with others rather than simply send electronic messages, groupware will enable the interchange of ideas, decisions, and documents. Groupware products can facilitate the functioning of long-term project teams (e.g., lawyers working in several cities on a protracted government litigation) as well as ad hoc groups (e.g., in-house consultants forming quickly to generate a proposal to a client).

Yet there is more to groupware than simply software. Workgroup computing demands a high-performance LAN, powerful workstations on each user's desk, and an underlying organizational theory about how people interact most effectively. This theory increasingly presumes that the command-and-control structure in place at many companies is giving way to an "adhocracy," chains of workers running horizontally, vertically, and diagonally across the organization. These nontraditional linkages of professionals and executives require and expect immediate and flexible means of not simply communicating, but of getting their work done.

One of the most active means of interacting in groupware is the bulletin board conference, enabling team members to post electronic files or messages for all colleagues to see. A lawyer in Washington, for instance, could outline his or her defense in an upcoming antitrust case, and the team members locally or in New York could comment and cite precedents. The chief lawyer, upon checking the bulletin board, would see not only the comments, but a record of who has responded and when. The software retains a history of all communications and replies, which is invaluable when a new lawyer joins the team. Rather than being briefed verbally, this lawyer can read the bulletin board's thorough log of the case.

In another area, groupware can function as the logical software residing between team members and the multiple databases on which they rely. When a permitted update to a database is made, groupware ensures that all team members receive the change and are working from the same information source. Calendaring, resource scheduling, group writing, managing electronic messages, and tracking the completion of tasks are some of the typical functions performed by almost every groupware package.

ROLE AND IMPACT OF STANDARDS

Two sets of standards will be followed by all vendors in the mid-1990s that supply complete IIS systems: the IBM SAA, SNA, DIA, DCA de facto series, and the ISO Open System Interconnection (OSI) model. All seven levels of OSI standards will be implemented by the mid-1990s. A significant number of other minor standards will be enforced by groups such as the apparel and auto industries and the government.

The major pressure for standards adherence will come from commercial customers. In Europe as well as the United States, governments will add their weight toward defining standards, often taking myopic nationalistic stands. Because most IISs will contain computer systems provided by several suppliers, to be fully integrated, the systems must be able to interoperate, freely exchanging data objects and in some cases program modules. The continued existence of the huge IBM mainframe base with its customers' commitment to IBM's standards will force other vendors, at a minimum, to maintain gateways into IBM systems.

To facilitate the exchange of text as well as nontext information found in compound documents, office automation systems will support a variety of standards for various data types. New formats for sound, animation, synthesized speech, and so on, will require standards that adequately describe capabilities without excessively limiting them. Use of proprietary file formats will fade as desires for broader information sharing overwhelm vendor loyalties. Standards for transferring revisable compound documents between otherwise incompatible applications programs will mature. Consequently, recipients will be able to edit text and other elements of a document sent to them.

Document translation software will automatically convert document files to match the receiving workstation's requirements. Document exchange will advance beyond today's limited, point-to-point conversion process; it will use common-denominator formats and transparent document exchange that embed conversion capability within the network.

Computer-aided acquisition and logistics support (CALS) will be the most widely implemented standard for compound document exchange (CDE). In 1990, the Department of Defense required all contractors to comply with CALS as specified in the 1804A Standard, which establishes the digital interface between computers exchanging information necessary to support weapons systems. The 1804A Standard addresses technical information, such as manuals with associated tables and drawings, and provides for transfer in a form directly usable by computer applications.

Another CDE standard, the Office Document Architecture–Office Document Interchange Format (ODA-ODIF), will be in early stages of acceptance in U.S. markets. With backing from the ISO, ODA will gain support in Europe first. Vendors such as DEC endorsed the ODA concept early because it allows for the incorporation of video and voice.

Office systems will use page-description languages (PDLs) to facilitate the exchange of noneditable versions of documents and portions of documents. These languages describe the appearance of pages containing text, graphics, and sampled images. They communicate a high-level, device-independent description of a document between a composition system and a display system or hardcopy device. Adobe Systems' PostScript will dominate the marketplace by a large percentage, beating out Xerox's Interpress, Imagen's Document Description Language, and other products, as the foremost PDL.

Standards for exchanging text files will extend beyond the current ASCII model that handles plain text with little formatting information. Text exchange standards will convey more sophisticated layout instructions. The Standard Generalized Markup Language (SGML), which describes text, and IBM's DCA will be prominent. DCA will serve as a common denominator for typographically simple text documents for the next several years. This IBM-developed document exchange standard will continue to enjoy support from many vendors of office automation products. IBM is, however, already discussing a broader, mixed-object document architecture (MODA), commonly dubbed "Son of DCA." IBM will probably produce this standard in the early 1990s in the form of an enhancement to its current DCA. The enhanced DCA (still named DCA) will remain popular through at least 1995.

COMPUTER-GENERATED GRAPHICS

Graphic exchange standards will not mature to the degree of text standards. Among the many overlapping standards for exchanging computer-generated graphics will be the Computer Graphics Metafile (CGM), which governs graphics other than vector; encapsulated PostScript files; and the Initial Graphics Exchange Standard (IGES), which handles vector graphics. The CGM standard integrates creation and delivery of graphic information. It captures graphic information into compact, device-independent, transferable files of a standard format. CGM will continue to serve as an industry standard for nonvector, graphic data interchange among mainframe, minicomputer, and PC environments. When sharing vector graphics, offices will most frequently rely on the IGES, which is a neutral file format for the representation and transfer of object definition data among CAD/CAM (computer-aided design/computer-aided manufacturing) systems and application programs.

The office automation industry will reach broad agreement on how to handle bit-mapped images. Almost all organizations will comply with the Consultative Committee on International Telecommunications and Telephony (CCITT) Groups III and IV facsimile standards. Vendors first applied these standards to facsimile, but will extend them for use on document image processors, intelligent copiers and general-purpose office systems.

The evolving Group IV standard will ultimately handle transmission of final form compound documents and will be complemented by Integrated Services Digital Network (ISDN) implementation. At present, Group IV specifies a mode of black-and-white facsimile operation that utilizes bandwidth compression techniques to transmit images at 200 to 400 dots per inch in less than 1 minute over public voice-grade circuits. Group IV enables essentially fault-free transmission since it contains error detection and retransmission. Furthermore, Group IV can handle whole pages of any size. Group III contains less powerful compression algorithms, transmits data more slowly, and lacks error recovery. Although Group III will still be the most widely supported image file format, its use will decline.

Despite the overall dominance of CCITT standards, other protocols will thrive in certain market segments. The Tagged Image File Format (TIFF) will be popular for publishing applications and will probably add adaptive delta compression of grey-scale data. Processing of color images will still involve disparate proprietary protocols. Until such color image standards take hold, PostScript output of cyan, magenta, yellow, and black separations must suffice as a color output file format.

Audio standards will still be embryonic. Before office systems can exchange sound freely, makers of digital signal processors must settle on sweeping standards for coding wideband speech and music. Audio standards seem most likely to emanate from voice mail market vendors. Broad adoption of voice standards will wait until ISDN becomes widespread.

A forerunner of audio capabilities to come may be the NeXT Computer System, which includes:

- Digital signal processor for high-speed processing of digitized sound and images
- Telephone-grade, 8 bit, 8 kilohertz voice digitizing chip
- 16 bit, 44.1 kilohertz audio output with two-channel stereo for compact disk quality.

Both red–green–blue (RGB) and National Television Study Committee (NTSC) standards will still be used for handling analog video images. However, resolution standards and protocols for video compression and frame capture will be too immature for office systems to exchange video easily.

Intel's digital video interactive (DVI) technology may become a standard for moving images, sound overlays, and graphics. Nonetheless, only a few offices will have an appetite in the mid-1990s for DVI applications, such as computer-based training.

INFORMATION RETRIEVAL SYSTEMS

Information retrieval systems are generally differentiated from standard DBMSs in that they primarily store and retrieve text and other unstructured information, compared with the highly structured data in the latter. Information service providers, such as Mead Data Central with its LEXIS legal text retrieval product, currently feature some of the most sophisticated systems on the commercial market.

Generally, however, information retrieval systems have not engendered much enthusiasm from mainstream businesses. Many companies have experimented with such systems and given them up as being insufficiently useful to be worth the expense. The current drawbacks stem primarily from the lack of natural language technology. The user cannot express and then refine relatively unstructured, ambiguous queries in a way that ensures receipt of the textual data of interest.

Most current techniques either return too much information, only partially accomplishing the task of filtering out the extraneous data, or do not return the particular information that most interests the user. The most successful systems deal with subjects in which precise terminology is common, such as the legal and medical professions. In both cases, the procedures have been rigorously codified in manual systems.

Over the next 5 years, there will be three major classes of information retrieval system developments:

1. Systems for retrieving information from a large and steadily growing library of "documents"
2. Systems for scanning a steady stream of incoming information (e.g., cable traffic, newswires) for data of interest to one or more people
3. Systems for composing and utilizing specially prepared information bases which allow users to more easily follow existing

relationships among the information elements and to form new
relationships as required (hypermedia systems).

Although these classes will evolve at different rates and be accepted
to different degrees in the commercial world, they will share some
technological developments. Most of these systems will be implemented on standard architectures. Mainframe computers will be the
primary machines utilized. Departmental systems, and sometimes
workstations, will be employed for information bases (e.g., those
containing document images) which, although physically large overall, contain relatively small numbers of entries (thousands to tens of
thousands).

Artificial intelligence boards or add-in processors will often
assist in the semantic analysis. Since they will be relatively inexpensive, these aids will add only a very small fraction to the overall
system's costs. Some information library retrieval systems will also
be implemented using massively parallel associative processing computers, such as Thinking Machine Corp.'s Connection Machine.

Enhancements in mass storage technology over the next 5 years
will encourage the development of very large information bases.
Databases measured in tens of gigabytes will be common, and databases having hundreds or even thousands of gigabytes will be set up
for special applications. Because of this easing of size constraints, a
wider variety of information objects will be routinely stored, such as
document images, photographic images (e.g., of houses for sale),
sound recordings, TV recordings, and charts.

Retrieval of noncoded or nontext elements will generally be
handled via a standard DBMS associated with the information base.
IBM already stores pointers to ImagePlus document images in DB2
databases. Via this route, SQL interfaces will be extended to information retrieval systems. In general, however, SQL will not be used
as a standard information retrieval interface over the next 5 years. In
fact, SQL will evolve into primarily a program-to-program interface,
with graphic-oriented, human-to-SQL translator programs being
employed as an easier human–machine interface. By mid-decade,

most commercial DBMS suppliers will have followed IBM's lead in providing indirect hooks for the storage of noncoded or nontext information elements in their systems. They will not, however, have incorporated generalized retrieval capabilities due to lack of a general solution to the natural language query formulation problem as well as little demand for such capabilities.

Information library retrieval systems will be closely related to the information retrieval systems of today. Library retrieval systems deal primarily with large text databases, often for commercial information service providers. Slow advances in the technology over the next 5 years will be mostly in the area of the end-user interface. AI-assisted semantic analyzers, expert systems combined with graphic interfaces, and, in some special cases, uses of systems such as the Connection Machine, will be the major advances. Fully inverted, automatic indexing will also be universal for text-based systems.

With increased use of document image processing systems, many commercial users will build up libraries of document images. Most such systems, however, will use standard DBMS information retrieval techniques to reach the documents of interest.

The general business environment has far more interest in information stream retrieval systems than in library systems. Even in the mid-1990s, the primary customers for such systems will remain information service providers, although stockbrokers and other financial institutions will be potential clients. Several large firms, such as Dow Jones, are experimenting with semantic analyzers and pattern analysis technologies to scan wire service and stock market reporting service stories for areas of interest. Besides alerting individuals of fast-breaking news stories that might be of interest, these firms are building up dynamic history files to identify and track trends important to business.

By the mid-1990s, most such systems will be implemented on associative processing computers with AI assists. However, technological advances will permit usable systems (with plug-in processing elements) to be implemented on PCs and departmental systems as well as on mainframes.

HYPERMEDIA SYSTEMS

Introduction of the Hypercard system by Apple Computer has done more to spark interest in hypermedia technology than all of the previous research. Thousands of amateur and professional application developers have focused their attention on developing "Stackware" programs for the Macintosh. Besides lowering the cost of basic hypertext systems, Apple has added new dimensions in the Macintosh by allowing the inclusion of other forms of data, such as sound, graphics, and potentially even moving images accompanied by sound tracks. This incorporation of data other than text demands applying the term "hypermedia" rather than the more conventional "hypertext."

Individuals will use hypermedia files at an increasing rate in the coming years, primarily as training tools or to accommodate new types of products, such as the electronic encyclopedia. In addition, there is a great deal of interest in the following:

- Cooperative concept generation for new projects and books
- An entirely new software development paradigm
- Major enrichment of published works
- An aid for information retrieval to assist medical diagnoses
- A major new education and training tool.

After the initial excitement dies down, the first two of these goals will be found to be out of reach, at least for the next 5 years. On the other hand, rapid development can be expected in the last three areas. By the mid-1990s, hypermedia systems will be employed primarily in publishing systems for the purpose of producing CDI-based, enriched publications. Such publications will be used by businesses in computer-assisted instruction courses, training and maintenance manuals, and overview reference manuals. Some software documentation will be published in this form, especially that intended for on-line use.

The major problem in meeting the first two goals will be the authoring systems. It is extremely difficult to produce effective hypermedia and authoring systems for very large, dynamic collections of information. These systems tend to expand very rapidly, making the finding of information almost as difficult as without them. Only a partial solution will appear by the mid-1990s; it will be possible to produce such authoring systems on a case-by-case basis, but at relatively great expense. Generic commercial solutions will most likely not exist at that time.

SOFTWARE ENGINEERING

In the 1990s, new system development tools and programming languages will emerge, and they will be very different from those common today. Use of COBOL for large system implementation will decline. FORTRAN will be modified significantly, but remain an important language for scientific applications. Imperative object-oriented languages (e.g., C++) for traditional applications, functional languages (Lisp and APL) for small-scale systems requiring complicated data types, and declarative languages (Prolog) for AI-type applications will grow in popularity.

Future systems will often be subdivided into small, cooperating processes. Workflow languages and LINDA-type additions to standard languages will be used to link cooperating parts of the system which may be written in different languages and run on different computers. Workflow languages generate large programs that exist above normal programs and determine how work flows among processors. LINDA is a set of subroutines that can be added to a conventional language to allow a special routine to coordinate cooperating processes.

Integrated CASE tools will evolve from today's primitive products, which cannot assist in the development of distributed or multimedia systems. In the next 10 years, these tools will aid in all aspects of developing the distributed multimedia applications environment. CASE tools, as envisioned now, will help improve the productivity of systems analysts and programmers, but will not significantly help in reducing the backlog.

Some CASE products will use AI techniques to help analysts design new systems and reengineer older ones. Some will be based on the object-oriented paradigm of design and development. By the mid-1990s, approximately 75% of system development organizations will use at least one niche CASE tool. By the year 2000, many developers will turn to integrated CASE tools and dialects of programming languages such as C++ and Prolog. Still, significant use of COBOL will last into the 21st century.

Application-specific fourth-generation languages (4GLs) and tools such as spreadsheets will proliferate as end-users develop workstation or workgroup applications. In fact, spreadsheets systems—master spreadsheets that draw information from numerous individual spreadsheets—will be developed. Salespeople might download their work to a server at headquarters, where the master spreadsheet picks out the appropriate information for recalculating. Dbase III, in fact, is not as much a database tool for an individual as it is a tool that a company can use to write a master database application for a group. By the mid-1990s, the end user will develop most small-scale systems on workstations using 4GLs, spreadsheets, and database tools.

Powerful forces are encouraging changes in current development techniques. IS departments must dramatically reduce the cost and time it takes to develop new systems. Furthermore, they must reduce the effort required to maintain and make slight changes to existing systems. In essence, IS management must give up executing a typical 2-year plan for developing even a modest-sized system; instead, developers must make and execute a series of 3-month plans. Such quarterly plans would allow the opportunity to correct the mistakes of the prior period, and thus more quickly adjust to changing business situations. When IS planning and system development have been reduced to a collection of 3-month tasks, the IS department will appear more responsive to the business.

Some other forces are also influencing how systems are developed. Most developers realize that COBOL and FORTRAN are not suitable for creating distributed processing systems, and extracting processing power from emerging parallel computers will be very difficult with either of these languages. Furthermore, many new uses of computers, such as AI applications, can best be developed using logic-based declarative languages, such as Prolog, or functional languages, such as Lisp. It is unlikely that such applications would ever be developed using COBOL or FORTRAN.

Many algorithms and applications, typically in the AI area, can best be described using a language such as Prolog. Declarative languages are ideally suited for developing programs to check data consistency or provide inquiry into complex databases. As more applications depend on AI concepts, the use of these languages will grow.

Even though the programming language ADA possesses some object-oriented features and some capabilities to develop a network of synchronized processes, its basic functionality is primitive compared with more modern languages, and its use will not expand in the commercial arena.

INTEGRATED CASE TOOLS

The term "CASE" initially described tools that helped in the analysis and design stages of software development. In the past 2 years, however, the definition has expanded to include tools supporting many other aspects of software development and maintenance.

Because of alliances, acquisitions, and business failures, the number of vendors selling CASE products has shrunk from 15 to about a half dozen, according to the research firm International Data Corp. The remaining companies can be better trusted by users to remain in the market over the long term. Still, the penetration of CASE products into mainstream use is being held back by several factors: the lack of metrics showing performance before and after the introduction of a specific tool, limited portability and flexibility, and the inability of one vendor's product to work with another's.

CASE tools now include ones geared to information strategy planning and code generation. Some include project management and others aspects of reengineering. Many vendors of 4GLs, prototyping tools, and code generators are marketing their facilities as CASE tools. Similarly, tools for maintenance of existing software have been included under the CASE umbrella. As a result, CASE tools can be thought of as any software that helps in any part of the development process.

The growing application backlogs, the maintenance nightmares, and the skyrocketing costs of systems development indicate that users need better system development techniques. By 1995, at least 90% of companies doing software development will have investigated CASE tools, and as much as 50% of them will have invested in the technology.

During the next 5 years, many new CASE tools will emerge. Some niche products will help automate one aspect of the system development process, such as planning, programming, or testing. Others will be integrated tools that try to provide assistance in the entire process. More comprehensive integrated CASE tools will continue to focus primarily on the development of information systems.

The niche tools will support small, isolable tasks of design conversion, development, and maintenance. Significant among them will be the tools that permit conversions of databases between one specifically defined DBMS and another, and between specific query languages and standard SQL. Semantic problems will prevent the development of any generic DBMS conversion tools. Niche CASE tools will support an increasing number of target hardware and operating environments, including mainframes, minicomputers, personal computers, workstations, and networks.

Integrated CASE tools will continue to target systems operating on large mainframe computers and using database management systems, particularly relational DBMS. These tools are currently targeted to COBOL code generation, but there will be growing support for the more popular application generators (including 4GLs) and for C, because of program portability. These systems will also be enhanced to take into account distributed systems and the growing use of workflow languages. ADA will not be supported by major CASE tools by the mid-1990s, because there is very little requirement for this language outside of the Department of Defense.

The significant progress being made on the development of data dictionary and data interchange standards may sometimes permit niche CASE vendors to provide integrated solutions. IBM's system development methodology, AD/Cycle Repository, will make it easier to integrate such CASE tools. Despite IBM's pressure, use of AD/ cycle products and the Repository will grow only slowly during the early 1990s.

The niche CASE approach will achieve significantly greater market penetration but provide relatively small productivity increases. The integrated CASE approach could bring about far higher productivity increases, but, because it requires major changes to an organization's culture, policies, and procedures, it will experience much lower market penetration during the next 5 years.

Many MIS managers will be reluctant to adopt CASE tools and new programming languages until they are proven. These technologies will seem abstract and not applicable to their operations. The cost of training staff in such a new methodology or language seems high in light of the need to retrain staff to maintain COBOL- or FORTRAN-based systems. The managerial problems of having two classes of programmers, those who know the "new ways" and those who know only "the old ways," will also discourage adoption of the new technologies.

Nonetheless, the bottleneck in developing and maintaining systems has become so serious that many aggressive companies will take the risk of leaving the old ways. Some firms that have adopted CASE tools are reporting increases in programmer productivity of 20 to 30%. Many managers will be willing to make sizable investments in training and organizational change to get such benefits, even though they are an order of magnitude smaller than initial vendor claims. The amount of this investment is difficult to judge, but certainly far exceeds the original purchase price. CASE expert Ed Yourdon calculates that a company spending $3.75 million for the hardware and software to outfit 200 professionals with CASE tools should expect to spend an additional half million dollars a year for training, support, and maintenance. Perhaps in part because of this heavy ongoing cost, 70% of CASE tools are no longer in use 2 years after their purchase, according to Yourdon.

Although CASE products will positively affect productivity, they are fundamentally aimed at the wrong problem. The real problem in software development today is less the productivity of programmers and more the labor-intensive systems definition phase. Development often spans 3 years, by which time the intended users' requirements have changed. The initial configuration never works correctly, which means time-consuming rewriting.

The old programming languages were designed decades ago when central processing unit (CPU) time was relatively expensive. The languages were optimized before running to minimize machine time. The economics have shifted, however. CPU time is now an insignificant cost of software development, whereas the major costs appear in the system design and implementation stages. Today, developers work on constructing monolithic integrated applications in which programmers spend Monday or Tuesday of each week simply catching up on the changes made by their peers the week before. What is needed is good functional decomposition of the system into modules, and CASE tools are not helping to achieve it. CASE tools do not effectively work in distributed systems, and they do not take into account implementation tools, such as workflow languages. CASE is mired in the old paradigm—the one big system being developed in traditional COBOL detail.

A programming language such as Prolog may help the software

development process, because code can be written at a higher level of abstraction. An inference engine (essentially an elaborate interpreter) compiles the system primarily at run-time. Although the application runs more slowly, dramatic increases in machine speed will more than compensate. Reservation systems cannot be written today in a language such as Prolog, but evidence indicates that they could be in 5 or 6 years.

CASE tools are in a similar state as the old line editors of 1970; it is hard to imagine what they will look like in 1995, but they will be dramatically different. CASE is surely no panacea. Regardless of where the solutions for development problems come from, however, they will end up being incorporated into CASE.

ARTIFICIAL INTELLIGENCE

Even by the mid-1990s, AI will remain primarily a software technology. No foreseeable commercial market exists for large, specialized AI machines, with the possible exception of neural network computers. Almost all AI applications will be implemented on specialized component processors, which are embedded in larger systems, or will be purely software-based systems implemented on standard-architecture computers.

The major AI applications will still fall into the "assistant" or "agent" classifications; that is, they will be applications intended to assist clerical and professional personnel in making repetitive, important, but common decisions. Credit application approval, credit card purchase authorization, device failure diagnosis, and factory floor and computer system resource utilization optimization will be some of the routine applications. In particular, AI will be applied to operating systems, DBMS, and network managers to improve information system control and security. Such applications will be fully integrated into the overall IIS, accepting input from standard software systems and producing output usable by other standard software systems as well as human users.

Neural network computers will remain in the embryonic stage of development by the mid-1990s. Their major function in the commercial marketplace will be for pattern recognition and signal processing applications, such as machine vision, natural language understanding, and other such advanced AI applications. Natural language translation and understanding will develop very slowly. The underlying science of computational linguistics is making little progress. The keyboard will remain the major command interface for workstations, although voice entry of limited commands and perhaps direct transcription of speech will be possible.

IMAGE PROCESSING

Over the long run, images as an information type will become as vital an element of information processing systems as data and more recently text have been. The full flowering of this possibility will extend into the late 1990s and beyond, but already a limited number of custom, expensive specific applications have been developed. These applications deal with the daunting tasks of managing huge volumes of engineering drawings, or coping with time- and cost-sensitive paper information flows, such as those associated with processing insurance documents.

The benefits of these systems include cost savings (reductions in clerical staff and other operational costs of storing and retrieving paper documents); higher productivity (less time wasted by expensive staff locating document-based information); and improved service that may translate to competitive advantage (e.g., more accurate and rapid tracking and response to customers in processing insurance applications).

Some benefits are application-specific, for example, the savings reported by Pacific Gas and Electric of $500,000 per closed-down day by shortening the outages of the Diablo Canyon reactor through providing more rapid access to the drawings needed for diagnosis and repair (250,000 drawings are involved in all). Until now, imaging systems have been largely stand-alone, that is, not integrated with existing information processing systems. As standard computing platforms advance in performance and decrease in price, there is a clear trend to implement imaging systems on these, rather than on proprietary platforms, and to seek to incorporate imaging systems into the mainstream of information processing.

Thanks to higher speed local-area networks such as **FDDI** (see Chapter 9), communication will be less of a potential bottleneck for operating bandwidth-intensive distributed imaging systems. Software is becoming the major source of value-added for these systems as well as the principal differentiating factor between competitors and the pacing factor for market growth and user acceptance.

In broad terms, the use of document imaging systems involves two major categories:

1. *Document filing*—which typically covers straightforward storage and retrieval of documents based on keyword indexes
2. *Workflow automation*—less common than filing systems today, which automatically handles such tasks as routing and scheduling work with the help of workflow software

Because of their greater potential benefits as the appropriate applications software is developed, the work flow imaging category should grow more rapidly than the filing category, especially in the mid-and late-1990s.

Early examples of document image processing systems from which new generations of products will emerge over the next few years include **IBM**'s Image Plus and Filenet's systems. Other major computer vendors such as Wang, DEC, and Unisys are also targeting these imaging applications.

The major functions of these systems will be to input, store, and retrieve images of hard copy documents. These systems will also handle simple image manipulation tasks, such as cropping, sizing, rotating, image merging, and image insertion into complex documents. By the mid-1990s, document image processing systems will represent the largest single portion of the overall image market.

Images will increasingly be associated with other information types (e.g., data, text, voice) to provide a multi-media applications environment that links the power of computers to the natural skills of humans and their desire to work with images as well as language, numbers and sound in creating, communicating, reviewing and analyzing information.

Machine vision technology will focus primarily on assembly-line inspection, and systems to do this work will be widespread by the mid-1990s. They will be able to inspect objects on rapidly moving production lines and compare them to predefined parameters of shape, size, and color. The prepared foods and discrete parts manufacturing industries already employ such systems. Simple AI techniques, including basic neural network-based systems, will be utilized to enhance the discrimination capabilities of such systems.

Scientific processing systems (supercomputers, minisupercomputers, etc.) will make heavy use of graphic input and graphic output (visualization) to meet users' needs. These specialized systems will be variations of the high-end scientific workstations featuring special graphic processing chips and specialized fiber-optic I/O channels to handle very high bandwidths.

More advanced image processing systems will also exist. They will enable operators to produce animated images and produce and modify realistic images. They will be utilized primarily by animation and film production companies, businesses specializing in satellite image processing, or military and intelligence agencies. The average large commercial enterprise will find little reason to use these systems.

The adoption of more powerful hardware, including graphics coprocessors, compression/decompression chips, and higher resolution displays, will make editing bit maps of still images much more economical and convenient. The most common applications for image editing will continue to be found in publishing, presentations, and document image processing. Functions will include thresholding, edge detection, rotation, cropping, sizing, text or image overlay, and pixel editing.

Character recognition systems will develop superb accuracy rates. Similarly, significant developments, primarily in software, will improve recognition of geometric objects (arcs, lines, etc.). Despite such progress, the state of the art in recognition technology will not be sufficient to allow office systems to identify objects such as buildings, vehicles, and faces. Only very specific and predictable applications, such as vision systems for identifying parts on an assembly line, will be able to interpret real-world images.

Editing of full-motion and animated video images will still be prohibitively expensive for most regular offices. The cost of producing 1 minute of image-edited video will exceed $1,000, a price few organizations will be willing to pay. Specialized companies such as Pixar will set the pace for animated video editing, specifically in moving images, editing techniques include captioning, zooming, and polarity inversion.

FUTURE SYSTEMS

Just as most of today's modern applications require an operating system, DBMS, and a transaction processing monitor, the systems of 1995 will require even more:

- Office automation technologies, including electronic mail, enhanced word processing, desktop publishing, full-motion video graphics and images
- Document image processing systems
- AI software and component hardware processors.

These applications will be composed of multiple cooperating processes running different systems. Response-time critical processes will run on the workstations whenever possible. Data-dependent processes will run on the mainframes or on application-specific departmental systems when appropriate. These systems will depend upon full connectivity of all elements and upon the interoperability of computers supplied by multiple vendors.

Yet even in the mid-1990s, however, many of today's application systems will still be operating, using what appears to be a very restrictive subset of the IIS's capabilities. This software lag will keep the IIS from realizing its full potential, cause end-users to complain about the restrictions on their systems, and keep local programmers very busy with the same 2- to 3-year backlog that exists today.

This note of realism stems from the realization that in 1995, IS departments will still face the traditional problem of too much to do with insufficient resources. As discussed in Chapter 3, companies must make many hard choices in terms of their rate of progression towards IISs, considering the modification or total rewrite of existing applications versus the development of new applications intended to meet pressing business needs. This realism should not be confused with pessimism. Aggressive companies can handle the challenges of building the appropriate infrastructure, balancing the short-term business demands for new, isolated applications against the long-term infrastructure building needs.

The vision of the highly competitive, information-supported integrated enterprise contains the seeds of the continued success for companies that adopt it. The struggle and the expenditure of management time and attention required to attain the integrated enterprise will be advantageous. As companies prepare the new infrastructure, they will also be paving the way for the organizational changes necessary for success in the 1990s. Such changes are much easier to make in an information-rich, flexible environment than in one based on isolated automated systems containing reams of inconsistent or inaccessible data.

Although the technological terms and concepts can be daunting, their effects can be clearly explained in simple business terms. Work will be needed on both management's and MIS's parts to form a much closer working relationship that is based on mutual trust and understanding. In that environment, the long-term versus short-term tradeoffs can be intelligently made. The vision of the integrated enterprise can be maintained in balance with the need to keep the business running today.

CHAPTER 7

BUSINESS COMPUTER SYSTEMS AND SOFTWARE

The increasing capabilities of every level of business computers will be almost breathtaking in the early 1990s. Although the numbers quantifying these changes may be almost unimaginable, the effects are not. By 1995, almost all personnel in an aggressive corporation will depend upon their workstations and supporting infrastructure to allow them to gather and utilize information with decided ease to support virtually every aspect of their everyday functions. Little will transpire in a business without one or more computers assisting, supporting, or actually carrying out the action. The anticipated price reductions and performance improvements will permit companies to afford automated support and, in fact, make it a necessity for competitive existence.

The interconnection of computers and applications will require commonality in the definitions of many financial business measures and terms, and a higher degree of compatibility among systems than is usually found in today's corporations. For example, "profit before tax" for each of a company's divisions must be defined in the same way (i.e., profit before or after corporate taxes, profit before or after depreciation, etc.). Parts identifications must be made consistent so that the same number does not refer to two different parts in two different divisions. The transition to the connected enterprise will

129

not be easy to manage and will be costly to achieve if many such incompatibilities have crept into an organization's manual and partially automated systems.

THE BUSINESS WORKSTATION

The PC of the late 1980s generally operated as a stand-alone machine, switching to a communications mode only when it exchanged simple messages with other devices. By the mid-1990s, the typical PC will evolve into an interface device between a worker and the network of resources available to him or her, with communications and cooperative processes taking place invisibly and automatically. This machine will go far beyond the current PC in capability; therefore, it requires a new designation—the business workstation.

Low-end workstations will attain speeds and memory capacities at least equal to those of the 80386-based PCs of the late 1980s. Much of this speed will help support ease-of-use features. In addition, large compact disk read-only memory (CD-ROM) disks will store libraries of programs and multimedia reference materials. All but the lowest end workstations will use graphic cards for clipping, scaling, and hidden-line removal.

High-end business workstations of the mid-1990s will be based mainly on Intel Corp.'s 80486 chip. (A follow-on chip probably will not come into general use until the latter portion of the decade.) These workstations will feature extensive graphics capabilities and throughputs just slightly less than today's Stardent graphic workstations. Displays will contain 1280×960 picture elements, which approaches the resolution limit of the human eye.

Figure 7.1 summarizes the characteristics of basic and high-end workstations of the mid-1990s. Prices will remain at current levels while power and capacity improve sharply. The low-end workstation will include an arithmetic-logic unit (ALU) with the power of today's fastest microprocessor (5 to 10 MIPS), whereas the high-end unit will run twice as fast. Both will feature flat-panel, addressable-matrix

Figure 7.1   Business Workstations of the Mid-1990s

BASIC WORKSTATION

- $4-8K (Aver. Config.)

- 5-10 MIPS

- 960 x 480 Display

- 4-6 MB Main Memory

- 50-300 MB Disk

- 0.6-1 GB CDROM

- Low-Cost Impact or Non-Impact Printer

- LAN Interface

HIGH END WORKSTATION

- $8-12K (Aver. Config.)

- 10-20 MIPS

- 1280 x 960 Display

- 8-12 MB Main Memory Boards

- 200-400 MB Disk

- 1-10 GB Optical Disk

- Output Page Imager of 400 Dots/Inch

- LAN Interface

- Add-On Graphics and Accelerator

displays offering resolution equal to that of current base CRTs. Standard storage will be much larger (50 to 300 megabytes per disk for the low end, 200 to 400 megabytes per disk for the high end), with optical disks potentially adding another 1 to 10 gigabytes.

SERVERS

Low-end servers will be derived from high-end workstation hardware, using the same types of microprocessors (80486 and successors) found in them. Servers will provide file storage, data sharing, electronic mail, and group services (e.g., desktop publishing, group calendaring, and draft document reviews). In its average configuration, a server will cost $15,000 to $50,000, little more than a high-

Figure 7.2   Servers of the Mid-1990s

– $15-50K (Aver. Config.)	• Add-On Signal Processing Accelerator and Gateway Boards
– 30-50 MIPS	
– 16-32 MB Main Memory	• Multicolor Large Format Imager
– 2-5 GB Disk	
– Multiple 10 GB Optical Disks	• Input Scanner
– Standard Instrumentation Interfaces	• Protocol Conversion Devices

end workstation. The server will operate at 20 to 30 MIPS and include 16 to 32 megabytes of main memory and 2 to 5 gigabytes of disk storage. The operating system will be DOS or OS/2 (Fig. 7.2).

High-end servers will be based on a new type of computer architecture. They will couple 2 to 32 standard building-block processors, such as the Intel 386, 486, or 860 chips. Special processors will provide I/O channel and caching capabilities. The servers will be designed to allow extremely fast access (12 milliseconds) and data transfer speeds (500 megabytes per second) for applications running on a LAN. The servers will be connected to two to six separate LANs, thus creating one large logical network. These high-end servers will support a few hundred users and 2 to 100 gigabytes of disk storage. OS/2 and Novell's Netware operating systems will be most common, although Unix will run on some. These machines will range in cost from $20,000 to $200,000.

DEPARTMENTAL COMPUTERS

Departmental machines (Fig. 7.3) are generally minicomputers possessing the power and I/O throughput of small mainframes. They can handle all the processing needs of a department or subsidiary of modest size with little or no communication to a mainframe.

Figure 7.3 Mid-1990s Departmental Computer

- $100-1,000K (Aver. Config.)

- 50-500 MIPS

- 32-50 MB Main Memory

- 1-20 GB Disk

- Multiple 10 GB Optical Disks

- Specialized Coprocessors

- Gateway to LANs and WANs

The architecture of 32-bit, bus-oriented minicomputers will continue to predominate in the mid-1990s. Tightly coupled multiprocessors in departmental computers will be common. Special application speedup cards and add-on processors for signal processing, graphics, and vector processing will be in widespread use by engineering and scientific users (see Chapter 8).

The high-end departmental computer will take on many characteristics of small mainframe computers, except their higher cost. Such features will include multiple processing and clustering capabilities, as well as an emphasis on effective transaction processing and data accessing. Departmental computers will not, however, attain the much higher I/O throughput capacity of their mainframe counterparts.

The footprint and base technologies of low-end departmental systems will rapidly evolve over the next 5 years to closely approximate the "desk-side" computers of the late 1980s. Multiple reduced instruction set computer (RISC) chips will form the processing units of many of these future systems, and the price–performance ratios will rapidly approach those of workstations.

Processing speeds will increase and costs will fall for departmental computers, but not as fast as for high-end workstations. As a result, the departmental computers will find themselves squeezed between high-end workstations or servers and small mainframes. Partly for this reason, the market share occupied by departmental computers will decrease, even as the actual market size increases.

MAINFRAME COMPUTERS

The mainframes of the mid-1990s (Fig. 7.4) will be based on advanced hardware architectures that are upwardly compatible from those of the late 1980s so that program compatibility can be maintained. Machine designs will be dominated by those from IBM, because most users will want to use evolved versions of the MVS/ESA operating system. IBM's future machines will come with an architecture based on the current 390 systems. The new I/O architecture will continue to evolve. Channels, which will continue to use fiber-optic technology and will become faster serial (20 megabytes per second) transfer devices. The backplane may also use fiber-optics and possess gigabyte transfer capabilities.

High-end machines will feature up to 32 processors, 48-bit addresses, and some of the object-oriented features of the IBM AS/400. The basic design of the machine facilitates its use in a centralized transaction processing system or as a high data-access rate file server.

Figure 7.4   Mid-1990s Mainframe Computer

- $2,000-10,000K (Aver. Config.)   - Multiple I/O complements
- 100-1,000 MIPS
- 1-5 GB Main Memory
- 200-400 GB Disk
- Multiple 10 GB Optical Disks
- Vector Facility, 100-400 MFLOPS
- Gateways to high speed LAN for connection to specialized processors and local LANs
- Fiber optic Bus

The top speed of the individual processors in a system will grow to more than 60 MIPS by the mid-1990s. Such an increase will contribute to an effective processing rate of 500 to 600 MIPS per system, compared to the 120 MIPS per system on the late 1980s' IBM 3090-600. The cost per MIPS will fall from $120,000 in 1988 to $20,000 by about 1995 (Fig. 2.8).

Enhanced versions of today's proprietary operating systems will predominate. Improvements will come mainly in usability rather than new function. Floor space and environmental requirements will remain unchanged, despite major increases in processing and memory capacity.

DATABASE MACHINES

Database machines will be used only in the highest rate on-line transaction processing systems of the mid-1990s. The growth in use of database machines has been slow because the major mainframe architectures, such as IBM's ESA, continue to provide sufficient I/O power for all but the most demanding situations. The most widespread class of database machines at present is SQL servers, which are intended to support relational databases on a PC LAN. Standardized SQL is used for communicating with users. IBM, DEC, and several others supply SQL servers. They will take many forms by the mid-1990s, from server-class DL1-based systems to large mainframes.

Using its 3990 controller within ESA, IBM separates a database into parts according to frequency of use, and stores the parts in a storage hierarchy. Teradata, the most successful maker of specialized database machines, separates a database among parallel processors according to frequency of use. IBM uses vertical separation; Teradata uses horizontal. Current research seeks to combine the two methods by taking advantage of uneven file reference frequency to distribute segments across parallel processors as well as down a storage hierarchy managed by each processor. Such processors may be necessary to support the 2,000 transactions per second throughputs expected of the larger systems in the mid-1990s. Already American Airlines' Sabre reservation system has reached that threshold. Another innovative database machine technology (e.g., from Nucleus International) separates relational tables into data dictionaries containing the values and bit vectors in two dimensions that represent the relationships. This procedure is useful for high-speed searching in slowly changing files.

Despite the experimentation and improvements, database machines will grow only slowly in popularity. SQL servers within PC LANs will be widespread, rendering specially designed database machines of limited utility. Their main use will be in niche applications with either high data throughput or high complexity.

OTHER TYPES OF COMPUTERS

Startup companies will continue to develop and commercialize computers with novel architectures, such as data flow, wave front, and neural networks. These machines may prove useful for some very specialized applications, but little commercial use will occur before the mid-1990s. By that time, some neural network computers may perform limited pattern recognition tasks for such applications as assembly-line parts recognition.

Internally redundant "nonstop" processors are already in widespread use for transaction processing applications and should increase their market share. The bulk of transaction processing, however, will probably still be performed on conventional mainframes and minicomputers. Their availability is already so high that many users are willing to assume that outages will be infrequent. Furthermore, in many transaction processing applications, the level of computing power needed exceeds what nonstop processors can provide. By mid-decade, even conventional mainframes will be capable of restarting within a few minutes after an error, thus meeting the extremely high availability requirements for most companies.

OVERALL PRICE PERFORMANCE IMPROVEMENTS

Figure 2.8 illustrated the incremental improvements in price performance that have taken place over the past 25 years from large through small systems. This steady progress of approximately 20% per year will continue. Since the mid-1970s, the price of smaller mainframe-type computers (the 4300 class, now called departmental machines) has tracked the price of mainframes at about half the cost per unit of computing.

SYSTEM SOFTWARE

Because users of operating system and database software have made significant investments in preparing programs and procedures dependent on them, they are reluctant to give them up. As a result, system programs remain in use for 10 years or more after the vendor has declared them obsolete and no longer supports them.

Vendors want to be relieved of the cost of maintaining old versions of their proprietary programs. Users want interoperability and transportability of software, and the public relations pressure on vendors to support standards is strong. Driven by these influences, SQL has already become a de facto standard for interchange of queries between different database systems, despite its shortcomings and lack of maturity, and despite the shortcomings of the relational database model itself.

Because of users' requirements, no operating system or DBMS that has not already been announced will be important by the mid-1990s. Some new operating systems and database products will be available, but they will all be interoperable with existing ones. The NeXT personal computer, announced in 1988 with an operating system called MACH, could be a significant product by 1993. MACH will be compatible with Unix, so it can be viewed simply as another implementation of that operating system. New database packages will be primarily SQL compatible and based on the relational model.

OPERATING SYSTEMS

All operating systems will become more robust, automatic, secure, and easy to use. Expert system techniques will focus particularly on ease of use, thereby reducing the need for system operators. Significantly more advanced security will be provided, reminiscent of the old Honeywell Multics system. New operating systems will consume even more of the system resources than they do currently, but few users will complain since mainframe performance will increase rapidly.

The pressure for interoperability of computer programs and the need by computer vendors to reduce their expenditures for development and maintenance of operating systems will mean that the number of widely used operating systems will slowly decrease (Fig. 2.7 (page 29)). Use of OS/2 and Apple OS will steadily grow because of the transition from stand-alone PCs and dumb terminals to communicating workstations. Some high-end workstations and most servers will use Unix. MS/DOS will survive in simpler systems, however, because of extensive user investments in it.

Departmental computers will use OS/400, the operating system for the IBM AS/400 series; Unix; or DEC's VAX/VMS. By 1995, 10 to 20% of servers will use Unix. Variants of Unix, of which there are almost 50 in 1990, will meet a single standard by mid-decade. The variants will not disappear, but they all will comply with POSIX (Portable Operating System for Computer Environments) and other standards necessary for interoperation. Both IBM and DEC have already changed their stances to become sincere supporters of a Unix standard. The federal government perceived that the key issue of what version to use is the applications interface and pressed for acceptance of POSIX. The government has insisted on "open" systems, which by definition are those with operating systems meeting the POSIX standard. Initially a time-sharing system, Unix is poorly structured for data-intensive applications, and its security capabilities need improvement. Adaptations satisfactory to the market will be made, however.

OS/400, the operating system for the IBM AS/400 series, is perhaps the best design for its purpose of any operating system on the market. IBM seems only belatedly aware of this fact. Its advantages, such as database orientation, were somewhat obscured until major new applications made them clear. Now that IBM has recognized its benefits, OS/400 will be improved steadily along with that of the hardware follow-on to AS/400.

Large mainframe servers and specialized parallel processors will continue to use proprietary operating systems. The trend in the high-end mainframe business is to MVS/ESA. ESA better matches market needs, such as security, multiple simultaneous modes of operation, very large DBMSs, high-volume OLTP systems, than any other mainframe operating system. Over time, MVS/ESA should sweep the field because businesses will require this functionality for current as well as future applications. Although numerous capabilities will be added to make MVS/ESA more robust, responsive, easy to use, fail soft, and secure, it will not change in any basic way during the next 5 years. Proprietary operating systems for other high-speed servers, such as parallel computers, will be based mostly on Unix or AIX.

DOS/VSE will inevitably lose share to MVS/ESA. Use of VM will also decrease, not because of replacement by another operating system, but because mainframe-based software development will give way to workstation-based development coordinated by a mainframe. Still, VM will be kept current since it will remain indispensable as the host in supporting multiple control programs.

VMS will lose share as DEC's emphasis on Unix increases and as all other vendors of proprietary operating systems will be forced to adopt either Unix or comply with IBM systems.

DATABASE SYSTEMS

Most users will steadily migrate to relational database packages, such as Oracle, Ingres, and Sybase. IBM users will adopt DB/2. Use of IMS, IDMS, and other network-based packages will slowly decrease. Disk caching, use of main memory, and other techniques will improve the performance of relational database systems. Peak SQL transaction rates may approach 1,000 per second.

SQL will continue to be modified and developed as a standard data query language. It will interconnect heterogeneous networks of files and, along with SAA or POSIX, improve the interoperability of application programs. Nonrelational DBMS will build SQL interfaces.

The capabilities of relational databases will be expanded so that they can handle new data types, such as images and voice. Some packages will provide object-oriented capabilities and rule-based data integrity and relationship features. By 1995, the most popular database systems will be able to operate in a distributed mode on a variety of processing platforms. The use of distributed processing will spread as it becomes clear that integrity, security, and control can be accounted for in this environment.

Special-purpose DBMSs will retain healthy market niches not mentioned above. Systems dedicated to high-speed transaction processing will still use IBM's TPF (or descendants) and specialized software by Tandem and Stratus. Peak financial transaction rates for such systems will reach 2,000 per second (in lotteries and credit approvals). Specialized database systems will also support supercomputers, AI systems, and some image processing systems.

PATTERNS OF SYSTEM SOFTWARE USAGE

Figure 2.7 (page 29) shows the pattern of system program use expected in a typical Fortune 500 manufacturing company of the mid-1990s. Other types of organization will usually be subsets. General management, marketing, and finance are grouped together because they will probably have similar uses, primarily financial-oriented applications and reports. System software uses in engineering and manufacturing are distinct and even differ somewhat from one another. Manufacturing handles control applications of machines and processes as well as applications involving scheduling of operations.

Engineering needs high compute power for design and simulation applications. Central data processing provides mainframe and departmental server services for them all.

GENERAL MANAGEMENT, MARKETING, AND FINANCE

The stand-alone PC will become obsolete, generally replaced by integrated workstations that communicate transparently with the corporate network. The majority of these will use OS/2 as the operating system, but many will still run evolved versions of MS/DOS, using Microsoft Windows as their graphical interface.

The evolution to OS/2 will be slow for several reasons. On the technical side, native OS/2 applications will not appear quickly because of the complexity that software developers face in writing code for the new use interface and for the overall operating environment. This effort represents a major investment for the developers, who often can more profitably utilize their resources by developing more capable versions of their existing packages running under DOS.

From the users' perspectives, OS/2 provides an easier-to-use interface and multi-tasking but offers no other desired functions. At the same time, OS/2 prevents them from using some of their favorite utility programs, such as the Fastback file backup and the Norton Utilities file recovery. Users can also experience problems with locally written applications, some of which will not run under OS/2.

From IS management's point of view, OS/2-equipped PCs are much more expensive than DOS-equipped systems because of the increased main memory and processing power required by the newer operating system. By 1990, no blockbuster new application, such as the spreadsheet of the late 1970s, had appeared that would run only under OS/2 and not under DOS. Thus, although a few power users have talked their way into getting what they want, management has not been convinced that OS/2 is required for the general masses.

The Apple operating system will be used in a significant minority of cases. The database manager of choice will usually be relational, such as Microsoft's version of DB/2 or Oracle.

To support network processing applications, aggressive companies will move quickly into the OS/2- and DB/2-compatible environment. These applications, often homegrown or developed by system integrators, will be designed so that the time-sensitive parts run on the PC, while the data-intensive parts run on mainframes or servers. Many of these applications will draw on images or multimedia information which use the capabilities to the best advantage. AI-based components will also be integrated into these applications to free users from the mind-numbing stream of "no-brainer" decisions, leaving them more time to handle those matters in which human judgment is required.

These applications will not only make a user's life easier, but will allow him or her to provide customers with more accurate, faster, and higher quality service. American Express has already implemented this kind of application in its purchase-credit approval area. The company was able to substantially reduce the size of its credit approval workforce, thereby saving money.

Departmental systems will usually be application specific, that is, contain the programs and files for an application or region, but interoperate with the network. IBM's AS/400 product line will be the most widely used, with its proprietary operating system and database manager. VAX systems and, to a lesser extent, systems from other vendors will also be employed.

ENGINEERING AND MANUFACTURING

Because of their long-standing commitments to DEC and other vendors, engineering and manufacturing users will resist IBM standards. Their present vendors, however, are in the process of evolving from proprietary software to Unix and SQL standards. The secondary tier of vendors is already adopting these standards. The more conjectural question is DEC's policy. Although VMS will still be supported in the mid-1990s, market pressure will force DEC to become an increasingly vigorous Unix supporter. More than half of its users will have adopted Unix by then, particularly those in engineering and manufacturing.

Engineering users will almost always require Unix and Oracle in the workstations they buy, as well as in the minisupercomputers that will be widespread in the mid-1990s. The situation in manufacturing will not be so straightforward. Some workstations in this environment handle mainly administrative work, and thus will be provided by central data processing and most likely use OS/2. Many manufacturing facilities are already deeply committed to VAXs running VMS, and a sizable percentage will still use them in the mid-1990s. In virtually all cases, however, enough standardization will occur in the next few years to permit network interoperability (via SQL, as noted above, and communication standards).

CENTRAL DATA PROCESSING

In 5 years, the data processing center will be even more IBM-standard than it is now. Integrated workstations will be employed primarily for data entry, software development, and system monitoring. They will typically use OS/2 and rarely require internal databases.

The server-class departmental systems provided to the entire organization as part of the centrally controlled network will usually employ OS/2 and its version of the DB/2 database manager. These two will be the primary server system programs of SAA, which will have been adopted by most users. OS/2 appears to be a powerful tool for controlling the server environment.

Mainframes will almost always use MVS/ESA; by the mid-1990s, its advantages over earlier operating systems will be overwhelming. Although DB/2 will be the most common database manager, users needing high throughputs who are satisfied with the structure of IMS will continue to use it. When they do, they will employ some sort of bridge to the SQL intercommunication standard.

CONVERTING TO THE IIS

Business computer systems are becoming richer in function and more complex in the brands and types of products they include. Most users will choose more than one operating system and DBMS because the surviving systems will come with varying capabilities and can interoperate; however, some users will need application portability among different classes of processors in the networks. These users may standardize on POSIX-compliant Unix despite the relative clumsiness of that operating system.

The system programs with decreasing market shares will not suddenly disappear. Most operating systems and DBMS in widespread use today will remain in the mid-1990s. Some will be enhanced to be compatible with interoperability standards and late-model hardware. Experience shows that it takes many years to eliminate a once-popular system program from the marketplace. Also, there is money to be made in supporting the remaining users, at least for a while.

Maturity does not preclude improvement. During the coming years, all surviving operating systems will be required to become more versatile in the breadth of applications handling. By 1995, they all should be capable of turning a computer system into an information repository manager and assigning its resources to batch and transaction processing, office automation, and workstation support.

Also, the surviving system programs will be steadily improved with "self-consciousness," user-friendliness, self-measurement and self-management, data security, and self-protection. These enhancements will be driven by the market forces described earlier, as well as by increasing network complexity and security consciousness among users. Expert system techniques have already proven to be especially applicable to self-consciousness functions, and a great improvement in the hardware price–performance ratio will accommodate the steady increase in systems overhead.

Self-consciousness functions will be extensions of the current resource scheduling algorithms and the user interface "agents" that were available in the late 1980s. Normally, these functions will be expressed in the form of increased self-scheduling of systems and interfaces in which the default responses to varying situations are based on past user behavior. Shared machines (e.g., mainframes and departmental computers) will increasingly be able to set their own processing schedules to optimize the allocation of scarce resources. These algorithms will dynamically change priorities, reschedule jobs, and automatically take care of unexpected emergencies or rush work without human intervention.

Major functional enhancements are required for Unix (and to a lesser extent other major operating systems) to better meet user needs related to mid-sized and larger machines:

- To support applications that simultaneously use several processors in the same machine. Since many newer computers will be based on multiprocessors, some users will develop applications that show modest degrees of parallelism in trying to use the processors simultaneously. Most operating systems today include only awkward capabilities to work in this way. The next 5 years will bring more user-friendly interfaces for multiprocessing.

- To support machine clustering and workload balancing. With the advent of distributed processing and high-speed LANs and/ or hyperchannels, workloads can be spread among separate computers linked together. The capabilities currently exhibited by the VAX cluster and Tandem systems will be extended to other operating systems.

- To support high I/O rates. Any mainframe and mid-sized computer can be used as a file server in the future. As a result, all machines will need to sustain very high I/O rates. Vendors must enhance most of today's operating systems to sustain the I/O rates needed for image, voice, and other advanced applications. This task is relatively easy.

- To support security needs. With the growing awareness of the threat posed by computer hackers or even more malicious corporate spies trying to obtain sensitive information, most organizations will expect improved security capabilities to be embedded in the operating system.

Database packages will change greatly over the next few years as well. Users want to be able to:

- Use more complex data types, such as images, voice, lines, surfaces for CAD/CAM applications, and so forth
- Sustain high-speed transaction rates nearing 2,000 transactions per second
- Distribute databases so they can take advantage of the power of workstations, transparently use information at other business sites, and provide wider bandwidth access to data.

Users are confused as to how to define a distributed database management system (D-DBMS). At the very least, a D-DBMS must provide a seamless interface to data that is stored on multiple, geographically dispersed computers. Transparent access occurs when the user does not need to know or specify where each piece of data physically resides. The D-DBMS of the future will eliminate most of the current complexities of using distributed data and will provide greater control over data creation and increased data availability throughout the company.

D-DBMSs are a natural fallout of the evolution to the IIS; that is, companies moving toward IIS implementation will naturally develop applications that utilize D-DBMSs. A general principle of good computer application design is to keep the data as close to the end-user as economically possible. This principle holds because closeness generally reduces the response time for user queries and

operations and makes the application less sensitive to communications malfunctions. In some cases, this closeness actually reduces
the cost of implementing the solution because of the inverted price–
performance ratio of current systems (the smaller the machine, the
better the price–performance).

Before the strong movement toward IISs, and the concomitant
effort toward interconnecting all computers in a company, most
large databases had to be centralized, that is, situated as far from the
user as possible. Mainframes were the only computers with OLTP
monitors (e.g., CICS) capable of handling the high transaction rates,
and the only machines to which all users of the application were
connected. With the advent of the IIS and D-DBMSs, companies can
design their large applications, paying more attention to the basic
"close-to-the-user" principle.

Most databases will be distributed according to geographic criteria. Data concerning a given customer will be located at or close to
the company office with which the customer normally does business.
Operations that affect the local database will also be sent to a central database (either on-line or in batch mode at night) to provide a
backup, to store information that can be used to generate company-
wide reports, and to act as a database for other applications that
must operate on the same data.

This distribution will provide a company with additional advantages. Users will feel more ownership of "their" data, and therefore
be more inclined to take better care of it, which helps prevent data
corruption. Also, they will be able to obtain more timely reports
(many of them generated on-line) without fearing that they will slow
down the operation of the entire company by overloading the central database.

Since an application in a IIS can access data located anywhere
in the network, companies will be able to maintain up-to-date pictures of a customer's total interactions (e.g., order rate, outstanding
credit balance, expected delivery dates for current orders). This customer snapshot will permit a company to provide more timely and
complete service.

Although location transparency of data access seems to be a simple idea, it can be provided in varying degrees of complexity. For example:

- Query transparency is achieved when an application running on any node can read any logical data item without being told on which node the item physically resides.

- Query update transparency is achieved when an application running on any node can update any logical data item without being told where the item is physically stored. At this level, the data access activity has been expanded to encompass updates to the data as well as queries, which requires more careful synchronization of activities.

- Transaction transparency is achieved when any action involving data residing on several nodes either executes all of its transactions or does not execute any of its transactions. In other words, the action is a single indivisible unit. This capability is important for any transactions that must read or update physical data elements residing in different nodes. Support for transaction transparency is the most critical characteristic in a D-DBMS since it means that all transactions, both query and update, will maintain the consistency of the database just as a single DBMS will. Most current products, unfortunately, do not yet provide transaction transparency.

- Replication transparency is achieved when the D-DBMS can support the execution of any action through the use of physical copies of a single logical database. This feature is important when an organization decides to copy data for backup or performance reasons onto several different nodes.

- Schema transparency is achieved when the database administrator for a given computer node may make local changes to the database definition in a way totally transparent to users on all nodes.

- Systems transparency is achieved when the database system may run on different vendor platforms using different operating systems.

In the late 1980s, some vendors (notable Oracle Corp., Sybase, Relational Technology, Inc.) began claiming to sell distributed database systems, which, in fact, are network file systems. In a network file system, each node operates a separate database and can process inquiries or updates only for single records. In a full-fledged distributed database system, SQL queries can be executed at any node, even when requiring data from several different computer nodes. A D-DBMS should have a heuristic optimizer available which will choose an intelligent accessing strategy and, in some cases, send queries to the remote databases, assemble appropriate information, and do joins with data collected from other nodes in the network.

Although traditional DBMSs and current D-DBMSs have significantly improved the ease and speed of user access to key data, they do not provide adequate support in two areas: capturing operations performed on data and handling complex entities. Object-oriented database technology is based on an approach to organizing information that structurally accommodates the storing of complex entities and operations. The objects are structures that contain both entity descriptions and the operators that may be legitimately performed on the entity. Applications that frequently access and modify complex objects, such as CAD/CAM and manufacturing applications, demand these more sophisticated database capabilities.

For example, some 3D CAD packages use a constructive geometry mechanism for design. A desired part can be built up by performing multiple operations on simple, basic parts, such as cylinders, boxes, cones, and so on. In an object-oriented database, the description of these basic parts, along with the equations describing the mathematical operations that can be done on the part, can be stored only once in the database and referred to by the records describing the more complex parts that have been designed. This arrangement, which saves considerable disk space, allows corrections or enhancements to the descriptions of the basic parts to be made in one place, with automatic updating done to the descriptions of the complex parts in the database.

Traditional databases lack these capabilities because they were designed to support typical business applications that require simple objects and a limited number of operations, such as insert, modify, and delete. Object-oriented database systems place operations alongside their related data within the database so applications can get to these operations without reimplementing them. Localizing complex operations within the database improves software mainte-nance by confining updates to one location. Both data and the opera-tions allowable on them are immediately visible, making it easier for end-users and application programmers to work with the database.

Object-oriented database systems offer significant improve-ments over traditional systems in a number of applications. Object-oriented database vendors appear to be making positive strides in CAD/CAM and CIM (computer-integrated manufacturing) areas, and their systems will be in widespread use by the late 1990s. The improvements will allow users to more easily and quickly design new products, thus decreasing time to market and enhancing product quality.

Whether they implement true D-DBMS or simply network file systems, user organizations with any kind of IIS will achieve im-proved responsiveness and efficiency. In either case, they will be able to automatically exchange information worldwide among net-work nodes about incoming orders and the means of filling them most efficiently. In many industries (e.g., brokerages), companies must implement IISs to remain competitive with each other. The challenge of staffing the development activity will grow as object-oriented and distributed databases add to the complexity of systems. By reducing the number of system programs they support, however, user organizations will be better able to manage the development and implementation of increasingly complex IISs.

ORGANIZATIONAL IMPLICATIONS

Organizational applications will arise among the system develop-ment groups in the various parts of the enterprise, whether divisional or functional. Often divisions, functions, and national organizations operate autonomously. They may continue to do so as far as application programs for local use are concerned, but they will lose their autonomy in the selection of network-related computers, software, and standards. The more integrated a network is (especially if it employs a D-DBMS), the more consistency must exist among its nodes. Local system development groups must give up some of their freedom of choice, whereas corporate-level central groups, which have often been only advisory in nature, must become the decision makers and implementers of the network.

Managing these changing roles has already proved difficult in some organizations. Many companies have permitted divisions or functions to have great autonomy in defining data elements and in choosing database management systems, computers, standard applications (e.g., payroll), and so on. It is often very difficult to settle who will have to change their definitions and/or systems to become consistent and compatible with the overall corporate standards that must exist if an IIS is to reach its potential.

Often implementation of the new roles requires attention from senior line management. In some instances, a veteran executive, trusted to "get things done" when change is needed, is put in charge of information systems during the design and implementation of the basic IIS. The CIO's role thus shifts from being implementer to being visionary and negotiator.

Organizations implementing any form of IIS will face formidable training problems. Systems development and operations people must become proficient with the machines and programs selected for the network. They must help train the users—engineers, salespeople, manufacturing managers, distributors, and many others—in the principles, operations, and limits of the new system. The global conversion will, in many instances, be a more ambitious change than the organization has attempted before. Great care must be taken with the phasing, simulating, layering, and formal training employed.

New risks accompany these IISs. They have more points of entry than earlier systems because IISs are designed to serve employers and customers more responsively than before. Thus, IISs are more vulnerable to criminals and vandals than their predecessors, and system security becomes of greater concern. There is also an increased exposure to system failure, because the organization is more dependent on its IIS than it was on its previous architecture. This risk can be alleviated by providing backup hardware, redundant communication paths, and off-site data storage. Nevertheless, the IIS may prove to be unsatisfactory because corporate political or business conditions change in unexpected ways. There is also risk that an IIS may fail (i.e., workstations become inoperable, transactions cannot be performed) because migrating a key component, such as a DBMS or operating system, from an old to a new version is done incorrectly. Tight integration of components increases the difficulty and thus the risks of making changes.

These new risks are serious, and many line managers are carefully weighing the potential effects on the company. At all costs, they must ensure that critical operations remain running. The speed with which many IISs will be implemented is tied to the rate at which the IISs earn the trust of management.

CHAPTER 8

ENGINEERING
AND SCIENTIFIC
COMPUTING

Engineers will be among the first users in the early 1990s to benefit from Integrated Information Systems. These highly paid professionals are already familiar with workstations, the main entry point into the IIS, and will take every opportunity to save time and maximize their contributions to joint projects. The current environment for engineers and scientists is based on uncoordinated use of independent minicomputers, workstations, and, in some cases, supercomputers or minisupercomputers. The integrated environment of the 1990s (Fig. 8.1) will be characterized by:

- Heavy reliance on workstations
- Sharing of data and drawings among all engineers and scientists involved in a project
- Easy access to outside data sources, such as standard engineering specifications and published scientific research
- Easy access to high-speed processing power
- Growing use of very powerful, relatively low-cost parallel computers with a variety of architectures
- Expert technology embedded in many engineering applications.

Engineers and scientists will rely on workstations to provide the major part of their required processing power. These machines will be used:

153

Figure 8.1   The Computing Environment of the 1990s

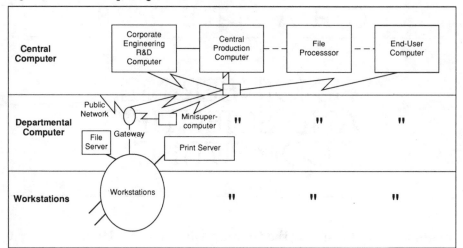

- For PC-type applications, such as word processing, spread-sheets, and symbolic manipulation of mathematical formulas
- To prepare engineering drawings
- As the primary vehicle of communication with customers, coworkers, and suppliers
- To access fileservers containing project information, such as drawings and calculation sheets
- To access the power of computational servers located at the departmental or corporate level
- To formulate problems and review, with graphs and pictures, the results produced by the computational server.

Engineers spend less than 20% of their workweek doing actual designs. The bulk of their time involves writing memos to clients, scheduling work, looking up standards, and so on. Therefore, to improve the productivity of engineers, computer systems must do more than tackle the CAD-CAM or numerical computation side of the profession. The most effective engineering workstation will enable its user to communicate and publish, as well as simulate, manipulate, and calculate. The engineer should be able to call up the American Society of Mechanical Engineers, for instance; search for needed specifications or drawings; and print them in his or her office for attachment to a design.

Standard capabilities of the near future will include transmitting and publishing formatted compound documents containing numerical, textual images, and drawings. Document image processing, as well as extensive visualization and animation capabilities, will become important. Scientists use these features to interpret in pictures the results of simulating natural phenomena, such as weather patterns.

Supercomputers and minisupercomputers will provide high-speed power for computationally intensive problems. By the mid-1990s, 100 gigaflop supercomputers costing $20 to $50 million will be available as corporate shared resources in aggressive companies. And 10 gigaflop minisupercomputers costing less than a million dollars will be found in the research and development (R&D) centers or engineering departments of large corporations. File servers will be located at the departmental level, providing the major repository for drawings, documents, and other types of information needed by large R&D or engineering projects.

KEY TECHNOLOGIES

We are on the threshold of a new era in high-speed computing architecture. Users are pressuring vendors to design computers that operate much faster than today's mainframes, and nearly as fast as supercomputers. But users want this computational power at a cost no more than a minicomputer or small mainframe of 1990, a few hundred thousand dollars to $2 or $3 million. Users need higher speed computers to deal with problems in areas beyond the reach of today's mainframes, such as engineering design, financial analysis, logistics, and software design and development. Some subject areas, such as weather forecasting, computational fluid mechanics, very large scale integrated (VLSI) circuit design, and molecular modeling, require computers that can perform from 100 to 1,000 times faster than even the speediest machines of the late 1980s.

During the early 1990s, switching speeds of silicon CMOS and ECL (Emitter-Coupled Logic) circuits will continue to decrease, chip density will increase, and power requirements will decrease at the rates of the last 10 years. Improvements will begin to slow near 1995 as theoretical limits are reached. GaAs (gallium arsenide) will be used to handle some critical applications, such as those only the fastest supercomputers can address. The cost of designing, developing, and manufacturing advanced custom circuitry will grow, especially in comparison to readily available merchant chips. Also, the speed advantage of custom chips relative to merchant chips will not be as great as in the past. The speed and functionality of microprocessor building blocks, such as the Intel 860, Transputer, Mips, and SPARC chips, will increase dramatically while the cost will remain in the few hundred dollar range.

These changes indicate that the fundamental economics of computing is evolving. Traditionally, a factor of 10 improvement could be garnered by applying state-of-the-art techniques along with customized circuits. Today, vendors can produce at very low costs commodity processors that operate nearly as fast as the best customized circuitry.

HISTORICAL PERSPECTIVE

From 1945 to 1990, the problem-solving capability of the fastest computers has improved approximately 10^{11} times. This extraordinary increase has resulted from faster computers as well as algorithms that require fewer steps to solve a given problem. In fact, computer speedup and algorithm effectiveness have improved at comparable rates (Fig. 8.2).

The increased computer speed has itself occurred because of the evolution of faster building blocks:

Figure 8.2   Improvements in Solving the Poisson Equation on a 64 × 64 Grid

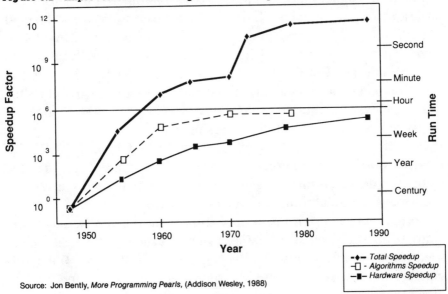

Source: Jon Bently, *More Programming Pearls*, (Addison Wesley, 1988)

- Vacuum tubes (1950s)
- Discrete diodes and transistors (1950s to 1960s)
- Small-scale and medium-scale integrated circuits (1960s to 1970s)
- Large-scale integrated devices (1970s and beyond)
- Very large-scale integrated device (late 1970s and beyond).

The second factor that has contributed to increased computer speed is the improved architecture (organization) of the overall system, including such features as:

- Parallel add and multiply circuits
- Overlapped access to memory
- Separate I/O processors
- Instruction pipelining.

From the 1950s to the early 1970s, high-speed computers were based mostly on the use of internal parallel operations, for example, interleaved memory access and instruction pipelining. From the programmer's viewpoint, however, operations were performed sequentially. The logical integrity of the von Neumann model of computationalism remained intact. A few commercially available machines in the 1960s and early 1970s did not strictly adhere to the von Neumann model and provided multiprocessing capability for those who were willing to exploit it. By and large, however, computers were based on sequential processing.

With the introduction of Control Data Corp.'s STAR, the floating-point attached processor and the Cray 1 in the early 1970s, computer designers introduced architectures that used parallelism (multiple functional units and vector operations) in a way visible to the programmer, a significant departure from the von Neumann architecture. These vector machines can be considered the first widely used commercially viable parallel computers. In the late 1980s, scientists and engineers accepted vector processors as an effective way to carry out high-speed computing.

TECHNICAL FORECAST

Dramatic changes will affect engineering and scientific computing technology in the 1990s. Supercomputers will reach speeds of 1 teraflop by the end of the decade, and 10 to 100 gigaflop computers will be available for under $1 million (Fig. 8.3).

The effort to develop faster and more cost-effective engineering and scientific computers is progressing simultaneously on two fronts. Some companies are using a traditional vector processing architecture with faster circuitry; others are harnessing a large number of high-speed, low-cost commodity processors into one parallel computer. By 1995, nearly all computers used for engineering and scientific applications will be either vector or parallel computers. Some vector and parallel computers will also be devoted to computationally intensive business applications (Fig. 8.4). There will be little use of parallel computers in traditional data processing applications, however, before 1997.

Figure 8.3   Forecast of Peak Speeds of Vector Processors

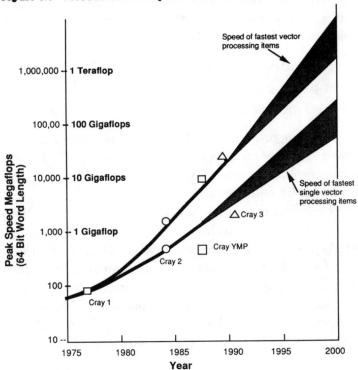

Figure 8.4   Typical Future Uses for Parallel Computers

Heavy Use in the Early 1990s for Engineering/Scientific Applications	Heavy Use in the Mid-990s for Business/Commercial Computationally Intensive Applications	Only Slight Use in the 1990s for Business/Commercial Transaction/Database Applications
Finite Element Analysis	Economic Modeling	General Ledger
Computational Fluid and Aerodynamics	Queuing Network Analysis	Payroll
Molecular Modeling	Linear Programming	Accounts Payable
Layout of VLSI Circuits	Portfolio Analysis	Sales Recording
Seismic Analysis	Production Facility Planning	Accounts Receivable
Oil Reservoir Analysis	Transportation Network Planning	Reservation Systems

Cray, Hitachi, NEC, and Fujitsu will continue to aggressively market supercomputers with traditional vector architectures. Speed improvements will be obtained in these processors by:

- Faster circuitry using less power
- Higher packing densities
- Low-level multiprocessing (8 to 64 CPUs per machine).

The cost of vector processors will stay comparable to today's prices. Use of lower cost vector supercomputer clones (e.g., from Convex) that can reach peak speeds somewhat lower than traditional super-computers, will be widespread.

Use of parallel computers with a wide variety of architectures (e.g., bus, hypercube, switch-connected, and very long instruction word [VLIW]) will grow in the next 5 years. Highly parallel comput-ers (2,048 to 10,240 processors) will be employed to solve certain kinds of problems (e.g., Navier Stokes equations for fluid flow) faster than traditional vector-oriented supercomputers. Moderately paral-lel computers will be in widespread use just prior to 1995 and offer significant price–performance advantages over traditional vector processors.

Figure 8.5 forecasts market share at mid-decade for each type of parallel computer and its relative actual (not peak) performance on four types of problems:

1. Naturally parallel (ray tracing, scene enhancement)
2. Domain parallel (solving elliptic partial differential equations and some A/I problems)
3. Little natural parallel (scheduling, combinatorial, and linear programming)
4. Serial FORTRAN-based algorithms (Dusty Decks).

Different parallel computers solve certain problems better than oth-ers. For example, multiprocessor computers can very effectively solve the partial differential equations that describe many physical phenomena, such as fluid flow. They are not as effective, however,

Figure 8.5 Effective Speed and Relative Marketshare in 1995 of Different Classes of High Speed Computers

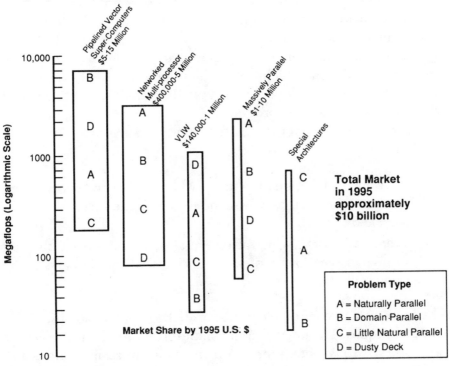

at running an old FORTRAN program not designed for a parallel computing environment. VLIW machines are better for that job.

CHARACTERISTICS OF PARALLEL COMPUTERS

The phrase "parallel computing" describes a variety of techniques for speeding up problem solving. Parallelism has been used since the early days of computing to improve the performance of serial machines. It has been achieved, for example, by interleaved memory access, use of special functional units that overlap traditional operations within the computer, and instruction pipelining. In these cases, parallelism has been transparent to the application software and programming.

A parallel computer is any machine that uses multiple processors simultaneously to solve a problem in a manner visible to the application programmer. A computational problem is divided into numerous parts, on which the several processors work simultaneously. Software developers must take the parallelism into account when writing application programs.

There are two approaches for using parallelism in computer architecture:

1. Data and instruction pipelining, which use several coordinated special units such as vector processors, digital signal processors, and so forth

2. Processor arrays, which use several processors, each obeying its own instructions and each working on different parts of the same problem.

The architecture common in most parallel computers combines the two techniques. The key parallel computers in use today are vector processors, VLIW computers with multiple functional units, and multiple processors. Vector computers are characterized by special instructions and registers that perform vector algebraic operations. These processors run faster because only one instruction decode is required for all the vector elements processed and operations can be pipelined. For example, adding all elements in one vector to all elements in another vector requires only one machine instruction, and the two vectors are streamed through an addition pipeline.

Vector computers have proved popular because most engineers and scientists can easily understand their design concept. Many algorithms for solving engineering and scientific problems can be formulated using the basic operations of vector algebra. Furthermore, old FORTRAN programs can often be reorganized and recompiled to take advantage of vector operations. However, it is only possible to speed up vectorizable code. For some problems, such as AI algorithms, which involve searching a complex data structure, this may represent only a small part of the computer program.

VLIW computers execute several instructions simultaneously on separate functional units. Each instruction specifies 2 to 28 operations. VLIW computers use advanced compiler techniques to find those operations that can be executed simultaneously. Speedups of 5 to 10 times on regular FORTRAN programs are possible, even when code is not vectorizable. Speedups of more than 10 to 15, however, seem unlikely by this approach. VLIW machines are most likely a temporary phenomenon in the market.

Many of the new parallel computers introduced in the last 5 years are multiple processors, which use from a few up to many independent connected CPUs. Multiple processors can be characterized by:

- The number and type of processors
- The method of interconnect—bus, network (2D or 3D rectangular mesh, tree, or hypercube), or switch
- The location of memory—shared, local to processor, or combination shared and local
- The method of synchronization—central control or message passing.

Many types of parallel computers have been built and marketed. Figures 8.6 through 8.10 diagram typical multiprocessor computers of today. Figure 8.11 shows cost and performance estimates for some typical models available in 1990.

Figure 8.6   Parallel Computing Sample Configurations

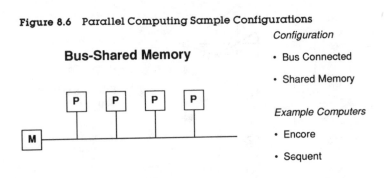

Bus-Shared Memory

Configuration

- Bus Connected
- Shared Memory

Example Computers

- Encore
- Sequent

Figure 8.7   Parallel Computing Sample Configurations (continued)

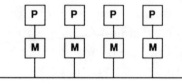

Bus-Local Memory

Configuration

• Bus Connected

• Processor Local Memory

Example Computers

• Several products under development

Figure 8.8   Parallel Computing Sample Configurations (continued)

Mesh

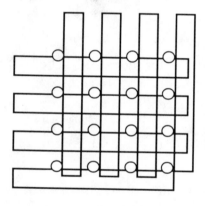

Configuration

• 2-D or 3-D Lattice

• Local Memory

Example Computers

• Illiac/V

• Wave Tracer

Figure 8.9   Parallel Computing Sample Configurations (continued)

Hypercube

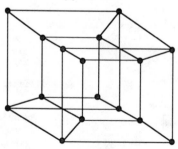

Configuration

• Hypercube

• Local Memory

Example Computers

• IPSC/2 (Up to 500 Intel 80386)

• N-Cube (Up to 1024 proprietary VAX-like chips)

Figure 8.10 Parallel Computing Sample Configurations (continued)

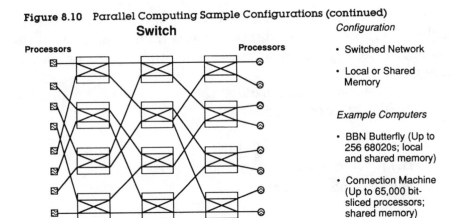

Switch

Processors   **Processors**

Configuration

- Switched Network

- Local or Shared Memory

Example Computers

- BBN Butterfly (Up to 256 68020s; local and shared memory)

- Connection Machine (Up to 65,000 bit-sliced processors; shared memory)

Traditional multiprocessors, such as the **IBM 390** high-end family, are not normally considered parallel computers because these machines usually run several job streams simultaneously, with each processor assigned to a separate job stream. Sometimes, however, large jobs are partitioned into a few tasks that can be run

Figure 8.11 Minisupercomputers (Parallel Processing Computers) Products and Technology

A Sample of Super- and Minisupercomputers

Computer	First Shipped	Architecture	Claimed Peak Speed (Megaflops)	Price Range ($Thousands)
Cray Y-MP	1989	6 pipelined vector processors	1,000-2,000	2,000-15,000
Facom VP 400EX	1987	4 pipelined vector processors	1,700	N/A
Hitachi S820	1988	4 pipelined vector processors	N/A	N/A
NEC 5X-4	1989	4 pipelined vector processors	N/A	N/A
N-Cube/10	1985	Up to 1024 processors; hypercube connection	500	N/A
Alliant FX82	1988	Up to 16 processors with vector capability, bus connected	188	250-1,500
Convex C240	1988	4 pipelined vector processors	200	350-1,000
Elxsi	1987	12 microprocessors; bus connected; shared memory	96	300-1,000
Encore Multivax 320	1988	National semi, bus, shared memory		130-700
Intel ISPC/2	1987	8-256 80286 processors; hypercube connect	400	300-1,500
Trace/300	1989	Multiple functional units with VLIW (28)		400-1,000
CM-2 Connection Machine	1988	Up to 65K bit sliced processors; switched hypercube	1,000-2,000	1,000-1,500
Sequent Symmetry	1987	Up to 30 80386 processors on a bus; shared memory	30	75,000-500,000
IBM 3090-600VF	1987	6 processor mainframe with attached pipelined vector processors	650	5,000-12,000
Butterfly	1986	Up to 256 Motorola 68020s; Switch connected, local and shared memory	100	200-1,500

independently and simultaneously on different processors of a multiprocessor system. In this situation, a traditional multiprocessor might be considered a low-level multiple-processor parallel computer.

The performance of a parallel computer depends on an effective matching of three factors:

1. The problem-solving algorithm
2. The programming language and compiler
3. The machine architecture.

The main goal is to appropriately partition and schedule a problem to keep all processors working on it all of the time. Without this efficiency, several processors may lie idle a significant portion of the job's run-time. In addition, programmers must reduce the delays in passing data from one part of the machine to another processor that needs it.

Problem-solving methods for parallel computers are just now being developed and tested. Some architectures seem better suited to solving certain kinds of problems than others. For example:

- The sustained problem-solving speed of vector computers is often much less than the peak capability
- Vector and VLIW computers seem best able to speed up simple variations of traditional serial programs (often FORTRAN based)
- Multiple processors using a shared memory and a bus interconnection seem to have performance and scale-up limitations for many problems.

Problem-solving speedups of almost 1,000 have been realized for a hypercube with 1024 connected processors with local memory.

Each type of computing has its advocates, but, in the long run, multiple-processor computers with independent memory should prove the most effective for a wide range of problems.

WORKSTATIONS

By the mid 1990s, high-end workstations will feature processing power nearly equal to a small mainframe of the late 1980s (25 to 40 mainframe-equivalent MIPS). Much of an engineer's work will be done directly on the workstation. This processing power, combined with large optical disk storage, will also make it possible for advanced workstations to visualize the outputs of supercomputer calculations at full video rates. Most high-end workstations will use vector coprocessing to solve computationally intensive problems cost-effectively.

One promising development for the early 1990s is the X-terminal. This machine, which is designed to use the X-Window protocols, essentially offers PC-like processing power to a user at only a few thousand dollars. No applications run on the X-terminal and no operating systems reside there. The X-terminal locally retains only the capability of displaying what it receives from servers on the network, which is where processing takes place. The X-terminal includes a high-resolution windowing interface and the ability to present sophisticated graphics. Because it can match much of a workstation's functionality at significantly less cost (about $2,000 compared with the workstation's $5,000 to $30,000), the X-terminal may grab up to 20% of the engineering workstation market.

COMMUNICATIONS

High-speed communications will be essential to engineering and scientific computing of the 1990s. LANs that can be used by workgroups to share information or provide access to departmental file servers and minisupercomputers will need transfer capacity in the range of 1 gigabit per second. This high rate will be used by engineers and scientists to transmit the large amounts of information required for drawings and data visualization.

Engineers and scientists will also need access to WANs to conveniently communicate with colleagues at different sites, as well as customers and suppliers. Wide-area transmission speeds in the range of 1 megabit per second will be needed for communication drawings, data, and images to suppliers, customers, and off-site coworkers.

SYSTEM SOFTWARE

The primary operating system for supercomputers, minisupercomputers, and engineering and scientific workstations will be a version of Unix. Some vendors may also supply proprietary operating systems for workstations so that they can be used in conjunction with their high-end computers. Most engineers and scientists, however, will be so familiar with the Unix environment that most machines will run this operating system.

Many variants of Unix will be available in the marketplace, but most will be POSIX compliant. The X-Windows user interface and PHIGS Plus graphics interface standards will be widely adopted and used.

DATABASE SOFTWARE

Engineering and scientific problem solving requires access to large amounts of information. Scientists often collect experimental data that they need to store and retrieve in various ways. Engineers who design complex systems such as aircraft, automobiles, and process plants also maintain huge amounts of information related to design. By the mid-1990s, all supercomputers, minisupercomputers, and workstations will include a relational SQL-compliant database package, which will be especially tuned for the high-speed data stripping kinds of access needed in engineering and scientific computations. It will, however, remain compliant with the SQL standards so that any information in the databases required for the commercial aspects of the project can be available to the businessman.

Although distributed database systems (see Chapter 7) will be widely used by the mid-1990s in general business applications, engineering and scientific users will not be so inclined to adopt a distributed processing mode of operation. They will be much more interested in extracting large amounts of data from a database and moving it to a minisupercomputer or workstation where they can work on the data for several hours before returning it to the central repository. Many characteristics of record synchronization that are important in commercial database packages will be much less so to the engineering and scientific community.

These users will, however, be much more interested in using object-oriented databases, which allow users to store structured information and processes for operating on this information as logical units in a database. Object-oriented database systems should slowly gain acceptance and come into moderate use by 1995.

PROGRAMMING LANGUAGES

Growth in the use of parallel computers will depend on the development of parallel algorithms and languages to describe them. A vast and growing scientific literature describes algorithms suitable for parallel computers. Many experimental languages have been demonstrated that make it easy to describe parallel algorithms. These developments, however, have not yet been widely disseminated into the scientific and engineering community. Furthermore, most users have developed large amounts of software written in various dialects of FORTRAN, and it would be extremely expensive for them to rewrite these in another programming language. As a result:

- Vector-oriented languages such as FORTRAN 88 and APL2 will become more popular
- Dialects of FORTRAN and C (possible using LINDA) will be developed to more easily describe concurrent activities

- Languages based on message passing for concurrency control, such as OCCAM and Concurrent C, will grow in use
- Parallel versions of Lisp and Prolog will become widely used.

APPLICATION SOFTWARE

A wide variety of standard applications will become available for the engineering and scientific computing environment. In addition, reworked and improved versions of all the standard packages, such as systems to solve large sets of linear equations, to fit curves to experimental data, and so on, will be reengineered and available.

Personal assistant systems for engineers and scientists will be available on workstations. These applications will include spread-sheets, database packages, expert shells, and engineering drawing packages. The applications will be integrated so the user may develop an intelligent document that contains text as well as drawings. Changes to one part of the document will be automatically reflected in other parts. Such personal assistant systems will also allow the user to prepare compound documents for publication or transmission to colleagues, customers, or suppliers. Many of these applications will have intelligent assistant AI modules built into them to prompt the user, learn his or her habits, and provide ways to help improve the user's productivity.

New CAD/CAM systems incorporating AI techniques will be created by the mid-1990s for a workgroup environment requiring sharing of text and drawings. These systems will be heavily oriented around the concept of parametric design. Users will be able to describe key characteristics of items they need, and the AI features of the system will size and generate preliminary designs. The final detailed design will be developed through further interaction with the engineer or scientist.

All of the standard scientific and engineering applications, such as finite element analysis and fluid flow analysis, will be made more user friendly and run on a wide spectrum of vector computers. These packages will slowly migrate to multiple-processor computers, but only after certain architectures prove to be commercially successful in the marketplace. Not until the mid- to late 1990s will standard analysis packages, such as ANSYS and FIDAP, be widely available on multiple-processor machines.

PREPARING FOR THE FUTURE

The market for high-speed computers, servers, workstations, and LANs will be chaotic during the 1990s. The variety of new computer architectures in use will make it possible for the first time to cost-effectively solve certain kinds of problems. For example, the parallel multiprocessor computers, such as the N-cube, will model physical processes, and massively parallel bit-sliced computers will handle database and text searching.

The dominance of the high-end vector processor vendors, such as Cray and several Japanese companies, will be broken by the growing use of multiple-processor computers, as will the dominance of the mid-sized engineering and scientific manufacturers, such as DEC. Several small parallel computer manufacturers will produce machines that are much more cost-effective than traditional high-end minisuper-computers.

The most interesting development relates to IBM. Since the early 1970s, IBM has essentially ignored the high-end engineering and scientific market. Only in the mid-1980s did it begin to participate in this sector by introducing the vector facility for the 3090. IBM has been fairly open in describing several experimental parallel computers in their labs and has taken a financial position in a vendor developing a moderately parallel computer. Every indication is that IBM plans to reenter the engineering and scientific market with a parallel computer in the early to mid-1990s. When it introduces a 64-processor machine, IBM will legitimize this type of computing, and the market for high-speed computers will explode.

UNDERSTANDING PARALLEL COMPUTERS

By the mid-1990s, the majority of high-end engineering and scientific applications will be running on workstations and computers that use parallelism in some way. As a result, engineering and scientific users should begin to learn about these machines and develop applications for them. In the long run, multiple-processor machines with independent memories will prove to be the more general-purpose type of computers. Examples of this architecture can be found today in the N-cube and IPSC computers. If a company anticipates needing inexpensive high-speed computing in the few years, then it should begin today to understand parallel computing. The first step into the future would be to acquire a small parallel computer in order to train programmers and application developers.

CHAPTER 9

NETWORKS AND COMMUNICATIONS

It has not proved possible, nor is it likely to in the next 5 years, for an aggressive corporation to satisfy its computing and communications requirements with products from one vendor, or even with products conforming to one communications architecture. Organizations pioneering the use of information technology will increasingly seek special-purpose computers to meet some of their needs, particularly machines designed for parallel processing and graphics. No matter which computers they choose, users will expect and demand that they can share data and programs. This capability is a must in the early 1990s, as many companies are seeking to improve efficiency and effectiveness in delivering products and services and, in some cases, to create competitive advantage through innovative uses of information systems.

In the past, communications networks were created ad hoc to handle data processing applications as they arose. Aggressive companies will now reverse the situation: They will set up basic, flexible communications structures from which users will draw capabilities as needed. The communications architecture will arise as a utility alongside the applications-oriented information systems structure.

Interoperability requires an environment that supports process-to-process communication among a set of heterogeneous computers. It provides a consistent way for a local process to carry out a set of tasks with other processes on a number of different computers.

Applications on these machines can perform their tasks by adjusting for individual system architectures, data management facilities, or other specific system characteristics. This requirement is more difficult and demanding than many networking products can currently satisfy. They typically concentrate on the details of delivery—how to exchange data between programs. A fully interoperable environment, however, must be separate from communications details, or rather capable of functioning not only with a range of diverse computers, but also over a variety of underlying communications infrastructures.

Some characteristics of the "ideal" environment for interoperation include:

- The ability to handle rapidly changing patterns of interaction between computers. This characteristic implies some degree of distributed control and communication to allow computers to deal with each other directly rather than through a centralized control point.

- An infrastructure of services to support interoperability. For example, the amount of information that users require in an interoperable environment can grow rapidly, making it impossible to replicate all information within each node. Computers will retain frequently used information locally and exploit remote services to store the remainder (e.g., directory and other user information).

- The use of virtual resources. A common representation of objects, such as files, processes, and terminals, must be supplied that can be defined and manipulated consistently. Local resources are required to transform the virtual resource into an actual representation that can be used by a local process.

In addition to continued technical progress, the development and implementation of computer networks will be influenced by external political and commercial forces, which include:

- Continuing pressure by users in favor of vendor-independent network standards (to increase their bargaining power) and by governments worldwide to limit the dominance of foreign-owned suppliers (i.e., IBM in Asia and Europe).

- Incentives to interconnect previously independent data systems to implement interorganizational EDI.

Three principal network standards have emerged to provide the backbones to make interoperable communications networks out of multivendor systems. SNA, OSI, and TCP/IP compete with, and yet complement, each other. Variations exist within all three suites of protocols, and they are all evolving. At the same time, the lines between them are blurring, thanks to gateway products connecting one with another, and to the mutual incorporation of specific protocol standards.

The market penetration of vendor-independent standards, such as OSI, will be paced largely by political, rather than technical, issues involved in reaching agreement. (The outcomes of these issues cannot guarantee market penetration of a standard, but they can delay or even stop it.) The emphasis in standards making is shifting to the higher levels of the OSI model (i.e., the application level), and several important OSI-based products should be well established in the marketplace by the mid-1990s.

Nevertheless, the computer networking environment of the first half of the decade will be heterogeneous, with both vendor-proprietary and vendor-independent standards. Furthermore, new applications and demands will arise as networks increase in both size and throughput requirements, for which some established standards will be inadequate. Therefore, both users and vendors will seek new standards that can support higher throughputs. They also will pay more attention to schemes for network management and control, and to procedures for security and privacy. These are becoming increasingly critical as networks proliferate and become an essential element of the infrastructure that supports applications that are the lifeblood of many businesses.

Finally, the development of distributed network computing (i.e., the partitioning of an application across several networked computers) will be paced over the next few years by progress in specific applications, including compiling large software systems or designing products for which complex calculations may be needed to simulate the effects of an engineering design change. In such cases, dramatic decreases in run-time can be achieved which will produce highly visible benefits, such as a reduction of time to bring a product to market. But distributed network computing presents a much more complex challenge to software developers than traditional distributed processing, and it is not expected to find significant use in mainstream corporate MIS applications by mid-decade.

IBM'S SYSTEMS NETWORK ARCHITECTURE (SNA)

Although SNA is established in a well-known set of products that originated in an era of computing dominated by centralized mainframes, it is now evolving in line with the movement to distributed computing. Through 1995 and beyond, SNA will continue to play a major role in networks in its newly emerging form because of its present widespread use and the great availability of, as well as investment in, SNA-based networks and applications.

From its original implementation in 1974 as a hierarchical relationship between mainframes and unintelligent terminals, SNA is being transformed into an architecture capable of supporting an environment in which remote intelligent equipment can be linked not only to mainframes, but also peer-to-peer with each other.

This low-entry networking is being created through the gradual implementation of two related protocols, namely Logical Unit (LU) 6.2, which establishes logical connections between cooperating programs, and Physical Unit (PU) 2.1, which makes possible point-to-point physical connectivity between peer nodes without mainframe involvement. LU 6.2 enables programs in workstations and midrange processors to exchange data directly, without logging onto a mainframe or requiring PCs to act as dumb terminals.

Thus far, not many users have demanded LU 6.2, because few applications have been written using it and the LU 6.2 software occupies several hundred kilobytes on a PC. Use will be stimulated on PCs and workstations as OS/2 is installed and as more applications that can support the protocol become available. Also important will be the incorporation of PU 2.1 into a widening range of IBM products, without which true peer-to-peer connections will be lacking (it will still be necessary to involve VTAM [Virtual Telecommunications Access Method] in communicating between processors on different networks).

In terms of handling truly distributed processing networks, future configurations of SNA will seek to combine the advantages of hierarchical control and management of thousands of nodes and devices with the peer-to-peer capabilities of systems based on PU 2.1 and LU 6.2 protocols. NetView, IBM's network management system, will play a key role.

SNA has become and will remain a de facto industry standard by virtue of IBM's strengths in the mainframe market. Other vendors must provide connections into and out of SNA networks if they want to be considered serious contenders in the marketplace. Indeed, competing product development groups often debate whether to allocate greater (and earlier) resources to implementing SNA or OSI capabilities. Proponents of the former argue that there are much greater revenue opportunities, certainly in the U.S. market, in selling products into SNA networks.

In recognition of the customer demand for open systems in the United States, Europe, and elsewhere, IBM has committed to the development of SNA/OSI gateway products. Nevertheless, SNA will remain the company's fundamental offering for distributed communication. The heavy investments by users in SNA products will therefore be protected.

IBM's initial emphasis in providing SNA/OSI interconnection involves conversion of the protocols of one system to the semantically equivalent protocols of the other (Fig. 9.1). In this way, an SNA and a non-SNA network can be interconnected using OSI as an

Figure 9.1 SNA/OSI Interconnection (Gateway Approach)

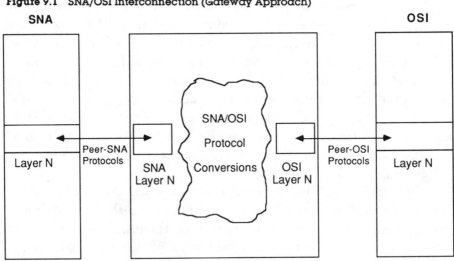

intermediary. A disadvantage of this gateway approach is that it may introduce significant additional delays in overall throughput, which may be unacceptable in time-sensitive interactive and transaction processing.

In the late 1980s, IBM announced several products that will eventually serve as the basis for a full range of links to the OSI world, including the OSI/Communications Subsystem. This IBM OSI software will eventually include FTAM as well as the currently incomplete standards for network management (CMIP, or Common Management Information Protocol) and OSI Directory Services (X.500) that were still in development at the beginning of the 1990s. The IBM OSI/Communications Subsystem will also be able to interconnect SAA systems and applications. Thus, IBM is positioning itself to be able in the long run to respond flexibly to market demands for OSI and/or SNA communications under the overall umbrella of SAA (Fig. 9.2).

An earlier interim IBM product, X.400 Open Systems Message Exchange (OSME), works directly with VTAM on a System 370 processor. OSME includes selected OSI protocols at the middle and upper layers that can be packaged with the X.400 application to

Figure 9.2   Coexistence of OSI and SNA

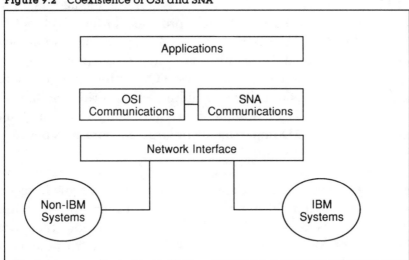

provide a full OSI stack that can be implemented on top of SNA's lower three layers. OSME will provide some capabilities that were first made available in Europe by IBM through different products.

One may argue that by extending the approach adopted with OSME, IBM may over time adopt a different approach to OSI interconnection than the gateway approach described above. Namely, interconnection could be accomplished by implementing one protocol in the products of another protocol (e.g., OSI protocols in SNA products, and vice versa). For both commercial and engineering reasons, however, IBM is unlikely to follow this path as its principal networking strategy.

TCP/IP

The TCP/IP protocol suite attracted an initial following because of its adoption by the U.S. Department of Defense. It has since found widespread commercial application, and the general business sector began to dominate TCP/IP shipments at the start of the 1990s.

TCP/IP has benefited from its symbiotic linkages with two other standards: Ethernet, which provides lower level network standards for it, and the Berkeley Unix 4.2 operating system, developed at the University of California. Many development engineers have transferred their enthusiasm for TCP/IP into the commercial arena as the protocol of choice for linking engineering and technical workstations. TCP/IP environments are most commonly found in the engineering and R&D departments of large corporations because of their commitments to Unix.

TCP/IP's addressing scheme and large communications overhead are well-known limitations. Thus, as networks grow in size and throughput demands increase, TCP/IP will eventually be eclipsed by OSI as the preferred multivendor conduit. Even now, the governments of the United States and several foreign countries dictate use of OSI. The U.S. government's OSI Profile GOSIP has become binding on governmental bodies, although there are plenty of exceptions to allow TCP/IP networks to be grandfathered. The great advantage and reason for the continuing substantial interest in TCP/IP, even in Europe, is that it is a set of proven standards supported by products from dozens of vendors.

Hence, although TCP/IP most likely will be superseded by OSI, when and how this transition will take place is uncertain. No current OSI products support the range of capabilities needed to connect large numbers of engineering and development workstations, for example. On the other hand, OSI applications are now enjoying intense development while TCP/IP applications are not. Nevertheless, the role of TCP/IP in providing multivendor connectivity will continue to be significant well into the 1990s. Even aggressive users of information systems are likely to be cautious in their approach to OSI, demanding proven products. Furthermore, users are not likely to scrap TCP/IP investments very rapidly, but rather to implement mixed TCP/IP-OSI networks, with OSI virtual terminal gateways and other methods to enable terminals to access all resources within these networks. Initially, these hybrid networks will continue to run the TCP/IP protocols. The hybrid transitional environment will be common in the first half of the 1990s. By 1995, the OSI standards will dominate.

OPEN SYSTEMS INTERCONNECTION (OSI)

OSI is not a product, but rather an internationally recommended reference model intended as a conceptual framework for the design and comparison of multivendor network backbone systems. Each of OSI's hierarchically organized seven layers consists of protocols that guide the performance of certain data communications functions. Not every layer is complete, and each may offer several protocol options.

OSI's lower layers have been dominated for some time by X.25 packet switching standards for public data networks and by Ethernet LAN standards (IEEE 802.2 and 802.3 protocols). Progress in developing a full suite of upper layer protocols has been slowed by the complex international committee work involved and the controversial attempts by individual vendors to gain acceptance of their standards within OSI. IBM submitted LU 6.2 as the basis of a standard for transaction processing (TP). This proposal was rejected once, for political, competitive, and technical reasons (e.g., the desire for full duplex, which LU 6.2 does not provide). The eventual OSI TP standard will, nevertheless, deliver functional services that are compatible with LU 6.2 in many, if not all, respects.

Delays in bringing OSI products to market stem from the plethora of parameters and features offered by several specifications. This permitted diversity causes problems with interoperability among products from different vendors.

OSI developments that will have the greatest impact over the next 5 to 7 years include the coming of age of products based on specifications such as X.400 and FTAM, as well as the steady expansion of the OSI platform to cover directory services (X.500), virtual terminal capability, TP, network management, and security. IBM has announced its long-awaited Repository, which may conflict with acceptance of X.500. The Repository will not be a robust platform until 1993, so no forecast of its impact is possible yet.

As image-intensive and other bandwidth-consuming applications are developed in both general office and engineering environments, increasing attention will be paid to the throughput limitations of OSI's overhead. These create bottlenecks in the overall speed of execution and response time associated with these applications. These bottlenecks will influence the transport and lower level layers and stimulate the introduction of new, more powerful lower level communications standards, such as fiber distributed data interface (FDDI) and its successors.

DEC AND OTHER COMPUTER VENDORS

During the 1980s, networking capability became a basic requirement for most computer vendors. At the minimum, it included connecting products from their own range as well as some minimal linking (e.g., 3270 emulation) to IBM systems. DEC, in fact, owes much of its growth during this decade to its networking strengths, as well as to, its single, scalable VAX/VMS computer architecture.

DEC's Digital Network Architecture (DNA), which is implemented through DECnet products, has gone through several major changes since its introduction. Because it was developed later than IBM's SNA, DNA is closer in its layering structure to OSI (Fig. 9.3). Also, given DEC's origins in the minicomputer business, DNA was originally conceived in a context of distributed rather than hierarchical, centrally controlled processing.

In contrast to IBM, DEC has committed itself to a plan to integrate OSI standards into DNA. DEC announced DECnet/OSI Phase V in 1987, and a number of DEC OSI products were available at the end of the 1980s. At the same time, DEC has been one of, if not the, leading supplier of connections to SNA networks through DECnet/SNA gateways, which provide protocol translations to Layer 6.

Figure 9.3   Comparison of Network Architecture Layers

OSI	SNA	DNA
		User
Application	Application	Network Management
Presentation	Network Addressable Unit Services	Network Application
Session	Function Management Data Services	Session Control
	Data Flow	
Transport	Control Services	End-to-End Communications
	Transmission Control Services	
Network	Path Control	Routing
Data Link	Data Link	Data Link
Physical Link	Physical Link	Physical Link

Other computer vendors, such as Unisys and Groupe Bull, have developed their own network architectures that in general make use of OSI concepts. These vendors are expected to migrate to OSI standards as these become established.

NETWORK MANAGEMENT AND DIRECTORY SERVICES

Network management and directory services are two of the most difficult and still relatively embryonic areas of development in computer networks. The challenges that they generate grow exponentially as networks themselves continue to expand in size and complexity.

No single, unified network management scheme will meet the needs of corporations by the mid-1990s. The range of equipment and environments involved (mainframes, workstations, LANs, WANs, PABXs, modems, etc.) is simply too vast. Aggressive companies will establish clear interfaces between local, regional or metropolitan, and wide-area networks to permit seamless interconnection among them and facilitate fault detection, diagnosis, and repair. Most organizations will still use a variety of network management capabilities, including independent minicomputer-based systems, modem management schemes, and diagnostic capabilities supplied in conjunction with host processors.

A number of management and control schemes will be employed, with different but interconnected primary domains of responsibility. Users will increasingly emphasize the need for these diverse schemes to exchange basic information so that, for example, faults can be localized.

The principal components of network management can be categorized as:

- Problem management
- Performance management
- Accounting management
- Configuration management
- Change management
- Security.

The four principal approaches to multivendor computer network management that have emerged thus far are IBM's NetView, which, although far from fully developed, was the first announced, potentially comprehensive network management scheme; DEC's Enterprise Management Architecture (EMA); AT&T's Universal Network Management Architecture (UNMA); and Hewlett Packard's Open View. The latter three are based on OSI, whereas NetView is based on SNA. They will all provide interfaces through which they can exchange data with devices from other vendors. Also, there will be specifications for programming interfaces to support network management applications written by third parties. IBM has already begun to offer this capability through NetView/PC.

Since NetView is System 370 resident, it enables IBM to continue to exploit its position as the leading mainframe vendor, even in an environment of distributed processing. Even in this kind of environment, or perhaps especially so, some central mechanism has to keep track of a network's evolution.

The OSI-based network management systems will be paced by progress in key OSI standards. One is CMIP, whose management information base is the same as that of the Simple Network Management Protocol (SNMP), thereby facilitating future migrations from TCP/IP to OSI networks (Fig. 9.4).

Given the product and market heritages of the respective vendors, it is not surprising that initial user interest in AT&T's UNMA is biased toward the telecommunications network end of network management, including long-haul circuits, end circuits and PBXs, while NetView is favored for managing SNA networks, rather than telephone networks or local-area networks supplied by DEC or Novell.

Figure 9.4   OSI Protocols: Status and Expectations

Protocol	Description	Product Availability
X.500	Provides information on names, addresses, routing, & other objects needed for global networking	Early 1990s
FTAM	Describes how to create, delete, read, & change file attributes, as well as transfer & access remote files	Available
Manufacturing Message Service	Command and control language to communicate with manufacturing devices, e.g., robots, programmable controllers	Available
Message Handling System		
• X.400 1984 Version	Standard for interchange of electronic mail between diverse common carriers & computer systems	Available
• X.400 1988 Version	Revision to include security, mailboxes, & physical delivery	Available
Network Management	Framework, service, & application layer protocol for passing information between managers & the resources they manage	Early 1990s
Office Document Architecture (ODA)	Specifies structures for the exchange of editable documents	Early 1990s
Virtual Terminal (VT)	Allows for the transmission across the network of terminal-oriented messages, e.g., keyboard input, screen updates	Available
Security	Security architecture & mechanisms that add application authentication & transport encryption to basic OSI reference model	Early 1990s
Remote Database Access	Facilitates access to databases from intelligent workstations & other database environments via a client / server relationship	Available

Similarly, initial interest in DEC's EMA and Hewlett Packard's Open View is concentrated among those companies' installed bases of customers, although theoretically these systems should ultimately be capable of managing networks dominated by computing products from other vendors. None of these systems offers a complete suite of capabilities and products for multivendor network management yet, and in all likelihood it will be several years before product lines become firmly established. Many users will probably install more than one major network management system to handle different major segments of their overall information system infrastructure.

Given the time required to reach agreement on standards and to develop network management applications that use these protocols, multivendor network management (in the sense of functions over and above those attained through use of multiple separate network management schemes) is not likely to become a reality until at least 1995. As with computer networking in general, there will be both SNA-based and OSI-based implementations.

Directory services also will continue to depend on some central mechanism for keeping track of changes and updates, even if directories themselves are partitioned and distributed in different locations in a network. Although CCITT X.400, an international standard for electronic message handling systems, has become a relatively mature protocol with a reasonable range of products to implement it (particularly in Europe), it will become truly widespread only by offering a directory service. In the early 1990s, a rapid expansion of electronic messaging will occur as this kind of service becomes available.

Directory service must meet several constraints, such as unique names, distributed naming, distributed updates, rapid response time, continuous availability, and worldwide interconnection. Distributed naming is required because no local system can hope to verify the uniqueness of names for the whole world. Furthermore, it is not practical to guarantee the accuracy of the data, or at least its primary copy, unless it, too, is maintained in a decentralized fashion.

Large investments are required to meet these constraints, and they can be justified only if protected by standards. Hence, the X.500 standard, whose 1988 version is setting the basis for the realization of international services using a worldwide naming scheme, is of critical importance. It can be used to support name-to-address mapping and, therefore, effectively a worldwide addressing capability.

As SNA has moved to a more distributed, peer-to-peer networking environment, the directory services it provides must exhibit similar characteristics to those of X.500 (e.g., the use of distributed local directories) rather than reliance upon a single central directory. As, and if, the X.500 standard is implemented in key markets, then it may be supported by IBM so that SNA users can participate in worldwide messaging services. On the other hand, IBM may choose to compete with X.500 using its long-awaited Repository product. The outlook is unclear.

THE COMMUNICATIONS ENVIRONMENT
FOR NETWORK PROCESSING

Traditional networking limits interactions between computing systems to file transfers and the exchange of messages. Users must be registered separately and independently at each system, files cannot be uniformly named and accessed throughout the network, systems must be managed independently, and processing bottlenecks at one location cannot be eased by transferring the load elsewhere. In contrast, a network processing environment seeks to permit the sharing of data and processing power among the components of the network. A single application can run on multiple processors located in different places.

The future network processing environment will comprise hardware, software, and data components that are connected by a network and provide a uniform core set of services with characteristic global properties. These globally available services need not be installed on every system in the network processing environment, but they must be globally available.

The characteristics of the ideal network processing environment are likely to include at least the following:

- Global availability of services, even when failures occur
- Global access to facilities, so that the same functions and performance are available throughout the network subject to constraints imposed by security and the capabilities of the local-network access
- Global distributed management—that is, components throughout the network can be managed from anywhere in it, using a single management interface (again, subject to considerations of security)
- Global names, so that the same names, with a consistent naming format and structure, should work everywhere in the network
- Global security, with user authorization and access control in use throughout the environment.

To be practical and acceptable, the network processing environment must:

- Operate transparently over LANs and WANs
- Run in environments of heterogeneous hardware and software
- Grant applications programs independence from lower layer communications protocols
- Be scalable and capable of supporting very large networks (more than 100,000 systems).

Also, the performance of applications in a network processing environment will have to be competitive with stand-alone systems.

The realization of such an environment poses challenges that go well beyond that of allowing any user in a multivendor environment access to any application on any computer where that application is executed on a one-processor system. The concept of a distributed application provides that a complex application can be partitioned among two or more processors. The reason may be to take advantage of available processor cycles in a multiprocessor network if the local capability is fully occupied, and/or to ensure that different subroutines in the application are run on those machines whose architectures are best suited to handle them.

Achieving this latter objective of improved effectiveness requires a perspective that in one way diametrically opposes the philosophy that has driven the development of networking products over the past 10 years. Considerable efforts have been expended to separate the networking from the programming or applications environment. Yet the development of effective distributed applications demands a high level of understanding of the variety of machines involved in a network and the ability to determine which subroutine may run best on which processor, and which tasks can be handled across the network.

The level of understanding required by the applications developer of both processing systems and the network is extremely high. The first uses of distributed network computing, therefore, are likely to be very specific and technical in nature, such as the design, analysis, and simulation of engineering-intensive products, or the development of a large software system. In both contexts, substantial benefits can be gained from improved run times—to rapidly simulate the effect of design changes, for example, or to compile different parts of a large software system simultaneously.

Despite the theoretical efficiencies of distributed network computing, mainstream corporate MIS applications, such as payroll, will not run in that environment in the foreseeable future. The technical risks are too high, including potential information loss, lack of consistency, and errors. The embryonic nature of the technology and the lack of standards to link diverse machines for interprocess communication will hold back distributed network computing from handling many large data processing applications.

Two major forums for dealing with standards are the Network Computing Forum (NCF), which was inspired by Apollo's Network Computing System (NCS) architecture, which was inherited by

Figure 9.5 Network Computing System Architecture

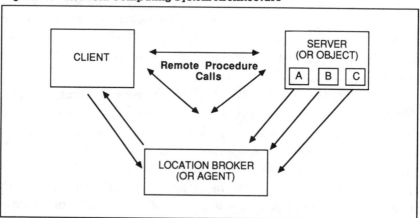

Hewlett-Packard on its acquisition of Apollo, and the Open Software Foundation (OSF). IBM has joined both, and DEC the latter. The next generations of Unix are likely to include NCS-like distributed features. With NCS, complex applications can be partitioned. Users or clients request services from the repository of server routines (or objects) available around the network (Fig. 9.5). A location broker acts as an intermediary bringing together clients and appropriate servers; otherwise, users would require detailed knowledge of available servers and their locations. The clients, servers, and brokers communicate using remote procedure calls. A key mechanism in future standards will be an ability to allow remote procedure calls to interact.

THE ROLE FOR PABXs

Through the mid-1980s, controversy raged over whether PABXs or LANs would become the dominant local-area communications vehicle. For nonvoice communications, the LAN camp has clearly won. The reasons have little to do with any fundamental technological issue. LAN suppliers (including broadline computer vendors and LAN specialists) were simply better at understanding the data applications of customers and marketing to them. No strong applications requirement developed to integrate voice and data functionally, which might have favored PABXs as a core communications vehicle.

PABXs will continue to provide occasional dial-up access to remote databases or processing resources for PCs or workstations. In some configurations of the IIS of the mid-1990s, direct PABX-to-computer links may handle specific applications, such as permitting cooperation between voice mail and electronic mail systems. This cooperation may involve not only cross-notification of messages waiting on the two systems, but also information conversion to deliver an electronic mail message, for example, to a voice-mail box.

It has already proven useful in some environments, such as telemarketing, for PABX switching functions to be controllable within a common applications framework. An outside call can be forwarded to a service representative, together with a screenful of information relating to the calling customer. This capability necessitates the establishment of PABX application interfaces that can support requests from an applications processor to initiate its call handling and feature control functions, as well as to provide call progress and status information. Several major computer manufacturers and PABX vendors are cooperating to promulgate such standards, such as those incorporated in DEC's Computer Integrated Telephony (CIT) and AT&T's Adjunct/Switch Application Interface (ASAI).

The impetus for these developments is coming as much from the data processing as from the communications side of the information equipment suppliers industry. By 1995, a few leading PABXs may incorporate SS7 interfaces. Although most PABXs will still employ digital circuit switching techniques, a few advanced systems will be based upon fast packet switching technology, which is inherently more suited to handling a range of data traffic speeds, including megabit-per-second flows.

It should also be noted that telephone companies are enhancing and aggressively marketing Centrex service (local-area communication based upon telephone company rather than customer premise-based switching) as an alternative to PABXs. Traditionally of interest only for large installations, Centrex is being extended to attract even small and medium businesses. It is also being expanded in capability to handle data traffic, for example, and to provide wide-area Centrex (in which a number of separate sites in an area are tied together logically so as to appear as one integrated local-communications system to users). Centrex data capabilities are more likely to compete with PABXs than LANs.

LOCAL-AREA NETWORKS

After several prolonged false starts, LANs have now definitely entered the mainstream of information processing. Central to their acceptance has been the development of robust network software. Most LANs were originally purchased to enable PC users to share expensive peripherals, such as high-speed printers and hard disks. LANs are increasingly becoming components of an architecture that is designed to permit the integration of many diverse desktop devices, so that information and processing resources can be shared among all varieties of computers.

The picture for LANs is becoming much more complex because putting an application on a network frequently requires the pulling together of software and components from many vendors to achieve not only internetworking but also interprocess integration.

Principal LAN developments to be expected over the next 5 years include:

- Expanded support by network services on the same LAN of a broader range of desktop computer platforms with different operating systems (OS/2, Unix, and Macintosh, as well as MS-DOS)

- Further integration of LANs into corporate networks of minicomputers and mainframes (notably SNA and DECnet)

- Development of a new generation of applications that allows users to access information anywhere on the network

- Advent of higher speed LAN transport standards (e.g., the 100 megabit per second Fiber Distributed Data Interface (FDDI)) to support applications and network environments for which currently popular standards, such as the 10 megabit per second Ethernet and the 4 or 16 megabit per second token-ring LANs, are inadequate.

Furthermore, as OS/2 matures, specialist vendors of LAN software will face added competitive pressure from the emerging OS/2 LAN Manager products. It is too soon to forecast that future versions of OS/2 will be the dominant LAN managers, however. The products are still too embryonic and the competition very intense.

TRANSMISSION MEDIA

As underlying transmission media, both copper and fiber-optic systems will be important in networks of the early 1990s at the expense of coaxial cable. Radio will also be employed to meet specific requirements, for example, satellite transmission for point-to-multipoint applications as in very small aperture terminal (VSAT) networks, or terrestrial mobile radio for field service staff who may need access to information while away from a home base.

Fiber-optics has already become the medium of choice for long-distance point-to-point communications of almost all kinds, as shown by the existing and planned installations of fiber-optic cables by all major common carriers. The capabilities of fiber-optic systems continue to advance substantially, with capacities in the range of 1 gigabit per second per fiber pair expected in the early 1990s.

Fiber-optics is also of great interest for very short-haul applications, such as carrying high-speed data between computing systems in a local LAN. The FDDI standard of 100 megabits per second is well advanced in implementation, and there are already proposals to launch work on a standard above 1 gigabit per second.

Despite all of the interest in fiber, copper systems will retain their place in LANs. The convenience and low cost of twisted pair make it attractive for handling speeds up to 1 megabit per second, a reasonable capability for a LAN, particularly in the framework of newer premise wiring schemes from IBM and AT&T. Many non-time-critical office environments do not need speeds higher than 1 megabit per second. Hybrid installations uniting copper "drops" with fiber-optic trunks combine the strengths of both media. Indeed, FDDI-compatible copper-based systems have been developed for short runs to and from workstations.

Broadband coaxial cable systems are likely to be attractive in environments in which their bulkiness is not a detriment and their ease of tapping and mechanical robustness can give them an edge over fiber cable. Examples are found in manufacturing installations where the power-bandwidth characteristics of coaxial cable are sufficient to support high data rate paths (e.g., 5 megahertz or 5 megabits per second per channel, with independent channels for video, data, and even voice if necessary).

WIRELESS COMMUNICATIONS

During the 1990s, wireless communications will assume a role that is at times complementary, at other times central, to providing the networking infrastructure needed to support information-based applications in the integrated enterprise. This communications medium includes, but will go well beyond, the mobile cellular telephones that became widely accepted business tools during the 1980s (Fig. 9.6).

By the end of the decade, wireless communications will extensively penetrate user and location market segments. The long-term technological possibilities are exemplified by the European RACE Project 2029, whose goal is "connection of mobile and portable equipment to the integrated broadband communications network."

Figure 9.6   Applications of Wireless Communication

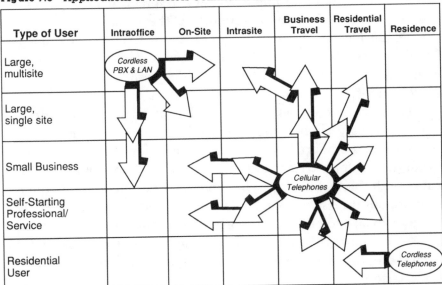

Type of User	Intraoffice	On-Site	Intrasite	Business Travel	Residential Travel	Residence
Large, multisite						
Large, single site						
Small Business						
Self-Starting Professional/ Service						
Residential User						

This project involving 23 companies aims at a $70 personal communication device capable of accommodating voice, image, and data traffic up to 2 megabits per second. Trial service is forecast for 1995 in the 1.7 gigahertz band.

Personal wireless communications will meet several needs in the integrated enterprise. The efficiency and effectiveness of intrinsically mobile employees, such as traveling sales staff, field service engineers, and others, can be substantially improved when they are able to receive and send messages and access information from anywhere.

A striking example of the application of wireless technology for these purposes was provided by IBM and Motorola at the end of the 1980s. IBM installed its own radio network and provided its field sales force with Motorola hand-held terminals that communicated via radio with mainframe and other information storage and processing systems. The application was so successful that, in 1990, IBM and Motorola formed a joint venture called ARDIS to offer use of this network to third parties.

Another notable example, Federal Express' package tracking system, is a key element in supporting the company's quality of service. Besides tracking packages, Federal Express monitors the location of its trucks and can redirect them via two-way radio communication to improve load factors, which results in a visible economic benefit.

Truckers, barge operators, and pilots of small business aircraft will increasingly choose a mobile satellite link to headquarters, as the price of on-board terminals falls to a few thousand dollars. Burlington Motor Carriers and United Van Lines are equipping their trucks with the technology, which not only permits instant communication, but tracks the vehicle's location to within a mile. The driver uses a keyboard to enter a message, which bounces off a geostationary satellite more than 22,000 miles away down to a ground station. From there, the message is routed over telephone lines to corporate headquarters.

In addition to the wide-area terrestrial radio and satellite links, a number of local or on-site radio-based applications can be very valuable when connected to fixed communication and processing facilities. Wireless key and PABX systems allow employees to carry their telephones with them as they move around a site and thus remain reachable. In 1989, AT&T introduced a multiline cordless telephone for business (the Merlin MLC-5), which is the forerunner of these systems.

Onsite applications in the data area are also of great interest. For example, in the warehousing environment, portable radio terminals can be used to eliminate paper picking lists. In shops, these terminals can verify that the prices shown on products or shelves correspond with the figures contained in the store's point-of-sale terminal system.

During the 1990s, aggressive organizations will increasingly seek out and implement radio-based personal and portable communications applications as part of their overall networking capabilities. They will do so to avoid wasting the time of expensive workers and to enhance the effectiveness of intrinsically mobile activities.

Truckers, salespeople, and company representatives of all types will be instantly reachable, even when they may not want to be.

PUBLIC NETWORKS AND COMPUTER NETWORKING

ISDN is the highly touted and frequently misunderstood basis for emerging and future public telecommunications networks. ISDN will be characterized by end-to-end digital communications paths; a set of standardized user interfaces to permit single-point access to a range of voice, data, and other network services; and a powerful common channel signaling system (SS7 or CCITT No. 7), which provides the foundation for a range of new and enhanced network service offerings. By the early 1990s, SS7 will be deployed throughout the major long-distance networks and cover more than 80% of traffic originating locally.

The most promising applications that exploit the ISDN infrastructure, or the intelligent network, as it is more usefully called, have to do with using the capabilities of SS7. SS7 is used to provide very flexible access to a range of information services, a variety of enhanced call-handling features (e.g., automatic callback), access to variable amounts of bandwidth upon demand, and increased security. Thus, although computer vendors (in contrast to telecommunications equipment suppliers) have thus far paid only limited attention to ISDN, it is very likely that by the mid-1990s, SS7 interfaces to a range of computer equipment will have become available, either directly or via the user D-channel. This channel is available to users to send data and/or signaling information from user terminals to the nearest public network access node.

Despite the spread of private or leased-line networks in aggressive organizations, public network facilities must form part and parcel of their overall communications infrastructure. Because businesses will not be able to reach all of their partners via leased lines, they will demand public networks that offer similar capabilities to private ones. Hence, users will require the power of SS7.

The current versions of ISDN are known as narrowband ISDN, which is a set of enabling technologies that provide a common user interface to a range of different network services at rates of up to 1.544 megabits per second (or 2.048 megabits per second in Europe). Thus far, telephone companies and other public network operators have not developed large-scale markets for the use of ISDN technologies, many of whose capabilities have been implemented by sophisticated U.S. corporate customers within the context of their private networks, independently of public ISDN standards.

The development and implementation of standards for narrowband ISDN have largely taken place independently from progress in mainstream information processing, such as the advent of very powerful workstations. Hence, the specific ISDN interfaces now available lack clear connections to emerging data communications needs. Nevertheless, ISDN will become a key technological infrastructure of public networks in the 1990s because of the increasing operational efficiency that it makes possible for these networks.

First-generation or narrowband ISDN as a transport or access mechanism is not on the critical path of development of computer networking or, even less, of computer applications. A large and growing number of PCs, workstations, and other intelligent devices will be installed by the early 1990s when the offering of ISDN interfaces becomes widespread. ISDN will be able to run within OSI, SNA, or other protocol stacks at lower layers as an alternative to link control standards such as IEEE 802.2. As, and if, market demand develops, computer and semiconductor suppliers will provide terminal adapters to enable existing voice and data terminals, controllers, and other devices to connect to narrowband ISDN transmission lines. Several had been introduced into the market by 1990.

A number of public network technologies under development go well beyond the capabilities of narrowband ISDN and address potential needs for broadband wide-area communications channels that will operate at extremely high speeds, tens of megabits per second and even higher. The need for and value of these broadband networks derive from a confluence of applications and facilitating broadband technologies in the spheres of data processing and data communications equipment and systems, as well as public and private telecommunications network facilities.

For many large organizations, the mainstay of distributed computing facilities has been hierarchical wide-area data networks, such as IBM's SNA. These networks are built around a multitier structure of mainframes, minicomputers, and PCs, with extensive distribution of processing services throughout the network. Many organizations have developed several networks over a period of years, leading to islands of automation built on different architectures. Although the communications traffic of these individual computing systems may be combined for economic reasons over a shared transmission backbone, often with a multiplexer network, relatively little interaction has occurred between the diverse subnetworks. IBM system users, for example, have not generally accessed applications or done their work on non-IBM hosts.

As these disparate hierarchical networks have been growing, however, there has been a rise of increasingly powerful workstations and of multimegabit per second LANs to which they are connected. These workstations have tended to be more highly standardized or vendor-independent than minicomputers or mainframes, thanks to the phenomena of Unix in technical computing and MS-DOS in commercial data processing.

Although they were often initially installed to satisfy individual computing needs, these workstations and PCs have increasingly been interconnected via LANs to permit the economic sharing of specialized or scarce services and resources and to allow their users to cooperate with each other in shared tasks. As the number of these LANs has grown, so has the demand for long-distance or wide-area and metropolitan-area links that enable LAN clients to access information and computing resources that may be located in another city, country, or site within the same metropolitan region.

Also, because a workstation user may wish to make use of information and processing resources that may be located in several different subnetworks (e.g., a design engineer may want to access pricing and other technical information on parts owned by several other divisions within a firm), the demand for transparent functional cooperation is developing far beyond the simple sharing of information transport facilities. With few exceptions, however, the speeds inherent in LANs and in modern workstations have been substantially greater than those readily available in intersite or wide-area transmission networks.

Furthermore, the power of the workstations, and of the applications they support, has risen much more rapidly than the capabilities of most commercially available LANs. For example, when the popular Ethernet LAN was conceived in the 1970s, its standard speed of 10 megabits per second seemed, if anything, like overkill. Yet in CAD applications of the late 1980s, users often found they had to limit an Ethernet population to five to ten workstations. Larger numbers must still be segmented into smaller LANs interconnected by bridges or routers.

These schemes can work well, provided that the traffic flow between LAN segments is small, which in turn implies that workstations in different segments cannot easily share frequently used servers. The tradeoff between throughput performance (the number of workstations on a LAN, which has to be kept small) and cost (the ability to share servers among many workstations) is, thus, not very satisfactory.

In short, there is a lack of balance between workstation and network performance, which, in the latter case, is deficient in both LAN and WAN speeds. In the 1990s, a number of LAN and WAN technologies and facilities will become available to enable organizations to redress this imbalance, which is becoming especially acute for widely dispersed, communications-intensive firms. The value of these new facilities will be fully realizable only as, and if:

- New communications protocols are developed that are suited to high-speed transmission networks
- The concept of a distributed computing environment is implemented to permit the effective sharing of computing and

information resources across a network that includes processing systems of disparate internal architectures from a variety of vendors.

The advent of broadband networks will encompass several technologies, including higher speed LANs, MANs, and WANs. As conceived by public network operators, broadband ISDN (BISDN) aims to support a very wide range of communications applications for its customers, whose traffic characteristics are likely to vary widely by application. BISDN will make the overall task of network planning and management extremely problematical, unless much more flexible networking structures can be implemented than those that prevail today. BISDN differs from narrowband ISDN not only in terms of its available bandwidth, but also because it is conceived as an ultimately truly integrated multipurpose network. Narrowband ISDN, however, is essentially an integrated access mechanism to a variety of different networks.

WIDE-AREA NETWORKS

In the wide-area, or long-distance, network arena, major service capabilities will be introduced in the next 5 years that depend on the realization of broadband transmission and switching and multiplexing technologies, known respectively as Synchronous Optical Network (SONET) and Asynchronous Transfer Mode (ATM).

SONET is an optical fiber-based transport and multiplexing concept that exploits the huge bandwidths available on fiber links. Bandwidth can be allocated to overhead functions that provide SONET with extensive network operations and management capability. SONET standards are also vitally important to ensure that reliable and maintainable optical connections can be established between network elements from different vendors and transmission facilities owned by different carriers and private companies.

The evolution of SONET continues, following the Phase 1 standards that were drafted in 1988. In particular, standards specifying several rates and the format for the SONET interface have been set at approximately 50, 155, and 622 megabits per second in the Synchronous Digital Hierarchy, or SDH. Major continuing standards efforts that should come to fruition in the early 1990s pertain to operational functions and network management that are essential if the benefits of this new optical interface are to be realized.

SONET will be introduced into networks over a number of years, beginning in the early 1990s. In the first stage, it will be introduced in point-to-point systems, much as optical fiber transmission systems were first deployed. In the second stage, optical interfaces will be integrated into network elements, such as circuit switches, digital cross-connect systems, and add–drop multiplexers. Additional services will be introduced and made available via optical interfaces, for example, new switched high bandwidth services.

In addition to the public network operators, perhaps only several dozen U.S. companies today have sufficient intersite communications traffic to justify the use of SONET services on a dedicated basis. Boeing Computer Services envisions that, by 1993, SONET will replace the slower T1 links as the digital transport and interconnect between its huge databases of aircraft designs and CAD/CAM workstations spread throughout the corporation. The retailer J. C. Penney is exploring SONET as a means of dispersing data and images among its 1,000 stores. For instance, a store manager could view the new season's styles on a workstation and then order directly over a LAN.

On the switching and multiplexing side, ATM deals with the rules for dividing up the usable capacity (or bandwidth) of a transmission system interface and allocating it to user services. The current rules used in digital communications networks, known as Synchronous Transfer Mode (STM), allocate time slots within a receiving structure or frame to a service for the duration of the call. An STM channel is, therefore, identified by the position of its time slots within a synchronous structure.

In contrast, specific periodic time slots are not assigned to a channel in ATM. Rather, usable capacity is segmented into fixed-size information-bearing units called cells (in principle, variable-size units could also be considered). These cells, each consisting of a header and an information field, can be allocated to services on demand. An ATM interface structure thus consists of a set of labeled, and not time-positioned, channels. These labeled channels, in contrast to STM channels, do not have to be restricted to a small set of fixed-rate values.

The principal reason for preferring ATM over STM is that ATM switches and multiplexers are less dependent upon considerations of bit rates for particular services. ATM is likely to be more suitable than STM for handling a mixture of both bursty and continuous-bit-rate services. Various hybrid stations involving combinations of ATM and more traditional STM switching have also been proposed. It should be noted that the word "asynchronous" in ATM does not refer to the transmission technique used (which can, indeed, be synchronous, such as SONET), but to the freeing of service channels from a time-defined position within a synchronous transmission structure.

The intention by public network operators to introduce ATM is motivated in part by the perceived need to accommodate a variety of telecommunications services with widely varying traffic characteristics. On the other hand, a major consideration for the public carriers is how to migrate smoothly and economically from today's networks, with their huge investments in existing plants, to the network of the future. The cost benefits of prolonging this migration as long as possible must be weighed against revenue opportunities that may be lost. For instance, large customers may find alternative ways of meeting their broadband applications needs that involve limited or no use of public carriers' facilities. These important users may need to act on their applications more quickly than the carriers can respond.

Implementing both forward-looking and backward-compatible solutions will be far from trivial tasks for both carriers and users. By the mid-1990s, only a few BISDN-like networks will likely be operating. They will serve pioneering customers, whether the networks are provided by the public carriers or implemented with customer or third-party-owned equipment. Equipment for private use may be developed more rapidly than that for public networks (albeit not necessarily to public network standards), and entrepreneurial suppliers may seize a perceived market opportunity without waiting for the results of lengthy public-standards setting procedures. This activity has already occurred in the realm of fast packet-switching multiplexers for use in private or leased-line networks.

METROPOLITAN-AREA NETWORKS

A metropolitan-area network, or MAN, is a high-speed network for voice, data, and video that provides inter-LAN or LAN-to-WAN connections to noncontiguous properties within a metropolitan area. The alternatives from which companies will be able to choose are likely to include the IEEE 802.6 MAN standard, which will be the basis of systems offered by telephone companies, and various private company alternatives based on fiber-optic loops installed in major metropolitan areas.

The 802.6 standard, known as Distributed Queue Dual Bus (DQDB), is based on a dual bus architecture. A scheduling algorithm can provide very high efficiencies under heavy loads, because contention has been eliminated from the system. Any given node sees some nodes on the ring as upstream and others as downstream. It can communicate with any other node by sending information on one bus and receiving it on the other. When a node needs a slot for transmission, it sends a request on the bus going upstream, so that each node learns how many slots are required by the nodes downstream from itself. Request signaling on one bus is thus used for access to the other.

An important potential application of the DQDB MAN in the early 1990s is to provide high-speed, switched LAN interconnection as an alternative to private or leased-line facilities. A service concept SMDS (Switched Multimegabit Data Service) has been proposed for telephone companies, based on the 802.6 standard, that would provide switched data transport at speeds initially of T1 and T3 (1.544 and 44.736 megabits per second), and eventually 150 megabits per second to be compatible with SONET speeds.

THE SHIFT TO PUBLIC NETWORKS

Broadband networks, and the prospects for access to practically un-limited bandwidth on demand, are not going to spring up overnight, or even over a 2- to 3-year period. Rather, broadband networking will steadily improve and penetrate the marketplace in the next 10 to 15 years. As a result of enduring political and competitive pres-sures, as well as the influence of existing installed bases, delays are likely to be encountered in implementing practical standards and procedures for the seamless interworking of networking facilities installed by different users and by the various public carriers.

Networks are not so much designed as redesigned, for the same reason as it is impractical for organizations to throw away their vast existing investments in software in favor of the latest computing technologies and applications.

In the first half of the 1990s, there will likely be a growing volume of higher speed LAN interconnections between sites that are based on backbone links made up of T1 and T3 trunks. Over the same period, the FDDI LAN technology will be introduced as a campus backbone LAN and as a means to interconnect token ring and Ethernet LANs. FDDI may also be used to provide mainframe-to-mainframe and mainframe-to-front-end connections within the computer room.

In metropolitan areas, IEEE 802.6 networks based on the DQDB technology will be introduced by telephone companies ini-tially running at T3 speeds, with the possibility of later extension to SONET speeds (155 megabits per second). These networks will be the public carriers' offerings to compete with other fiber-optic based networks installed and planned by private companies in many major metropolitan regions.

As experience is gained with broadband networking and new applications develop (e.g., color image processing), then the value of broadband multiple-purpose digital networking will become more apparent. Major telecommunications common carriers will attempt to satisfy these needs through their broadband ISDNs. BISDN-type capabilities, such as broadband on-demand services, will likely be exploited by a few aggressive organizations in the mid-1990s, the leaders in the interconnection of high-speed LANs and the development of new applications, such as imaging.

Competition in this BISDN arena, as in existing networks, will arise between privately owned or leased third-party and public carrier solutions. If the latter are to succeed in limiting or even reversing the growth of private networking in favor of public networking, not only will they have to work closely with customers to understand their emerging needs, but they will also have to cooperate with suppliers of computing and data communications equipment. Such cooperation in formulating and implementing future networks was lacking in the original narrowband ISDN.

For example, throughput analyses demonstrate that existing communications protocol stacks, such as TCP/IP, are not appropriate at broadband speeds. Several new protocols have been devised, such as XTP (Express Transfer Protocol), which has little overhead and can be processed quickly, and VMTP (Versatile Message Transaction Protocol), which is designed for fast response rather than high throughput. In general, it appears that multimegabit per second networks can be used effectively only if workstations have more intelligent network communications interfaces than they possess today.

For both technical and marketing reasons, public network carriers need to be involved with the development of these new schemes for broadband communication, if they are to be vendors of choice for providing broadband network service and support. They must maximize the likelihood that their public networks can be put to effective use for broadband applications, as the potential point of congestion for network-dependent applications shifts from the transport system (where it is today, certainly in WANs) to the processing of a communications protocol.

In theory, the tremendous and often unpredictable demands of broadband services should encourage the shift from private to public networking. The public carriers have much more bandwidth at their disposal than any private organization, so that they should, in principle, be able to accommodate unpredictable broadband applications within public network services more effectively than any private network.

The full flowering of broadband services and the resolution of these competitive issues will take place after the mid-1990s, once the viability of broadband networks and the value of business applications running on them have been established by pioneering organizations.

CHANGES TO THE ORGANIZATION

To achieve an integrated enterprise—the sharing of data and programs as needed wherever they may be physically located or developed—users must establish a very powerful and flexible network utility. The central information systems department of the 1990s will turn much of its attention to network management, orchestrating the communications systems that connect computers and people to each other. IS must create consistent user interfaces, set connectivity standards, and foster an environment in which applications can be added, removed, or modified without jeopardizing other applications or causing systems failure.

Aggressive organizations will be able to achieve a much clearer separation between data processing and data communications by the mid-1990s. Multiple functions carried out by a single computer (e.g., terminal support, database access, electronic mail,

WAN interface) can be divided among a number of specialized processors. On end-to-end broadband networks, servers need not be located on the same LAN as the clients they support, thus organizations can choose a more centralized approach to workstation support. In other words, broadband networking backs the belief that mainframes will not die. With their economies of scale and dedicated operators to provide backup and support, large mainframe-like servers will provide high performance comparable to that of local servers, provided that communications protocols appropriate to broadband speeds are implemented.

This type of networking naturally accommodates nonhierarchical flows of information—from desk to desk or person to person rather than from department to department. Such means of communication may either reflect or help stimulate changes in organizational structure.

The network should reflect the organization, however decentralized or centralized it may be. Even if a company is highly decentralized, however, its networks should still come under centralized control. In organizations that choose to decentralize information systems and place the development, operation, and maintenance of applications primarily in the hands of end-users, network management may, indeed, be the principal role of the traditional MIS department.

The network must be looked at not simply as a vehicle for linking computer systems, but more fundamentally as a means of linking resources. Sophisticated users recognize that connectivity itself is a multilevel phenomenon, involving physical, systems, and applications linkages.

The basic responsibility, or first level of connectivity, is to manage the physical network so that service is rarely, if ever, interrupted. Fluctuating and even unexpected demands must be accommodated with the minimum of disruption, either economic or operational. In this regard, a revival in public networking (if the telecom carriers seize their opportunities) may occur, because broadband networking inherently has to handle much greater variability and unpredictability in traffic patterns than does traditional networking. When, for example, a workstation is sending compound color documents or is receiving the results of a job run on a supercomputer for local display, peak-to-average traffic ratios between locations will be much higher than today's typical 5 to 1 or 10 to 1. Given this variability in demand, planning and operating a private WAN will become much more problematic, even for large, experienced companies. The vast bandwidths at the disposal of public carriers and their new "bandwidth on demand" services will make them an increasingly attractive option or, at least, a complement in a hybrid public–private network environment.

On the second level of connectivity, systems must be monitored for performance. Security and access passwords must be easily assigned or modified, and installing new applications should be a straightforward process.

The most formidable task occurs on the third level: permitting applications to exchange data freely with each other. To achieve enterprise-wide networking, certain basic issues must be settled, such as a directory of user names and resources, LANs, and LAN-to-MAN and LAN-to-WAN interconnection to achieve high end-to-end bandwidth. Resolution of these technological issues is necessary to deal with the overriding questions to which they are subordinate. These questions concern the interaction of people and resources and necessarily involve organizational factors, such as economic realities, corporate policies, and regulatory constraints within and across national borders.

In the most sophisticated organizations, these technological issues will not be left up to the networking and information systems specialists alone. Real-world network management does not proceed according to a well-defined life cycle, with planning and design, followed by implementation, then operations and maintenance, and then feedback to planning and design again.

Networks are not so much built as they are continually being rebuilt. New networks are constructed on old ones, and many networks feed into each other. Thus, the business of network planning, implementation, and management is much more a process than a one-time project.

In the aggressive company, networking will cut across traditional organizational lines, involving top management and users in key planning steps. Business managers, as well as program and project managers, will become part of strategic network planning and control. Any technical scheme for network management must take these people into consideration if it is to succeed.

If used properly, this emerging style of networking may enable organizations to reduce delays in their operations, for example, to speed up resources to customer queries. Investments in technology alone are unlikely to yield substantial benefits, however, unless users are willing and able to change business practices as well.

CHAPTER 10

HUMAN INTERFACES

In the Integrated Information System of the mid-1990s, most workers will find that using workstations makes them considerably more productive in their everyday work. Employees who are not supplied their own machines or who cannot master the ones they are given will contribute much less to a company's competitive well-being than those who are.

User interfaces will be key to the full acceptance of workstations, and of the whole IIS. Companies that mishandle this crucial technology—by holding onto old interfaces for too long, for instance—will keep stumbling toward mediocrity. By paying proper attention to good interfaces, competitors will sail ahead on the winds of productivity.

The search for the perfect interface has been confused by the appearance of new, "uninterested" computer users. These primarily professional personnel have proven to be somewhat computer-phobic and resistant to formal training that would make them more comfortable. They readily revert to their pencil-and-paper procedures at the first frustration. They make clear that they are not interested in becoming proficient computer operators; they simply wish to carry out their assigned duties more easily, rapidly, and effectively. At best, they consider computers unavoidable necessities in their work lives.

These computer resistors have stymied designers for years. Once such users master the basics of a new system, they soon criticize the "cumbersome" interface that allowed them to learn so quickly in the first place. If provided a design geared to experienced users, they complain that it was too difficult to learn, or to relearn after periods of disuse. Interfaces that combine features for both types of users are called too slow or too draining of processing and memory resources.

In the early 1980s, Apple Computer introduced the Apple Lisa PC, based on earlier work by Xerox PARC researchers (Fig. 10.1). This system featured a graphics-based, "desktop metaphor" interface. Although the Lisa failed in the marketplace because of its high price and slow speed, the interface lived on. Apple's second such product, the Apple Macintosh, appeared in the mid-1980s to an enthusiastic welcome.

As software developers designed new applications for the Macintosh, they adopted certain conventions for screen layout, control functions, and overall "look and feel." Applications that followed

Figure 10.1   History of the "Desk Top Metaphor"

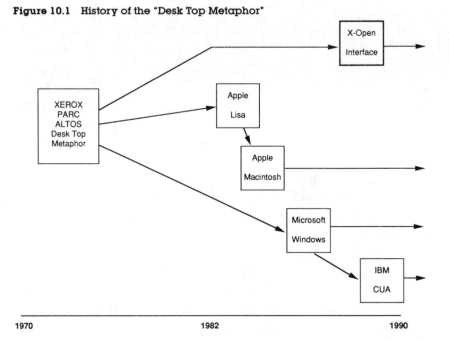

these standards generally became more popular than those that did not. This market acceptance quickly encouraged the use of the emerging standards.

IBM took this phenomenon into account during development of its SAA by including the Common User Access (CUA). This architecture (as yet not completely implemented) specifies screen layout as well as common control function implementation, and provides a level of screen size, resolution, and capability independence not found in the Apple systems.

Over the past few years, virtually every competitor, either independently or in consortia, has introduced a similar interface. Going by the names of X-Windows, Open Look, Windows, Motif, DECWindows, New Wave, NextStep, and so on, these interfaces have provided comparable facilities in roughly compatible form. Apple's lawsuit against Microsoft and Hewlett-Packard confused the market by casting doubts about its competitors' abilities to produce improved desktop metaphor interfaces, but no matter who eventually wins in a legal sense, neither Microsoft or Hewlett-Packard will be hindered in the marketplace.

WORKSTATION INTERFACES

By the mid-1990s, the desktop metaphor will be the interface of choice for all workstations except those dedicated to old applications. The interface will take a form similar to the HP New Wave product shown in Figure 10.2. The screen image presents a main desktop window upon which application windows can be placed in any position, possibly overlapping others. Icons represent various system functions, system resources, and application programs when they are not in use. Activating these icons with a pointing device expands them into an application window, which can then be worked on to carry out the user's desires.

There will be no standardization beyond this level of detail in the visual interface. Each manufacturer or consortium will develop

Figure 10.2 Appearance of Nested Windows in HP New Wave Interface

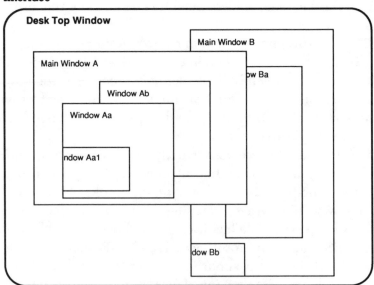

the details of its own interface to gain competitive advantage or to meet the special needs of its own base of users.

Two major communities will develop: scientific–engineering and business. The scientific community will choose interfaces based on the MOTIF (and X-Windows) standard. IBM has licensed the NextStep interface software from Steve Job's company, NeXT Inc., for its AIX systems, but that is only a minor move away from the above standard. The business community will employ interfaces based on the Microsoft Windows/IBM Presentation Manager standard.

Within each community, variations will continue to be supported, but they will not prevent users of one interface from easily switching to another. The major variations will come in the positioning of the action bar, the lack of a function key area, and the design and placement of the icons. All interfaces will feature the control and display elements shown in Figure 10.3, which is the design of the standard window for the IBM CUA. The various box and bar elements will govern window sizing and positioning, window scrolling, and program activation and control functions.

**Figure 10.3   Standard IBM Common User Access (CUA)
Window Elements (Source: IBM)**

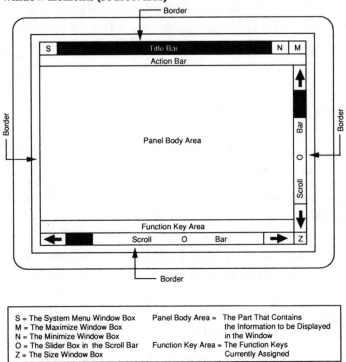

S = The System Menu Window Box   Panel Body Area =   The Part That Contains
M = The Maximize Window Box   the Information to be Displayed
N = The Minimize Window Box   in the Window
O = The Slider Box in the Scroll Bar   Function Key Area = The Function Keys
Z = The Size Window Box   Currently Assigned

By the early 1990s, all system suppliers will develop architectures, design rules, and kits to assist developers in implementing the interfaces within their individual applications. Vendors will also set up testing facilities to approve those applications that follow all of the rules. This approval process will encourage developers to provide a unified look and feel to each system and all of its associated applications.

One major goal of the rules and tool kits will be to insulate developers from changes in display and other system characteristics. Old applications will be moved without change among systems that have different display characteristics as well as to new-generation hardware. By the mid-1990s, this device-independence goal will be achieved, allowing users to upgrade their systems without the necessity of buying new application software.

Still, there will not be sufficient standardization to permit the
same application to be run on different brands of systems without
some alteration. The only exceptions are different systems using the
Unix interface standard and clones of popular brands of workstations.

THE FUTURE INTERFACE

Major advances in visual interfaces over the next 5 years will center
on three major areas:

1. Improving the interface to make it more user friendly for both
    experienced and inexperienced users
2. Incorporating video image (and sound) information, from such
    sources as Compact Disc Interactive (CDI) or Digital Video
    Interactive (DVI) optical disks and video cameras, into the
    screen interface
3. Improving the speed and reducing the resource consumption
    of the interface-supporting software.

AI assists at the interface will free the average worker from many
repetitive tasks, letting him or her concentrate only on those that
really need human intervention. Users will be able to mix live-action
sound and video with digitally generated text and graphics on one or
more of the windows in a high-end business or engineering workstation. Other advances will be less noticeable. In fact, the end-user
may note only that his or her system seems to run a little faster, that
almost all of the applications use the same controls for common
functions, and that sharing of data among individual applications has
not only become possible, but often easy.

The keyboard will remain the primary mechanism for users to
enter data and command options into workstations. Keyboard command entry is faster and less error-prone than other options, such as
voice input. With only minor modification to auxiliary PC keys, the
current QWERTY configuration will stay the overwhelming choice

for keyboard layout. Because almost all children in U.S. schools are being trained on the QWERTY keyboard, the pressures to re-design it into a more ergonomically effective form or to use another information input mechanism altogether have been reduced to almost zero.

Voice command input mechanisms will remain largely limited to users who work at hands-busy jobs or who have a handicap that makes using a keyboard difficult. Still, examples of voice input systems are penetrating mainstream commercial environments. Voice Trader from Verbex Voice Systems, Inc., targets the frenetic stock trading pit. Brokers at Shearson Lehman Hutton, Inc., were among the first to enter transactions by voice, such as "Buy 100 shares of IBM at 102." Verbex claims that the transaction gets entered not only more quickly, but at 98% accuracy, better than by keyboard entry or written note. In a very different setting, Burlington Industries, Inc., has installed a voice recognition system that has cut 25% the time it takes quality inspectors to log defects on the lengths of textiles passing by them.

Such systems are tailor-made for the particular application. The vocabulary in these instances can be restricted to a workable number of common phrases. Some current voice systems can handle about 1,000 words, but that figure is still only half of the number used by a person in a normal day. Says Jay Wilpon, a researcher in the speech research department at Bell Laboratories, "Unrestricted input in an unrestricted environment is not in the cards in our lifetime."

Voice I/O will continue to advance in terms of the machine's ability to discriminate speech and understand more words. Some predict that a substantial number of executives will use voice input as the interface to their workstations in the mid-1990s. Such a use will occur in situations where drafts of documents are reviewed and commented on or where directions are given to a subordinate. In these cases, the workstation will act as a convenient voice recording device, not to comprehend what is being said. The IIS will carry the voice annotation, along with the text or images that make up the document, to the recipient. For most professionals, voice I/O will remain a developing technical solution for which there is no real business problem.

Younger members of the workforce are, in fact, more comfortable writing or calculating on a keyboard than by any other mechanism, including pencil and paper. As these keyboard-trained workers become an increasing percentage of the workforce, the need for another technological solution, such as voice input, decreases.

Of course, some top executives have never learned to type. But these managers usually can rely on assistants to prepare information for their bosses' perusal. In aggressive companies, this information will come in the form of an executive information system. The interface will be customized to the executive's use and allow him or her to examine the details behind the charts and graphs shown by the system to better understand the causes of any unusual successes or problems. This information will be automatically updated from the main corporate operational databases.

Page readers and scanners will become increasingly important for entering hard copy data into workstations. These machines will be the low-cost form of the document image processing system discussed in Chapter 6. With all PCs interconnected in aggressive companies, the IIS will allow interested parties to simultaneously view useful documents without the infamous routing slip. Thus, one common situation can be prevented: important background information reaching the executive just after he or she has made an important business decision.

POINTING AND COMMAND INTERFACES

Perhaps the most difficult aspect of interface design is developing pointers and commands that satisfy experienced, inexperienced, and partially experienced end-users. Designers have settled on the concept of two complementary user-selected interfaces. The menu format accommodates infrequent users, and the command or function key setup satisfies experienced users.

The menu interface (including icons) leads the inexperienced user through the steps necessary to carry out a desired function. It normally employs the pointing device as an activator ("point and shoot"). For complex operations, a hierarchy of menus (first menu choice activating a second menu, etc.) is often employed. On the negative side, this interface requires the typist to lift hands off the keyboard, and sometimes requires the user to go through several nested menus before the desired function can be carried out.

The control or function key interface allows the user to rapidly activate functions without removing hands from the keyboard. It does, however, require the memorization of sometimes obscure key codes, which is a major disadvantage for inexperienced or infrequent users.

As shown in Figure 10.4, multiple variations of both types will coexist within the overall interface. Wherever appropriate, the menus will list the appropriate function keys for the fast interface,

Figure 10.4   IBM Common User Access Panel Control Mechanism (Source: IBM)

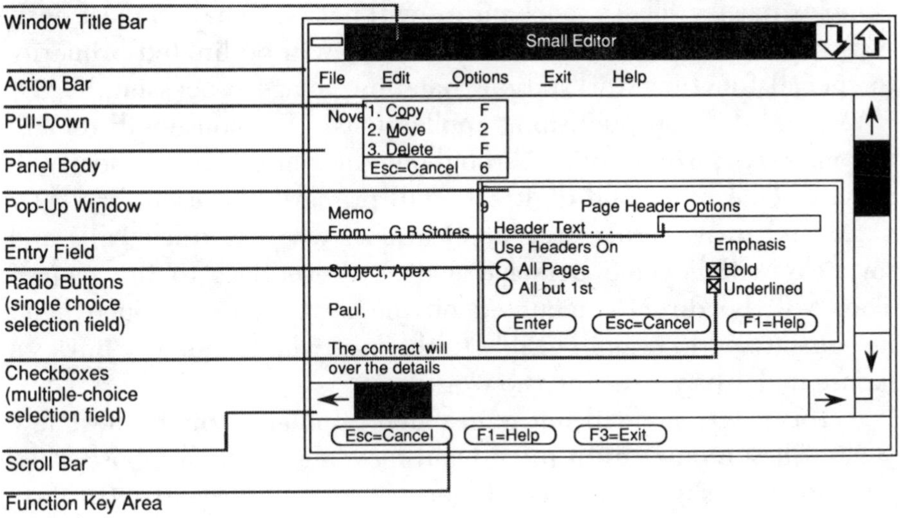

thus teaching the user the required codes by repetitive prompting. This mechanism allows users to move at their own pace and to easily retreat to the menu interface after a period of not accessing the specific application.

Specific function keys will take on common meanings for all applications within an individual supplier's interface. For example, IBM is specifying that in its CUA interface, the F1 key should always activate the "Help" function, and the Escape key should always move the user step-by-step back up the menu hierarchy when he or she does not desire to complete an operation.

A third interface will also be used to control the graphic elements of both the desktop and specific applications. For the primary window, this interface consists of the sizing boxes, scroll bars, and window positioning controls shown in Figure 10.3. Normally this interface will be directed entirely by the system pointing device, although elementary control will be possible using the pointing keys on the few nonintelligent terminals remaining in the mid-1990s.

Pointer and more complicated dial boxes will be used to create graphics and images on the screen and to control screen views of complex images. These mechanisms will not be found on most business workstations in the mid-1990s. They will be limited primarily to special function workstations handling image processing, CAD/CAM, and desktop publishing applications. The mouse will remain the major pointing device throughout the period, but others will survive. Dial boxes and digitizers will primarily be used for CAD/CAM and image processing applications, whereas track balls and joysticks will become personal choice alternatives to the mouse. They will be directly mounted on the keyboard to reduce hand movement and to remain visible to the user who frequently buries a mouse under paper during the workday.

Touch screens will not gain much popularity in the next few years. They require even more hand movement than a mouse, subject users to slight discomfort because of the large electrostatic charges on CRT screens, and cannot replace the keyboard for data input. Only in public places will touch screens remain a primary means of activating computers.

INDIRECT AND PROGRAM-TO-PROGRAM INTERFACES

In contrast to the physical aspects of the user interface, the underlying logical issues are proving more difficult and even more critical in the development of the fully seamless interface desired by users. Designers must consider the mechanisms used to:

- Interchange information among software systems that are designed to interoperate
- Interchange information among software systems on an unplanned, ad hoc basis
- Utilize and control resources across a geographically distributed system.

At present, most PC applications employ specially crafted clipboard and cut and paste interfaces to pass information. Unix and now OS/2 implement a facility termed "Pipes" which permits programs to dynamically pass information in a standardized form. However, the programs must be designed to cooperate in this fashion and must agree beforehand on the amount and format of the information to be passed.

Over the next several years, these relatively simple facilities will be enhanced to permit more flexible and dynamic passing of information. These refinements will be achieved primarily by implementing related applications as a single task with multiple threads that can operate independently of each other but that also can share memory segments and files. In addition, programs will use Application Program Interfaces (APIs) supplied by the developer to provide standardized interfaces for the information contained in their specific programs. These APIs, which are currently being developed, will permit standardized access to system facilities and standards for various types of information passing among unrelated applications.

By the mid-1990s, most commercial software application developers will provide standardized interfaces (using the API facilities) to permit static and dynamic as well as planned and ad hoc access by other programs to their RAM-resident data. By that time, most programs will use sufficiently common database and file structures that controlled access to their files will be easily implemented. It is these technological advances that will form the underpinnings of the client–server and network processing modes of computing discussed in Chapter 4.

INTERSYSTEM INTERFACES

All vendors state as a goal the implementation of a single, seamless user interface that will permit users to easily access data and employ resources anywhere within an interconnected corporate system. They are actively working in two major areas to reach this goal: overall system architecture standards and definitions, and distributed resource sharing mechanisms.

IBM's SAA architecture (Fig. 10.5) has, simply by its existence, spurred competing vendors to develop software standards across their product lines. DEC already claims a full set of standards as a result of its declared "single-system" product strategy. In reality, DEC seems to have a two-operating system, two-interface strategy, whose incompatibilities the company has not yet fully papered over using its Network Application Services (NAS) approach. Other vendors, such as Hewlett-Packard and Data General, have evolved architectures similar to SAA.

By implementing such architectures, vendors will standardize the major application program interfaces for all of their own system storage and communication services. This standardization is especially important for IBM, which offers several architecturally different systems. For example, under the SAA DDM scheme, the company is aiming for almost total compatibility between its

Figure 10.5   IBM SAA Structure (Source: IBM)

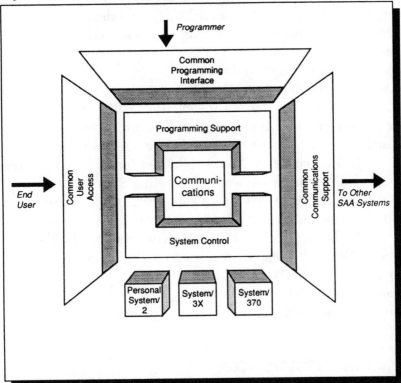

PS/2-based OS/2 Query Manager and its mainframe-based Query Management Facility (QMF). This compatibility will include exchange of objects as well as a single callable interface. It will allow a PS/2-based program to direct a specific query to any computer in an interconnected system without requiring a translation that might be inexact.

The utility of client–server and network processing capabilities will be enhanced by IBM in its products, allowing all levels of SAA-compatible systems to act as servers for all workstations and permitting the same program to migrate to different levels in the processing hierarchy.

These architectural definition and implementation efforts will generally be completed by 1995, but the various vendors' definitions will not yet be completely compatible. It will still be easier to share information within a single manufacturer's product line than across different vendors' machines. Although its basic existence will not be threatened by this situation, the IIS will not be able to reach its full potential until later in the 1990s.

A significant amount of work is currently underway in defining standardized resource sharing mechanisms. IBM has been putting major efforts into its LU 6.2 communications protocols and associated software, such as the Advanced Program-to-Program Communication (APPC) facilities. The Apollo division of Hewlett-Packard has been developing its Network Computing System (NCS) and Sun Microsystems its Open Network Computing (ONC) facilities, both intended to meet users' distributed resource sharing needs.

Standards, such as the ones being contemplated by the Apollo-sponsored Network Computing Forum (NCF), are aimed at smoothing resource sharing across multiple vendors' products. Both the IBM and NCF standards will be widely adopted by the industry over the next several years.

LAYING THE GROUNDWORK

The move toward an integrated user interface will be slow over the next 5 years. By the end of the period, the visual interface should be relatively standard. Most programs will use minor variants of the icon-based, desktop metaphor. The command interface will also be generally standardized in terms of such features as scroll bars, window sizing, and some frequently used function keys.

By the mid-1990s, it will be easy for a software developer in an aggressive company to create applications that span multiple nonhomogeneous, geographically separated computer systems while presenting a seamless interface to the end-user. It will still be difficult, and sometimes impossible, however, to interchange information on a completely unplanned, ad hoc basis among programs that are not designed to interoperate. By this time, however, all of the architectural groundwork will have been done, the directions set, and the actual implementation well on its way.

A significant percentage of the software required to provide the seamless interface will reside in the workstation. The remainder will be spread across the rest of the overall integrated system. Only via skillfully crafted architectures and standards as well as carefully implemented software and protocols can the ultimate interface goal be met.

In addition to this infrastructure software, a large number of specialized routines will be developed to provide standardized access to specific, heavily used applications that are not themselves standard. Many of these programs will still be in use in the mid-1990s. Local programmers must provide the finishing touches to the seamless interface for each organization. This requirement will not change until well into the next century. Thus, the seamless interface will be implemented, but at a great cost in terms of local programming effort to support and maintain it well beyond the 1990s.

The need for a common user interface is a subtle but vital part of an aggressive company's IIS strategy. Truly effective client–server and network forms of computing depend upon the existence of such an interface at the deeper levels.

At the physical user interface, conversion to the new desktop metaphor is important in order to gain wider acceptance of PCs as part of users' standard operating methods, particularly at higher levels of management. By one estimate, in 1990 55% of the white-collar workforce in the United States still work without a PC. Greater acceptance and use of PCs are necessary because electronic mail and computer-aided conferencing increase productivity only when all of the involved participants can communicate. As long as even a single important team member does not use a PC regularly, the entire group will stay at the lowest common working denominator—the printed word. Therefore, paper continues to flow unabated until all people are comfortable working in the electronic media.

CHAPTER 11

SECURING
THE IIS

Since the 1950s, IS directors have restricted user access to the machine room, backed up files, and considered their security adequate. In the early 1990s, many are changing their minds for two reasons. First, the growth of network information systems, particularly for Electronic Data Interchange, requires many companies to open their data networks to dial-up and other connections to outside organizations. Because these external groups are linked to still other individuals and companies, the effect is to expose the data network to virtually any workstation in the world equipped with a modem and operated by a clever user. No longer can aggressive companies operate in a leased-line environment where all terminal points come under physical security management. Second, the widespread publicity given to network penetration by hackers and the epidemic spread of certain software viruses have attracted the attention of many general managers. For the first time, they are asking IS the question, "Are you sure our systems are secure?" The answer often must be "no"; the technology used today by the attacker is ahead of that used by the defender.

Notwithstanding an increase in general management concern, most CIOs continue to believe that their antagonists possess only limited means, and thus limited ability, to penetrate corporate systems. The attackers are viewed as individual thieves, vandals, or hackers—perhaps clever, but with limited resources. Even managers concerned that competitors may attempt to enter their systems doubt that they would engage in "serious" crimes or invest inordinate resources toward their ends.

Furthermore, few companies have room for security experts on their already overloaded staffs. Outside auditors will remain the main force pressing for appropriate controls. For their part, IS directors will buy packaged complexes of hardware, software, and management practices (the latter as automatic as possible) as long as these products can be trusted. The criteria for establishing trust will be compliance with guidelines fixed by standards associations and the U.S. government, based on the research of the National Security Agency.

Unlike its role in most aspects of computer technology, the U.S. government has taken the lead in fostering and assessing computer security technology. Commercial users and manufacturers have been content to follow its lead partly because they do not wish to invest any more than necessary in developing new technology. More important is the question of legal liability. If sued, companies would rather defend their use of standard and approved techniques than the creative but little-used ones, even though the latter may be superior. A company might well have to publicly explain its security practices in the 1990s if, for instance, a thief steals money from a customer using that firm's computer.

Key components of computer security technology have already been developed and proved. The Data Encryption Standard (DES) has been thoroughly verified as a means of encrypting all but the most secret messages. The processing required by the DES can be performed by inexpensive microchips that intervene between each information appliance and the communication line to which it is attached. The frequently changed keys needed by the DES chips at each end of a communications link can be generated by standard software packages and distributed automatically through a network, using approved and standardized software. In an IIS, companies can use a single key management system to govern encryption–decryption at all links in a network.

IBM's announced Repository, which will appear in stages in the early 1990s, allows a distributed system to act as if it has a single head. Thus, access control can be handled from one spot, a significant security advantage.

Software packages and operating systems are frequently written with the presumption that users must provide passwords before the system will respond. Many DBMSs employ the concept of "ownership," where every access to any data element must be personally granted by a designated employee of the organization owning the file. This person must put into the system explicit permission before a given password can access the data element.

These techniques, and perhaps a few additional ones described below, will be used almost universally in the commercial computer networks of the mid-1990s. They will be sufficient to push the technology of the defense ahead of all but the most determined attack. Even though the IIS potentially magnifies threats, it also possesses the capability of minimizing them by enabling the application of security across whole systems. The IIS can, in fact, be more secure than almost any system today.

TYPICAL SECURE SYSTEMS OF THE MID-1990S

Figure 11.1 shows two communications networks, connected respectively to a master file processor and a user support processor. These correspond to the mainframe tier of computers shown earlier in Figure 4.1 (page 68) in networks in which security has a high priority, such as those in financial institutions. The network in Figure 11.1 applies to a company that must provide access to its master files through the public switched net. In organizations employing only private nets with leased lines, no encrypted gateway would exist between the processors.

Both processors will contain secure operating systems, accompanied, if necessary, by hardware options. They will be versions of the operating systems the organization would otherwise choose,

Figure 11.1   Typical Secure Commercial Network of the 1990s

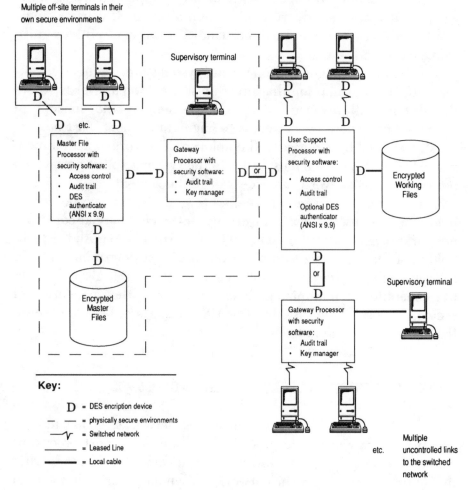

and they need not be the same. By the mid-1990s, all major operating systems will be available in versions secure enough for most users.

The network connected to the master file processor will be the physically secure one. It will consist of leased lines (or lines within the organization's premises) attached to terminals in secure premises belonging to the user. Access to the terminals will be controlled by password and biometric identification, probably a fingerprint reader. DES encryption devices will appear at each end of the communication lines.

The master file processor will contain access control software that verifies user and terminal ID, authorize the specific request, and perform callback and time out if appropriate. An audit trail processor will monitor activity. It will be a heuristic program, able to learn about typical use patterns and alert the security manager (via the terminal connected to the central gateway processor) if anomalies appear.

Message authentication will be applied using the DES according to existing standards. The purpose of this arrangement will be to guard against viruses or spurious messages and also to comply with financial industry rules where necessary. The master files will be kept in encrypted form, with a DES link between the master file processor and the file subsystem.

A minicomputer-based gateway processor will separate the two networks. Link encryption will be applied to traffic passing through. The heuristic audit trail processor will also act as the key manager, automatically generating the distributing keys for the entire system using public key algorithms. No transportation of keys will be performed manually, and users will not have access to keys.

The user support processor will provide connections to the switched public communications net. In many cases, all the connections will be to known sites with known telephone numbers and physical access control (top right of Fig. 11.1). In some cases, access will also be provided to uncontrolled sites, for example, to EDI correspondents who may call (bottom right in Fig. 11.1).

Where links are controlled, DES encryption will be applied; access control procedures will include callback as well as access screening. DES authentication may also be applied, although it will often be judged unnecessary for traffic not affecting master files and not likely to contain viruses. Working files will probably be encrypted.

Access via uncontrolled links will be isolated from the rest of the network and specially monitored to guard against viruses and fraudulent penetration. The switched net will terminate at a special gateway processor supervised by a person who approves any unexpected traffic. In addition to the usual gateway access control and audit trail, this processor will support whatever generic virus detection software the user may have installed. At a minimum, this software will search for suspicious text and code, particularly file modification commands.

SECURING WORKSTATIONS

Almost all workstations of the mid-1990s will be PCs capable of independent operation. This development is unfortunate from a security viewpoint: The old-fashioned terminal able to operate only on command from the attached host computer is easier to control.

Some organizations will force their workstation PCs to operate the way terminals do, either to provide security or to continue using old software. These companies will withhold I/O ports and hard disk storage devices. The workstations will be able to receive programs and data only as downloaded from an attached host or server. Extraneous material cannot enter the system except as keyed in by the operator. Such "diskless PCs" are already used in some networks.

X-terminals, which do no applications processing locally, are the newest version of the old dumb terminal mode of operation. Because they draw on a central server for processing applications, X-terminals can be much more easily controlled from a security viewpoint than a regular workstation.

In most cases, however, users will be endowed with full PC capabilities in their workstations. Furthermore, users will want at times to operate machines within the secure IIS of the company, and on other occasions to connect outside through public lines. The challenge is to prevent any malicious software, no matter how subtle, obtained from the public network from entering the secure IIS.

The approach depicted in Figure 11.2 will meet the challenge. The design concept rests on the use of removable cartridges, which will contain hard disks and programs in read-only memory (ROM) that must be physically inserted and removed to initialize and terminate use of the PC. This procedure, which burdens users

Figure 11.2   Secure/Public Terminal Design of the 1990s

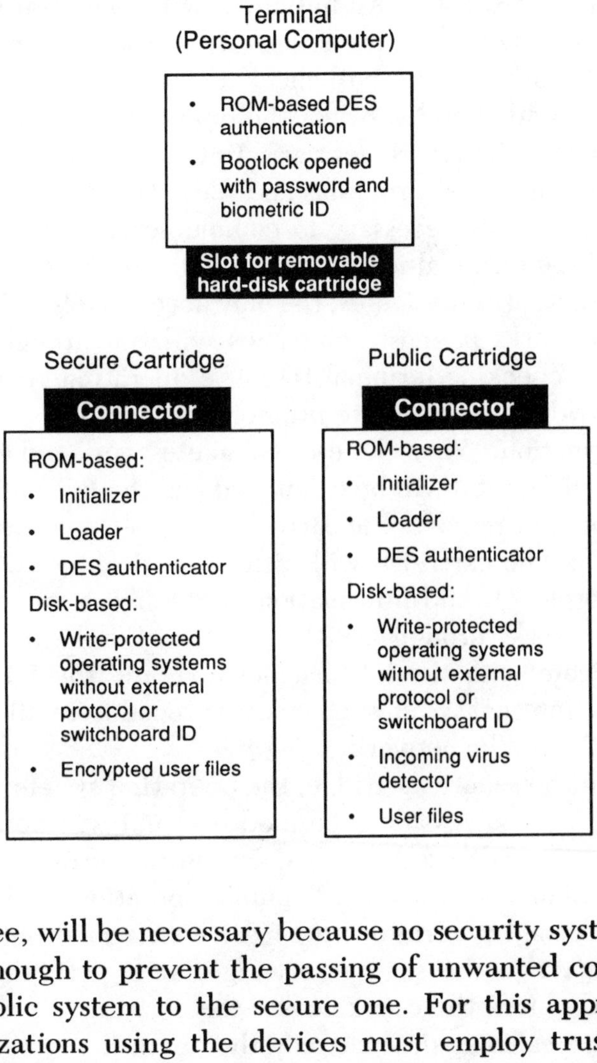

Terminal
(Personal Computer)

- ROM-based DES authentication
- Bootlock opened with password and biometric ID

Slot for removable hard-disk cartridge

Secure Cartridge

Connector

ROM-based:

- Initializer
- Loader
- DES authenticator

Disk-based:

- Write-protected operating systems without external protocol or switchboard ID
- Encrypted user files

Public Cartridge

Connector

ROM-based:

- Initializer
- Loader
- DES authenticator

Disk-based:

- Write-protected operating systems without external protocol or switchboard ID
- Incoming virus detector
- User files

to some degree, will be necessary because no security systems will be reliable enough to prevent the passing of unwanted commands from the public system to the secure one. For this approach to work, organizations using the devices must employ trustworthy staff who will guard their secure cartridges and not attempt to subvert the system.

Two types of devices will be used in this terminal: secure and public. The mechanical process of initializing will be similar for both. After a user inserts a cartridge, a bootlock system will prevent initialization until the user has inserted both his or her password and a biometric ID, most likely a fingerprint. If these identification markers are accepted, three unchangeable subroutines from the cartridge will be executed. An initializer will then clear all memory to zero, a loader will bring in the operating system from the cartridge, and a DES authenticator will check it.

Once loaded and verified, the operating characteristics of the secure and public cartridges vary. In the former, all operations involve encrypted user programs and files. The operating system will lack the protocols necessary to communicate with the public network and the terminal-identification data needed to connect to outside networks. (In the 1990s, the only access likely to be available to public networks in most companies will be through a local PBX capable of checking terminal ID.) The operating system on the secure cartridge will be write-protected so that the user cannot add this information. When the user completes work and logs off, a new authentication total will be calculated and the PC will be initialized before the user removes the cartridge.

The public cartridge will differ significantly. Although it will contain protocols and information necessary to gain access to the public network through a PBX, it will lack both the capability to communicate with the internal network and the ID necessary to access the internal systems. Hence, all procedures will operate solely through the public network.

As in the secure cartridge, the operating system will be write-protected so that it cannot be modified and will be authenticated when the cartridge is loaded. Once authenticated, the operating system will allow the user free public operation, with all incoming traffic screened by virus detection software appropriate to the user's activities. As in the secure cartridge, at log-off, the PC will be initialized before the user removes the cartridge. A new DES total will not be calculated, since only the operating system will be authenticated upon reload.

VIRUS DETECTION PRODUCTS

Many technologies likely to be part of the secure IIS and workstations of the mid-1990s are already available in embryonic form today. The

DES will frequently be used to detect intrusions, such as viruses and bombs. ANSI x9.9 will be the dominant method employed for this purpose, and will be common in software packages, electronic bulletin boards, and general-transaction (i.e., order-entry) applications. Commercial users in many fields will have strong incentives to adopt ANSI x9.9, specifically because of its approval as the financial transaction standard and widespread application history.

In cases where a DES authentication code cannot be provided at initiation of a message, detection and prevention technology will continue to be installed on an ad hoc basis according to the type of virus and specific user needs. The number and level of such discrete, non-DES applications will affect the future development of the "virus vaccine" market. At present, it is principally served by small, entrepreneurial firms that develop focused responses to each publicized viral outbreak. If the market remains in such a state, which is likely if widespread adoption of ANSI x9.9 proceeds as forecast, large software vendors will see few incentives to enter the field.

PERSONAL-IDENTIFIER TECHNOLOGY

The major personal-identifier technologies include biometric systems (i.e., fingerprint matchers, retina readers, signature dynamics sensors, face matching systems) and the traditional alphanumeric identifier methods. Although all approaches will continue to evolve, the three technologies that will most likely dominate commercial systems will be based on fingerprints, voice, and cards.

Fingerprint identifiers are already reliable and inexpensive (about $1,000 per unit). The disadvantages of early versions have been eliminated by, for example, storing characteristics of the user's fingerprint on a smart card by the user, rather than in a remote file subject to access delay. Such a system is also ergonomically easier to use than signature or retina systems. Hence, the installed base of fingerprint matching systems should grow rapidly over the next 5 years.

The prospects for voice recognition are less optimistic. Discrimination among people is not reliable because individual voices vary when people are tense or suffer from a cold or hoarseness, for instance. In systems set to provide adequate security, too many false rejections arise; however, systems set to minimize false rejections permit too many erroneous approvals.

Yet technological evolution in other areas could improve the viability, and hence the market potential, of voice recognition. In particular, users of ISDN will attain the capability of encrypting voice interchangeably with data and facsimile. The increasing interest in these areas could carry over to voice, renewing interest in it as an identifier.

Despite their appeal, however, neither fingerprint nor voice recognition products will dominate the market for identifier systems over the next 5 years. The traditional personal alphanumeric password will continue as the most commonly used identification method. Card-based personal identification number (PIN) technology, in particular, is already so widely accepted that, despite its weaknesses, commercial users will balk at giving it up. New technologies add cost and cause significant inconvenience to a system's users. Most organizations will need to be convinced by painful experience that the card and PIN are inadequate.

Retina scanners map the unique pattern of veins at the back of a person's eye and thus provide a highly accurate identifier. Few companies, however, are likely to require its employees or the public to step up to an eyepiece to be scanned before proceeding through a door.

HEURISTIC AUDIT-TRAIL SOFTWARE

Heuristic software will be a key component of the access-pattern monitors in the master, gateway, and user support processors. It will record use patterns, first for reports, then for simple matches to history, and ultimately to make expert system-based decisions about access control (especially when to permit variations from "normal" use).

The software will also help prevent damage and disruption from viruses or from any other unusual or accidental stimulus to the system. Enhancing its utility will be general advantages that extend beyond security concerns: its ability to perform functions on an unattended, 24-hour, 7-day basis (which is increasingly important as electronic data interchange mandates that systems operate on such a schedule); its effectiveness in minimizing the need for in-house access-control expertise; its ability to make systems self-diagnosing; and its association with all aspects of network management.

PERSONNEL ISSUES

The technology available now and in the next few years will meet the needs of all companies to secure the IISs and the workstations operating within them. In addition to the hardware and software features already mentioned, communications networks have become more amenable to electronic security management as **ISDN** has proliferated. Telephone, microwave, and satellite links are all more secure now, offering encoding methods and error-checking capabilities, which may increase users' confidence.

Technology alone can accomplish little, however, without cooperation from the people involved. Foremost, the system's users must comply with security procedures. When they select passwords and personal identifiers, for instance, they must choose ones that are not obvious (derived from employee number, birthday, etc.), even though nonobvious passwords are more difficult to remember. They must also refrain from hiding copies of passwords near their workstations. Auditors often report that a brief search of what they have come to recognize as typical "secret" hiding places often turns up passwords.

Employees must also be willing to change passwords, even though it is an inconvenience to remember a new one. Passwords that are not changed for a year or more lose all value. But in many organizations, reluctance to irritate the staff leads to a failure to switch passwords.

Users must also follow physical security guidelines. Both diskless and removable-cartridge workstations can be rendered insecure through mishandling. The diskless workstation can become an easy unauthorized entry point if users fail to guard the procedures that enable access to improper material. The fact that all material of value is downloaded from the host rather than retained in the PC then becomes a meaningless precaution. Likewise, the removable-cartridge workstation is only as secure as the protection provided for the cartridge. If the user does not always lock the cartridge in a safe when leaving the workstation, the system is left open to intrusion.

The basic problem of physical security is restriction of access—keeping people who have no need to know from learning about the system. Valued friends and customers must be kept away from the workstations unless they are authorized to use them. Strangers in halls or offices where they apparently do not belong should be politely challenged. Staff members do not want to do these things, but unless they do, security will be compromised.

The undeniable fact is that system security is an inconvenience and a constraint on user freedom. These drawbacks are particularly visible in a highly distributed system, in which users are accustomed to running their workstations and LANs as they please. Management must motivate users not simply to grudgingly accept security procedures, but to actively support them as necessary and reasonable.

The importance of the security measures should be carefully explained. Objections and suggestions should be solicited and accommodated wherever possible. Reinforcement should be provided periodically, even if users must take time off from their jobs to attend classes on security. There should also be enforcement, people and programs geared to patroling the system and its users for laxity. Enforcement, of course, also requires appropriate public discipline for security violators.

Security management is a more sensitive matter than it appears on the surface. Those responsible for planning and administration must be persistent perfectionists, but also good politicians and compromisers. Even the supervisory operators at the gateway processor depicted in Figure 11.1 must be more than technicians; they must posses the authority and judgment to permit an irregular activity when it appears to be in the interests of the organization.

No formal security procedure can anticipate all the conditions that arise in the real world.

WHAT COMPANIES SHOULD DO

Ideally, each user organization should undertake a risk management study to determine its exposure to and the cost of possible loss. Only then, the company can develop a tailored security policy. Yet few will perform a formal study for four reasons:

1. A perceived lack of resources will deter most commercial users from investing the time and effort necessary to conducting a security–audit/risk–management study, even though it could, in some cases, result in a simpler and less expensive security system.
2. Users will feel more comfortable with what they already use— the standard security systems that have been proven legally acceptable—than with any new one that has not been tested in a lawsuit.
3. The increasing presence of security enhancements as standard features or low-cost options on hardware, particularly in com- munication linkage devices, will encourage users to purchase off-the-shelf solutions.
4. A general desire to add security capability through technologi- cal, as opposed to staff, investments will augment the standard solution trend.

Even though no formal risk management study may be performed, however, all managers of Integrated Information Systems will have to pay adequate attention to risk. Outside auditors, if no one else, need to be satisfied. Personnel as well as physical security must be addressed, and disaster recovery plans devised and exercised.

In improving security through new technology, management must alter the basic structure of the software systems in use. The latest releases of operating systems probably have to be adopted along with related programs for access control, virus detection, and the like. New controllers and access devices that incorporate DES chips may have to be acquired. Such change is major and probably cannot be undertaken unless alterations are already being made for other reasons, such as implementing an IIS. Conversion to an IIS, therefore, should be viewed as an opportunity to convert to the technically secure system the organization feels will meet its needs for a decade or more.

If an organization is not prepared to significantly change system design, it can nevertheless evolve to a more secure environment by implementing some of the new access control and communications security technologies. In doing so, however, management should not delude itself into thinking that it has completed the job. If an organization's IIS does not incorporate the level of security technology shown in Figure 11.1, and if the system is not supported by appropriate personnel with physical security and backup procedures, management should limit the system's exposure to outside queries and inputs.

C H A P T E R   12

THE PROMISE
OF THE INTEGRATED
ENTERPRISE

If this book had been written in 1960, we would not have predicted the introduction of IBM's System 360 in 1964, which changed the landscape of mainframe computing and software use through today. If this book had been written in 1970, we may not have foreseen the rise of the minicomputer from companies such as DEC and Data General. And if this book had been written 10 years ago, we quite likely would have failed to see that a Personal Computer from IBM would soon sweep onto corporate desktops. Radical technologies or shifts in direction are essentially unknowable. This observation is particularly valid in the 1990s, as information systems and their interconnections approach the complexity of the human brains that design them. As John Hammitt, vice-president of IS at United Technologies Corp., has said, "I used to be able to take the experience of the past and project it into the future and largely succeed. That is not so anymore."

The inability to fix the future into a 5-year plan should not deter companies from preparing for what lies ahead. They must equip themselves well for the journeys that lie ahead, even if their course cannot be specified exactly or their destination end up different from their original target. Organizations that focus on developing the underlying systems infrastructure and flexible systems suggested in this book will be ready to take advantage of whatever new technologies develop. The corporation of the 1990s must be tilted forward on its toes, ready to move—not locked in step by a single vendor, style of computing, or even one architecture.

To lead the company into the future rather than follow it there, an aggressive CIO must break out of the usual modes of thinking and ask some unsettling questions to trigger new perspectives:

- Does the company's 3-month order backlog actually demonstrate product appeal or the inability of manufacturing and order systems to satisfy customer demand in a timely manner?
- What would the effect be on the whole corporation if isolated systems in various business units crashed for hours or days? If the impact is negligible, can these systems be placed at the bottom of the list in terms of maintenance and upgrades?
- What aspect of the way the company does business can never be changed? What stated or unspoken policies prevent such changes?
- Have any competitors achieved a market advantage in the last 10 years through deploying information technology? Are they likely to again?
- Do the customers really care whether they are talking to marketing, service, sales, or administration when they place an order, or could calls be handled by a trained representative with access to multiple databases and expert systems?
- Is there an expressed management directive, as at The Travelers Corp., that technology should be aggressively applied to all aspects of the business?
- Is the company becoming what Rosabeth Moss Kanter, the noted organizational observer, calls a "free-exchange culture"? Or despite all the talk of flexibility, is the organization still stuck in the command-and-control mindset?

An Arthur D. Little, Inc., survey of 112 senior executives revealed that 94% of companies are still hierarchically structured, down only 2% from 1980. From now until the year 2000, however, 96% of the survey respondents expect their organizations to be transformed into a more fluid information-based enterprise. Answers to these questions should not be driven by technology alone, although its influence must be taken into account. Business goals should determine all technological investments and any attendant alteration of organizational structure. For instance, if the goal is to take market share from a competitor within a year, then the company may need to be hoisted onto the bleeding edge of technology. Old structures may need to be demolished as strike teams are established to develop, test, and market products quickly.

In many instances, longer term business goals can generally be attained by the "fast follower." At 3M Co. in St. Paul, Minnesota, the operating philosophy is to stay about 6 months behind the leading edge, according to Chuck Anastasi, director of technology. Such a position lets others cut the trail but never get far out of sight.

THE COMPLEX TASK AHEAD

Even sophisticated and aggressive organizations will not find it easy to achieve the Integrated Information System of the middle or even the late 1990s. Companies will have to back out of blind alleys as they test options. The history of computing is littered with both failures and overambitious claims of technological panaceas, from the "user-friendly" pitches of the mid-1980s to the hyperproductivity claims of recent years by CASE and relational database vendors.

The IIS will be among the most complex of human creations. Its successful implementation will depend on the clarity of business vision at strategic and tactical levels, insight into the realistic capabilities of information technologies and vendors, and strong project management skills.

The inherent difficulties of building integrated systems lie in their specification, design, and construction, not in their actual production. Much of the complexity that must be mastered is arbitrary in that it arises from the many human institutions and systems to which the system's interfaces must conform. This complexity, which differs from one interface to another and over time, cannot be designed out by redesign of the system alone. The hope, or sometimes the demand, that all existing institutions and systems be changed simultaneously and radically to eliminate the complexities inherent in the interfaces they require is both naive and arrogant.

Furthermore, the overall IIS has to be part of, as well as a supporter of, a rich and dynamic matrix of users, applications, and computing platforms that are themselves continually changing. Even if it were somehow possible to create a clean and simplified environment, or tabula rasa, on which integrated systems can be built, it would soon degenerate into the typical complex mixture of all computing installations.

The descriptions of the IIS presented in this book are essentially conservative in that they do not presume the achievement of any technological breakthroughs or discovery of a "silver bullet." No single development in technology or management technique can guarantee even one order of magnitude improvement in productivity, reliability, and simplicity. However, a disciplined, consistent, and imaginative effort to develop, propagate, and exploit the many encouraging innovations underway should, indeed, yield the order of magnitude improvement that is the implicit potential of the IIS. The streets may not be paved with gold, but they are at least paved, so that progress is possible.

PART-TIME WORKERS

In this new business decade, wherever a process can be mathematically optimized, it will be. Where routine human judgment is required, expert systems will provide it. Nonroutine judgment will still be needed in most important areas: negotiating sales terms, delegating authority for decisions where the data is imperfect, choosing among options, coping with unprecedented emergencies, and so on. The human being will remain the supervisor of operations, the performer of operations that cannot be automated, and the decision maker of both first and last resort. Namely, he or she will still decide both what to do in the first place, and when and how to change established objectives and procedures in light of new information and new circumstances.

Some jobs will be lost. Records management and inventory control clerks, production schedulers, timekeepers, expediters, and other employees involved in routine operations make business systems work will become unnecessary.

Increasingly, people will be employed part-time by more than one organization. Thus, employers will tap the services of a larger number of part-time workers possessing a wider range of skills. The IIS will help manage this increasing complexity and guard against threats of information misuse and conflict of interest.

It will be possible to track the progress of both organizational units and cross-organizational project teams to which the employees are assigned. It also will be possible to monitor operations (time delays, work status, volumes of transactions) as easily as financial performance. In fact, management will have to be careful to avoid the overcontrol that can engender resentment among workers.

Systems will take longer to develop in manufacturing operations because of the wider use of robots. Data availability on the factory floor will be almost perfect, because a by-product of using robots is data collection. They generate for their own purposes all the data that an operations control computer will need for scheduling, dispatching, and inventory management.

How will employees deal with the unexpected, once so large an amount of control is turned over to automatic systems? If the systems run semiautomatically and grow more complex as they do so through artificial intelligence, what happens when they fail or suffer a disaster? Today, employees receive continual practice in coping with the unexpected because information systems are so limited. How does one distinguish when an expert system is giving subtly wrong advice that will lead to long-term problems, or even liability—particularly in the absence of the expert? How does one fix such a problem? Such questions will test the technological sophistication of any organization.

THE NEOTECHNIC ERA

"Technological presbyopia" is how economic historian Paul David of Stanford University describes the view that all the benefits of a technology have been achieved. Such was the vision, he says, of many observers in 1900 about electricity. Lighthouses, light bulbs, central generating stations, and electric tram service had been invented. What more could be left, people wondered?

In fact, the best was yet to come. The immense electrical network connecting cities and nations was just beginning to be built. Power costs had not yet dropped to relatively trivial amounts, which would make electric use affordable by all. Also, secondary motors had yet to penetrate the factory. Only with these developments later in the Age of Electricity did economic productivity soar. One dramatic example of how electricity changed the landscape is that motorized elevators enabled the building of skyscrapers.

In the late 1800s, manufacturers of electric generating equipment fell into an economic slump. Every user company that needed a generator had seemingly already bought one. Mainframe computers are much like the electric generators of old: Not much possible growth is left. On a broader level, however, just as simple household motors spurred a resurgence in electric generators, so too will powerful workstations and the basic component itself—the chip—spur tremendous use of computers in this decade.

Paul David recites the history of electricity in part to counter an observation about another field—computers—by people such as Robert Solow, a Nobel Prize-winning economist from MIT. Solow has said, "We see computers everywhere but in the economic statistics." More specifically, Solow and others question why the massive investment in computers over the last few decades has not resulted in a similarly massive productivity increase. Some skeptics would settle for any noticeable increase in economic productivity, massive or not, that could be linked to computers.

David responds about computers by analogy to electricity: "You don't get the full productivity effects until about two-thirds of the way into the diffusion process." How far along is the diffusion of computers? The history of general-purpose computing can be traced to the creation of ENIAC in 1946. Yet even after four decades, computer networks are still in their infancy. Workstations are only now attaining sufficient power to allow routine, truly personal computing at the desktop. Software is now beginning to be developed that can make using computers as simple and familiar as driving a car.

The true Information Age is still a few years away technologically, and may be even farther away psychologically. As Lewis Mumford, the eminent observer of the world and technology, noted in "Technics and Civilization," we have not passed out of the paleotechnic era and into the neotechnic. The tools necessary to implement the information-based neotechnic era are in our hands, but in our minds remains the attachment to the way things have always been done. Perhaps it is this legacy of an earlier management era that most constrains the effective use of information systems today and weighs down the buoyancy of the computer industry.

FAR-OUT TECHNOLOGY

This book forecasts the course of information technology through the mid-1990s. In many research labs, however, that time frame is too short-sighted. The far-out future of the next century promises a far richer table of technologies from which to choose.

For instance, in January 1990, AT&T Bell Laboratories, Inc., announced an experimental machine whose commercial use will surely not come before the year 2000. This optical computer calculates by means of pulses of light rather than currents of electricity.

The familiar circuit boards and silicon chips are replaced by lasers, lenses, and mirrors. Light beams in such a machine can intersect without interfering with the information that each is carrying. Optical computers could be applied in the 21st century to data-intensive areas, such as identifying faces in a security system, or machine vision.

Alan Huang, head of the Optical Computing Research Department at Bell Laboratories, compares optical computing's potential for storing and accessing data to the difference between going to a library to read a single book and reading all the books there at once. He envisions computers with 1,000 or even 10,000 times the processing speed of today's machines. He foresees optical communications switches of 1 terabit/second capacity, able to handle 100,000 high-speed data LANs or almost 200 million facsimile terminals.

At the Microelectronics and Computer Technology Corp. in Austin, Texas, scientist Douglas Lenat is trying to instill common sense into a computer one assertion at a time. His goal is to enter 100 million rules, basic facts, observations, and rules of thumb, essentially all the foundation knowledge information that the writers of an encyclopedia assume we already know. Such a vast knowledge base will far surpass the limited-domain usefulness of today's expert systems. In fact, Lenat is in one sense creating a supraprogram that could underlie all expert systems, providing the natural links to them all.

At MIT's Mobile Robot Laboratory, Rodney Brooks and others are doing the complement of Lenat's work—creating a physical feedback loop system in which "robot beings" know by doing. This method mimics how humans often learn, by interacting with the world rather than by deducing actions from rules. Robot beings require sophisticated vision, infrared and other sensing systems all under development today, including a touch-sensitive skin that can enable a robot hand to distinguish an egg from an apple. In Japan, Sony Corp. has come out with a notebook-sized machine that substitutes a pen and touch-sensitive screen for the keyboard as the means of data entry. This "pen computer" is a natural for Japan, where the

7,000 ideographs known as kanji render keyboard entry a problem of immense proportions. The computer turns written notes into characters that can be appended to an architect's drawings, for instance, or a musician's score.

Also in the realm of the small comes the "Private Eye" from Reflection Technology, Inc. A user wears a headset with an attached eyepiece 1 inch wide. By focusing on this display, the user can envision a 12 inch screen floating in front of him or her, presenting text 25 lines long and 80 characters wide. When perfected, such a product could help people who must work hands-free, such as on a factory floor.

Some of these "breakthroughs" will prove illusionary, of course, or perhaps irrelevant to real business needs. But they are only a sampling of the exotic technologies coming to life in labs throughout the world. The history of the computer is a record of phenomenal change—in machines, in business, in society. The wise corporate manager prepares for what he or she can clearly see coming but always keeps one eye alert to what looms indistinctly on the horizon.

GLOSSARY

ADA A specialized computer language promoted by the U.S. Department of Defense.

AIX IBM's standard version of Unix.

ANSI American National Standards Institute.

ANSI x9.9 American National Standards Institute's electronic financial network authentication standard.

API Application program interface; the formally defined programming language interface between a vendor-provided program and its user.

APPC Advanced Program to Program Communications; IBM's protocol for peer-relationship program-to-program communications under SNA. Also known as LU 6.2.

ASCII American Standard Code for Information Interchange; ASCII is a seven-bit-plus-parity code established by the American National Standards Institute to achieve compatibility among different computers and terminals.

ATM Asynchronous Transfer Mode; a set of rules for the SONET system.

BANDWIDTH The range of frequencies assigned to a channel; the difference, expressed in hertz, between the highest and lowest frequencies of a band. In general, the higher the bandwidth, the more the data throughput.

B-CHANNEL 64 kilobits per second information carrying channel specified in ISDN networks.

251

BIOMETRIC   ID security system based on intrinsic human characteristics, such as fingerprint reader or voice recognizer.

BISDN   Broadband ISDN; a form of ISDN that will carry digital
transmission at rates equal to or greater than the T-1 rate.

BRIDGE   A device for connecting two segments of a LAN. The bridge
manages the flow of message traffic between segments by reading the address of each unit, or frame, of data it receives.

CAD   Computer-aided design; the process of digitally creating engineering drawings and capturing part geometry using a variety of interactive devices and programming techniques.

CASE   Computer Aided Software Engineering; an umbrella term
for a collection of tools and techniques that promise gains in
systems analyst and programmer productivity. The two prominent delivered technologies are application generators and PC-
based systems that provide graphics-oriented automation of the
front end of the software development process.

CCITT   The International Consultative Committee for Telephony
and Telegraphy; the technical committee of the International
Telecommunications Union (ITU), which is responsible for the
development of recommendations regarding telecommunications, including data communications.

CDE   Compound Document Exchange.

CD-ROM   Compact disk read-only memory; optical data storage
based on the same technology and media used for audio CDs.

CENTREX   A set of communications services, provided by local telephone companies, that takes the place of local PBXs.

CGM   Computer graphics metafile; a device-independent standard
for image data interchange.

CIM   Computer-integrated manufacturing; the integration of manufacturing operations by "integrating" people systems, information systems, and manufacturing systems.

CLIENT   A workstation connected to a network, which can access
resources on a server. See also *server*.

CMIP   Common Management Information Protocol.

COMPOUND DOCUMENTS   A document containing more than one form of information, such as text and graphics.

COMPRESSION DECOMPRESSION CHIPS   Devices for reducing file size for faster transmission and expanding files for full information access.

CRT   Cathode ray tube; vacuum tube used in a video terminal screen.

D-CHANNEL   The 16 kilobits per second data signaling channel specified in ISDN networks.

DASD   Direct access storage device; typically, a magnetic disk device used on all classes of computers, but DASD is a more general term.

DATABASE SERVER   A system used to store and maintain one or more databases, and to supply responses to queries from workstations.

DBMS   Database management system; method of storing, updating, and retrieving information where many users access common data files.

DCA   Document Content Architecture; IBM's architecture for documents containing one or more data types (compound documents).

D-DBMS   Distributed database management system.

DDM   Distributed data management.

DES   Data Encryption Standard; a U.S. government standard widely used for computer security systems.

DIA   Document Interchange Architecture; IBM's architecture for interchanging compound documents.

DIP   Document imaging processing; systems integrated to facilitate the storage and retrieval of electronic images of paper documents.

DNA   Digital Network Architecture (DEC).

DRAM   Dynamic random access memory; electronic semiconductor memory requiring periodic refreshing to avoid loss of data; the most common form of main memory in current computer systems.

DUSTY DECKS   Existing FORTRAN programs which cannot be easily translated into modern languages.

EBCDIC   Extended Binary Coded Decimal Interchange Code; the data-encoding format for IBM mainframes.

EDI   Electronic data interchange; the electronic transfer of preformatted documents, such as purchase orders and bills of lading, between trading partners.

EFT   Electronic funds transfer; a computerized payment and withdrawal system used to transfer funds from one account to another and to obtain related financial information.

EMA   Enterprise Management Architecture (DEC).

4GL   Fourth-generation language; includes two categories of software development tools: application generators (for production applications) and information generators (for decision-support applications). Fourth-generation languages are relatively non-procedural and easier to use, but less precise and more wasteful of computer resources, than third-generation languages such as COBOL, FORTRAN, and C.

FDDI   Fiber distributed data interface; a low-level communications standard for fiber-optic networks.

FTAM   File Transfer, Access, and Management; one of several services provided by the OSI application layer.

GATEWAY PROCESSOR   Minicomputer dedicated to interconnect two otherwise incompatible networks, network nodes, subnetworks, or devices.

GIGAFLOPS   A billion floating-point operations per second.

GOSIP   Government Open Systems Interconnection Profile; sets of national networking standards based on the OSI model. National GOSIPs are not necessarily 100% compatible.

GUI Graphical user interface; includes not only the graphics library used by programs to display text and graphics, but also the user interface toolkit and style guide that provide a consistent look and feel across multiple applications.

HEURISTIC AUDIT Self-educating program that records patterns of usage.

HP-GL Hewlett-Packard Graphics Language; a specification to support H-P and compatible graphics plotters.

HYPERMEDIA SYSTEM Self-cross-referencing systems, such as Hypercard by Apple, that allows inclusion of data other than text. For example, an encyclopedia that provides in depth information on each particular subject that may include graphics or audio enhancement, usually used with a mouse.

HYPERTEXT SYSTEM Self-cross-referencing text-only system, usually used with a mouse.

IEEE The Institute of Electrical and Electronics Engineers, formed in 1963.

IGES Initial graphics exchange specification; a vendor-neutral method of representing parts, geometries, and product dimensions used as an intermediate system for transfer between specific computer-aided design products.

IIS Integrated information system; a completely interconnected system comprised of an operating system, DBMS, transaction processing monitor, OA (electronic mail, enhanced word processing, desktop publishing, full-motion video graphics), DIP systems, AI software, component hardware processors and their interconnections.

ILRS Information Library Retrieval Systems.

IMAGE PROCESSING See *DIP.*

IMS Information Management System; one of the current IBM database management systems.

INTEROPERABILITY The ability of multiple incompatible computer systems to cooperate in the execution of a single application.

IRS   Information retrieval system; system for cataloging vast amounts of stored data so that any part can be retrieved at any time.

ISDN   Integrated Services Digital Network; project undertaken by the CCITT for the standardization of operating parameters and interfaces for a system that will allow mixed (voice and various forms of data) digital transmission services to be accommodated. Access channels include basic (144 kilobits per second) and primary (1.544M and 2.048M bits per seconds).

ISO   International Standards Organization; organization that includes the interests of governments, users, and the scientific community in preparation of an international standard.

LAN   Local area network; system of multiple interconnected devices that operates in a maximum range of 50 kilometers and supports high-speed data transmission.

LINK ENCRYPTION   The coding of access, for security measures, to the transmission of data between adjacent network nodes.

MAN   Metropolitan area network; a system that provides interconnection among devices in a metropolitan area.

MEGAFLOPS or MFLOPS   A million floating point operations per second.

MIPS   Millions of instructions per second.

MOTIF   A set of user interface standards and software being generally adopted as the de facto Unix user interface.

NCF   Network Computing Forum; standard-setting organization for distributed network computing standards.

NCS   Network Computing System (Apollo).

NETVIEW   A communications network diagnostic and management system developed by IBM.

NEURAL NETWORK   A method of simulating the branching network employed by the brain to allow systems to create spontaneous relationships between data and operational elements, used for pattern recognition.

NFS Network file system; a method of sharing files across a computer network. Pioneered by Sun Microsystems, it is now a de facto standard in the Unix environment. NFS is built upon TCP/IP and Ethernet.

OA Office automation; the integration of all information functions in the office.

OCR Optical character recognition; technology that enables a scanner to "read" characters and convert them to digital form.

ODA–ODIF Office Document Architecture–Office Document Interchange Format; an international standard for the interchange of documents that may contain text, graphic, image, and data material.

OS/2 Operating system for PCs developed by IBM and Microsoft.

OSF Open Software Foundation; a software development organization sponsored by a large number of vendor and user member organizations, and developing an open, standard operating system environment, including extensions and subsystems, on a Unix base. The founding sponsors of OSF were Apollo, DEC, Hewlett-Packard, IBM, Bull, Siemens, and Nixdorf.

OSI Open System Interconnection; a seven-layer network architecture developed by the International Standards Organization (OSI) to enable any OSI-compliant computer or device to exchange information with any other OSI-compliant computer or device.

PABX See PBX.

PBX Private Branch Exchange; a telephone switch located on a customer's premises that primarily establishes voice-grade circuits (over tie lines to a telephone company central office) between individual users and the public-switched telephone network. The PBX also provides switching within the customer premises local area, and usually offers numerous enhanced features, including least-cost routing and call-detail recording.

PDL Page Description Language for laser printers.

PIN   Personal identification number; a number used by IIS users in conjunction with a physical identification device to gain access to an information system.

POSIX   Portable Operating System for Computer Environments; Unix-based standard under development by the POSIX committee of the Institute of Electrical and Electronics Engineers. In August 1988, the committee officially released the first installment of the standard (1003.1), a core set of system calls. Other pieces (e.g., real-time extensions) are also under consideration by various subcommittees. POSIX has been adopted as a Federal Information Processing Standard (FIPS), and is included in OSFs and X/Open's basic specifications.

PROTOCOL   A set of messages with specific formats and rules for exchanging messages.

RAM   Random access memory; a storage mechanism in which the time required to obtain data is independent of the location.

RDBMS   Relational database management system; a DBMS in which the database is organized and accessed according to the relationships among data items. In a relational database, relationships between data items are expressed by means of tables. Interdependencies among these tables are expressed by data values rather than by pointers. This allows a high degree of data independence.

RISC   Reduced instruction set computer; a computer architecture using a small set of instructions at the hardware level. RISC enables a powerful processor to be built from very high-speed, simple components.

ROM   Read-only memory; a storage method where information is permanently stored and cannot be altered.

SAA   Systems Applications Architecture; a collection of selected software interfaces, conventions, and protocols published by IBM in 1987. SAA will be the framework for development of consistent applications across future offerings of the major IBM operating system environments: MVS, VM, AS/400, and OS/2.

The four components of SAA are Common Programming Interface (CPI), Common User Access (CUA), Common Communications Support (CCS), and Common Applications.

SERVER A system that provides a well-defined service, such as a remote file access or gateway communications on behalf of one or more workstations.

SIVA System Information Value Analysis.

SNA Systems Network Architecture; a layered network architecture introduced by IBM in 1974. Originally, SNA supported only terminal-oriented networks with a single System/370 host. SNA has evolved to support multiple hosts, program-to-program communications, and peer networking of peripheral nodes.

SNADS SNA Distribution Services; a set of SNA presentation-layer protocols that provide store-and-forward message handling services for applications such as electronic mail.

SONET Synchronous Optical Network Standard; standards used by public telephone networks for fiber-optic public networks.

SQL Structured Query Language; sometimes pronounces "sequel," a relational data language that provides a consistent, English keyword-oriented set of facilities for query, data definition, data manipulation, and data control.

TCP/IP Transmission Control Protocol/Internet Protocol; a set of transport and network layer protocols developed over a 15-year period under the auspices of the U.S. Department of Defense. TCP/IP has emerged as the de facto standard for communications among Unix systems, particularly over Ethernet. TCP/IP implementations are available on products from more than 60 vendors, including DEC and IBM.

TIFF Tagged image file format; graphics file format supported by most desktop publishing programs.

TP Transaction processing; a procedure in which files are interactively updated and results are generated immediately as a result of data entry.

TRN   Token Ring Network; a LAN topology and protocol in which all stations actively attached to the ring listen for a broadcast token or supervisory frame. Stations wishing to transmit must receive the token before doing so, and when done must pass the token to the logically next station on the ring.

UNIX   A family of operating systems originally developed by AT&T, and known for their relative hardware independence and portable applications programming interface; a time-sharing operating system available on AT&T, VAX, Intel 80386, Sun, and many other computers, and widely used in technical and scientific computing applications.

UNMA   Universal Network Management Architecture (AT&T).

VIRTUAL PRIVATE NETWORK   Public network facilities that provide a customer with the effect of a leased-line network, even though the physical facilities may not be 100% dedicated to that customer.

VLSI   Very large scale integrated circuit; generally contains in excess of 10,000 logic gates.

VSAT   Very small aperture terminal; a spread spectrum satellite terminal that allows operation with a small diameter dish antenna at much lower cost than traditional satellite terminals.

VTAM   Virtual Telecommunications Access Method; in an IBM 370, a method to give users at remote terminals access to applications programs in a main computer.

WAN   Wide-area network; a voice–data communications facility connecting geographically dispersed sites via carrier-provided long-haul transmission facilities (e.g., interexchange carriers, leased lines, public packet-switching networks).

WIMPS   Windows, icons, menus, pointers, scroll bars; a style of graphic user interface originally developed by Xerox and popularized by the Apple Macintosh.

WMRM   Write-many, read-many; an optical storage technology with that characteristic. (Contrast **WORM**).

WORM   Write-once, read-many; an optical storage technology with that characteristic.

WORKFLOW LANGUAGE   A language designed to specify and control the flow of information objects (e.g., document images) around an IIS.

X-WINDOWS   A graphics architecture, application programming interface, and prototype implementation developed by MIT. X-Windows defines a client–server relationship between the application program and the workstation screen, where the application program is the client and the workstation screen is the server. This model facilitates cooperative processing between workstations and back-end applications processors. X-Windows has emerged as a de facto standard user interface graphics library for non-SAA environments. It is not, however, a complete graphic user interface.

INDEX

263